D1383914

IN THE
SHADOW
OF THE
RISING
SUN

IN THE SHADOW OF THE RISING SUN

Judy Hyland

AUGSBURG Publishing House • Minneapolis

IN THE SHADOW OF THE RISING SUN

Scripture quotations unless otherwise noted are from the Holy Bible: New International Version. Copyright 1978 by the New York International Bible Society. Used by permission of Zondervan Bible Publishers.

The hymn "Wide, Wide as the Ocean" on page 88 is copyright © 1917 by C. Austin Miles. Renewed 1945 by The Rodeheaver Company (A Div. of WORD, Inc.). All rights reserved. International Copyright Secured. Used by Permission.

Library of Congress Cataloging in Publication Data

Hyland, Judy, 1912-
　IN THE SHADOW OF THE RISING SUN.

　1. World War, 1939-1945—Prisoners and prisons,
Japanese.　2. Hyland, Judy, 1912-　.　3. World War,
1939-1945—Personal narratives, American.　4. Prisoners of
war—United States—Biography.　5. Prisoners of war—
Philippines—Baguio—Biography.　6. Missionaries—
Philippines—Baguio—Biography.　I. Title.
D805.P6H95　1984　　940.54'72'52095991　　84-12303
ISBN 0-8066-2091-9 (pbk.)

Manufactured in the U.S.A.　　　　　　　　　　　　　　APH 10-3260

　　　　　4　5　6　7　8　9　0　1　2　3　4　5　6　7　8　9

This book is lovingly dedicated
To my husband Philip,
who faithfully waited for me
during the five-year absence
and who has given immeasurable help
and encouragement in the writing.
To our children
Phyllis and Kenneth Larson
Lois and Louis Sonstegard
Ruth and James Forsythe
Rebecca and Charles Heikenen

I want to express deep appreciation
To daughters Phyllis and Ruth
for their helpful suggestions
and criticisms of the manuscript
To typists
Mary Duffy and Carol Johnson
To Kenneth Larson for the maps
To all my dear sisters
of the American Lutheran Church
Japan Missionary family
who have encouraged the writing of this story.

Contents

Preface

We spend most of our lives in yearning and planning for the future. As a young girl growing up in rural Minnesota I dreamed of a life as a missionary in the Orient. Since then there have been many moves, new assignments, and children to plan for. But there is a point when we look back and begin to assess the meaning of what has passed. Such a time has now come for me.

Three years ago my husband and I put our lesson plans away in the drawers, placed the last books on the shelf, and turned over to someone else the keys to the Student Center in Tokyo, Japan. For us an era had ended. Thirty years of living and working as Lutheran missionaries in Japan were over. Japan has been home to us and our four daughters, and today the Japanese are among our dearest friends. The beginning of our acquaintance, however, was not as friends but as captive and captor during World War II in the Philippine Islands.

The war affected all who lived through it, but in a special way it left indelible marks on the 500 of us civilians who were confined in Baguio Internment Camp. For 40 years I have used bits and pieces of the experience as bedtime stories for our children and often as illustrations in speeches and Bible studies. Now at the urging of many friends and of my family, I am gathering up the pieces.

The impact of those three years came back vividly in 1980, when I revisited Old Bilibid Prison in Manila. The chief of police let me wander freely through the cell blocks, the courtyard, and the concrete building where we had slept. Emotions and memories long lying dormant overwhelmed me. We had done a heap of living within those stone walls. I stood on the parapet of the second story and could see clearly the Far Eastern University from which the Japanese had opened fire on the advancing army of General MacArthur on the evening of February 4, 1945. I felt an inner conviction: "This story must be told."

The result is this legacy of 500 people who during World War II became the unwilling guests of the Imperial Japanese Army in the Philippine Islands. From December 1941 to February 1945, these 500—old and young, rich and poor, high and low, pious and irreligious—squeezed into stark barracks and shared food, work, and leisure. The experiment in chaotic communal living has left lifetime impressions on each of us who shared the experience.

Names and details are beginning to fade, and the journal which may have kept them alive in my mind was lost in an overturned truck somewhere on a mountain road in northern Luzon. However, there are names and personalities that can never be forgotten. Their names will appear on this manuscript, while some other names are fictitious. Locked up in my heart and memory are the group of rugged individuals who comprised our Lutheran family. Let me introduce them: a Christian businessman, Irwin Lerberg; his effervescent wife, Esther; their son Charles, a high-school boy; Carroll and Mary Hinderlie, whose faith and good humor never failed even in serious illness and suffering; Herbert Loddigs, whose active mind was producing new theories by the minute; his wife Edna, a quiet girl with deep resources of courage and talent; Herman and Ruth Larson, honeymooners whose desire for privacy was always

doomed to frustration. Then the single women: Ruth Joth-
en, a pretty, sensitive nurse; Gladys Anderson and Ina Heg-
gum, also nurses; Ruth Gilbertson, who had been a teacher
in China; Dorothy Ekstrand; and Esther Olson, my bunk-
mate, with whom I shared a rich prayer life and for a time
a comb and even a toothbrush.

What I want to share is not a tale of suffering and dep-
rivation. In a sense we lived a sheltered life in Baguio Internment Camp, where we were merely marking time and
bent on survival. We were separated from the agonies of
war that were the everyday reality of the Americans at
home—the personal sacrifices for the war effort, the news
of tragic defeats, and the daily lists of casualties. Nor can
our experiences be compared to the sacrifices and suffering
of our men on the battlefields.

This is not a record of events, for there were few days
which stand out as eventful. In fact, the only chronology
that is important is that we were captured in Baguio, Philippines, by the Japanese on December 27, 1941. We were
held in Camp John Hay, a rest camp for U.S. military in
Baguio, from December 29, 1941, until May 1942. Then
we were moved to Camp Holmes, a Filipino constabulary
in Baguio, where we remained from May 1942 until December 27, 1944. Finally we were moved to Old Bilibid
Prison in Manila, where we stayed until our release in February 1945.

The first three chapters of this narrative deal with the
events that brought us under the shadow of the Rising Sun.
This is followed by a fictitious account of a typical day in
each of the camps where we were held captive and with an
account of various aspects of our communal living. The chronology resumes again in Chapter 14 with our entry into Old
Bilibid Prison from which we were finally released on February 4, 1945.

During the three years of internment, our life went on
with monotonous sameness; each day was very much like
any other day. There were hungry times, as well as periods

when food was more plentiful. There were times of tension and also relaxed periods when life was enjoyable.

As I look back at those events after a span of 40 years, I recall the education of children, the care of babies, our efforts to live above monotony and boredom—our efforts to survive. The focus of this narrative is the impact that this interlude of three years during World War II had on 500 people who were confined to a life behind barbed wire, their lives out of their own control and lacking any realistic hope of a life beyond. Yet most survived.

In T. S. Eliot's play, *The Family Reunion*, Harry, who has just returned from years of roving about the earth, is trying to make his family understand what has been happening in his life during his wanderings. They cannot understand, for they have lived in exactly the same mold all these years and nothing has happened in their lives.

Harry speaks:

All that I could hope to make you understand
Is only events: not what has happened.
And people to whom nothing has ever happened
Cannot understand the importance of events . . . .
Of the past you can only see what is past,
Not what is always present. That is what matters.

The events of Baguio Internment Camp are not important. What happened in our lives and what continues to bring meaning in the present—that is worth remembering.

1

Detour
to the Philippines

I grew up in the small town of Erskine in northern Minnesota with a population of about 500. We had no radio or TV, very few books, and only a shabby movie theater, which I was forbidden to enter. We made our own entertainment, swimming in the summer and skating all winter. Our one window to the outside world was the tawdry carnival that appeared every summer. I remember how I became almost ill with excitement when I saw those carnival trucks and heard the calliope on the merry-go-round. I was mesmerized by the fat lady, the man who swallowed swords, and the freaks who appeared outside the sideshow tents. These people came and went from an unknown world beyond our little humdrum village.

A more wholesome influence was that of some excellent high-school teachers who introduced us to the world of good books and in many ways raised our cultural level. Through their well-selected books, we took exciting journeys into the past, and new worlds were opened to us.

We were also given an exciting view of distant lands and strange cultures by the missionaries who visited in our home every year. We heard of foot binding in China, child marriages in India, and adventures with wild animals in Africa. Since my home was very mission centered, world missions became part of my life plans when as a high-school student I committed myself to Christ.

Thus, on October 5, 1940, along with nine other Lutheran missionaries, I set out for China aboard the *S.S. President Coolidge.* Soon after embarking, warnings came from the State Department that we could not enter China because of the worsening conditions there. Our mission board, therefore, directed us to go to the Philippine Islands to study Chinese and wait for conditions to change so that we could go on to China to take up our mission work there.

The voyage to the Philippines was a series of misfortunes. During the first night at sea a Chinese passenger was murdered. On the third day a sailor fell from a ladder and broke his neck. A few days later we encountered a typhoon that left 70 passengers wounded, some seriously.

Despite the ill-fated voyage, we arrived in the Philippines on October 29, 1940—10 young people full of hope and enthusiasm. We were all optimistic about our ability to master the Chinese language and harbored a strong conviction that the situation in China would improve with our coming. We soon realized that in hot, humid Manila studies would lag, so we gladly accepted an offer to rent some Presbyterian mission cottages in the city of Baguio in the mountain province of Luzon.

There we opened a school of the Chinese language—10 eager students, but no books and no teachers. As a group we were prone to act on impulse. Carroll Hinderlie promptly recruited a woman missionary from Hunan, China, to be our teacher. She was a nice woman with good intentions, but, unfortunately, she spoke the Hunan dialect whose tones differed radically from the Peking dialect, which we were setting out to learn. On the first day of our school, in a flurry of hit-and-miss pedagogy, we floundered on "Jesus Loves Me" and a lesson in brush writing!

At the close of that session we called an emergency meeting and decided we must have another teacher. A day or two later, Herb Loddigs went out for a walk and returned with a rambunctious woman from Canton, China, who was living in Baguio. Unfortunately, she spoke Chinese with seven or nine tones. Her attitude toward our books, which had arrived from Peking, was condescending, for they taught only four tones. A few days later we recruited a third teacher, a gentle woman from Shanghai, who spoke with a dialect of only five tones. There was considerable confusion of tones until Herb, who had been reading a book about the Chinese language, made a dogmatic pronouncement that Chinese was really atonal, so we could ignore the tones! Our Cantonese teacher worked on the premise that if we spoke loudly and fast enough, the tones would somehow fall into place. So we proceeded, and as far as I know, Herb is still shouting atonal Chinese!

A few months later, when the language school from Peking evacuated to Baguio, the genteel Peking teachers were dumbfounded on hearing our loud atonal Chinese. We decided that if we ever did get into China, we had better all go to the same community and teach the nationals our brand of Chinese before we attempted to evangelize them!

Thus the late months of 1941 rolled by. We were completely submerged in language study, quite unaware of the world so soon to collapse about us. There were surely signs and rumors of impending conflict. However, in October 1941 Francis B. Sayers, the U.S. High Commissioner to the Philippines, met with us and assured us that we should remain where we were and cause no panic by sudden exodus. "The United States will take care of her nationals. Have you not seen Corregidor? No enemy can pass that barrier."

And so we settled down to language study until we were rudely aroused from our quiet academic life by an attack from Japanese bombers over the city of Baguio. News of the disaster at Pearl Harbor reached some of us simultaneously with that first bombing raid. That was December 7 (December 8 in the Philippines), 1941, and that is where this story really begins.

2

Surrender to Uncertainty

By the summer of 1941 the fear of imminent war between the United States and Japan had been growing. We knew war was coming, but we refused to really believe it. We seemed to think that if life went on as usual, somehow the spectre of war would disappear or at least recede into a distant future. We blinded our eyes to the preparations that the large Japanese community in the Philippines were making.

Late in December a Presbyterian couple and Ruth Jothun and I had taken a trip into the Bontoc mountains north of Baguio. All through those isolated regions we had noted small Japanese *tiendas* (stands) stocked with only a few hands of bananas and very few pineapples and coconuts. Obviously, business was not their motive for being there. After the invasion it was discovered that the Japanese in the Philippines had been making very detailed maps of the mountain province. How different had been American preparation for war. When the U.S. forces in Baguio withdrew into the mountains, they had to borrow a Socony road map from a civilian in Baguio.

People from the gold mines were surprised to find that a carpenter who had been working at the mines near Baguio for many years was not only the first commandant of our camp but also one of the highest-ranking officers in the mountain province.

The sudden attack on Pearl Harbor and on the Philippines came as a complete surprise to many of us. We students of Chinese were playing ostrich, our heads buried in language books. On December 8 we were cramming for final exams at school. Oblivious of the catastrophe closing in on us, I was sauntering down Session Road memorizing Chinese proverbs when I met Herb, who asked, "Have you heard that Pearl Harbor has been bombed?"

Barely had the shock of that news penetrated when we heard planes overhead—17 planes, their silver wings gleaming in the bright morning sun. Not yet knowing the significance of that silver, we joined the Filipinos pouring out of stores and places of business and began waving our arms and cheering—until the bombs began to drop! Those were Japanese planes! We weren't to see an American plane again for more than three years.

The lovely city of Baguio, tucked in among the towering pines of the Luzon mountains, was totally unprepared for war. There was no public air-raid shelter in the town. Complete blackout was ordered, and a singing, yodeling city became dark and quiet. Rumors of strafings, invasion, and bombings ran wild. How should we prepare? Some packed their belongings and fled to the plains, seeking safety in the big city; others fled to the mountains. Some of us chose to stay in our homes—to wait and see.

A crisis like that quickly changes people. Some who ordinarily were calm became jittery, while others, who had seemed timid and weak, proved to have great inner stores of courage and unselfishness. Still others, who had had impeccable manners, shoved and pushed on their way to the air-raid shelter. Our Polish neighbors, who lived next door to us on the third story of an apartment house, became very friendly. We all needed one another. Whenever the air-raid alarm sounded, Mrs. Stlokawski, a very obese lady, would quickly don a beautiful fur coat and, clutching a large framed picture of the Virgin Mary, would struggle down the stairs to the air-raid shelter, often obstructing the traffic. All during the raid, she prayed loudly and fervently, but as soon as the raid was over, she would shed her fur coat, the picture of the Virgin Mary, and her piety—until the next time.

The three weeks between Pearl Harbor and Christmas 1941, were a strange interlude. We made some half-hearted preparations for Christmas. Emergency bags were packed and repacked nearly every day, because we were uncertain what to prepare for. We all took first-aid lessons. Wild rumors circulated, but really reliable news was scarce. The merchants in town boarded up their stores and stashed away their supplies. The men at the big Japanese bazaar across the street from our apartment house must have been having a good laugh, for when the Japanese occupied Baguio we found that the clerks in that store were all officers in the Japanese army.

During the day when the sun was shining we foolishly hoped that our U.S. troops would soon reverse the trend of the war. We did not know the whole truth of the debacle at Pearl Harbor and Clarke Field. Every day truckloads of young Filipinos were being rushed to the front. As they passed, they made the sign of victory. Every day little clusters of people gathered on the Baguio streets to discuss rumors and a possible course of action for us civilians. Should we hurry to the plains for protection in Manila, or should we flee to the mountains?

On the radio we heard that the Japanese were besieging Hong Kong. That city, like Corregidor, was an impregnable fortress and would surely stand, we thought. Then we heard that Hong Kong was without water. Without water a city could not live, and Hong Kong promptly fell. Hopes really plummeted when news came that Manila was under siege.

On Christmas Eve 1941, Baguio was in panic. Rumor was that Japanese troops were on their way up the mountain and would soon enter the city. Early in the day expatriates began gathering at the Bishop Brent School, an Anglican boarding school, hoping for safety in numbers. Ruth, the Lerberg family, and I had stayed at our apartment until early evening, but then we, too, went out to the school. We were thankful we had not gone earlier, for the place was bedlam. Children and adults milled about; all were frightened, and some were crying. People sat crowded together on the floor. One woman who had seemed very upper class sat under a table, sucking her thumb. The toilets were overflowing. We were told that the Japanese army would arrive in Baguio during the night. We all slept—or rather tried to sleep—stretched out on the floor with our clothes on.

Toward dawn I whispered to Ruth, "Let's go home." It was Christmas morning, and we thought of our unopened Christmas gifts, the shelves of food, and, most of all, the peace and quiet of home. Knowing there would be opposition, we stealthily gathered up our belongings and ran through the woods to Baguio. In the woods we picked up a fir tree that someone had cut, evidently for a Christmas tree. Whoever it was had perhaps been startled by an air raid. We reached our apartment house, dragging the tree, just as our cook and his wife arrived, carrying a live chicken. We all began preparing for a Christmas party. We set up the tree and trimmed it. By the time dinner was ready, other missionaries had returned from Brent School. It was a sentimental dinner, for we all knew that feasting would soon come to an end.

In the afternoon Pastor Subido of the Baguio Church called and asked if I would dare go with him to City Camp, where we had been having Bible classes on Sunday afternoons. The Japanese army was expected to arrive at any time, and City Camp was several miles from the city, but I was eager to see the people again and to bring them the goodies we had prepared for the Christmas party, so I consented.

We started off on foot with our Christmas parcels, but when we came to City Camp we found the place completely deserted. There was not even a chicken in the place. We were about to return when a boy came running across the hills. "We're all in the caves. Please come!"

So we walked over some hills to a mountainside where there were several large caves. There the people of City Camp had made themselves as comfortable as possible while awaiting the arrival of the enemy. We visited a while, enjoyed the cookies, sang some Christmas carols, read the Christmas gospel, prayed, and then hurried back to Baguio. We arrived home just as darkness was setting in. That service in the cave with Filipino friends remains a precious Christmas memory.

The next night we were awakened by a great deal of activity and clamor on the street just below our third-floor balcony. No, the invading army had not arrived. These were American soldiers who had been vacationing at Camp John Hay. They apparently were withdrawing to some place in the mountains, but no one seemed to be sure where to go. A young English woman, a mother of three small children, put on her bathrobe and stood at the intersection, directing the U.S. jeeps to where the military were reported to be assembling. During the ensuing three years, we often chided her for having directed the retreat of the American army!

The next morning a group of civilians was standing on the sidewalk discussing what we should do when a jeep drew up to the curb and an American officer got out. "Say, where is my army?" he asked the bystanders.

"Judging by what happened last night, they must have gone up to Lusud," someone said.

"Well, I guess I'd better go too," he replied. Then he turned to us. "Say, this puts you in a pretty bad spot. Well, try to make the best of it." That was the last we saw of the American military for three years.

The morning the military left, the American flag was lowered at city hall. Now there was nothing left to do but wait and pray. A group of Baguio citizens had gone down the mountain, hoping to meet the Japanese officials and negotiate for the safety of Baguio and to assure them that it was an open city. The next morning those operating the telephone exchange reported that communication with Manila had broken off; only Japanese voices could be heard at the switchboard. We were now truly under a new order.

About 7:00 P.M., December 27, the first trucks of Japanese soldiers arrived in Baguio with much shouting and rejoicing. Peeking through our blackout curtains we could see the Rising Sun flags on the trucks. Now we were indeed at the mercy of the Imperial Japanese Army. We heard the scraping of boots and the gutteral voices that were soon to become so familiar. All night in the hotel nearby came the sounds of celebrating and carousing, punctuated occasionally by a single shot.

We read Psalm 91:

He who dwells in the shelter of the Most High
will rest in the shadow of the Almighty.
I will say of the Lord, "he is my refuge
   and my fortress,
my God in whom I trust."
Surely he will save you . . . .
He will cover you with his feathers,
and under his wings you will find refuge.

We prayed and then went to bed—with our clothes on. I had expected to lie awake worrying, but I promptly fell asleep and did not awaken until morning, Sunday, December 28.

3

Life under
the Rising Sun
Begins

We awakened that Sunday morning, December 28, feeling that life would never be the same again. We dared not open our curtains, but did risk a quick peek once in a while, which revealed only a few soldiers with fixed bayonets patroling the streets. We had no radio, so we did not know what was happening. We repacked our emergency bags and waited.

About 5:30 in the afternoon a Filipino boy who had been in my Bible class came to our door, very agitated. He said that he had just heard on the radio that all Americans must report to the city hall by 6:00 or they would be killed. So we women, with only our purses in hand, set off in haste for the city hall. As soon as we set foot on the sidewalk a Japanese soldier sprang out from somewhere and stopped us. "Who are you? Are you Americans?"

"Yes, we are Americans," we answered.

We were immediately put on trucks and taken to Brent School, where the enemy aliens were being held. The place was extremely crowded, and more and more people were being brought in. Most of them were already hungry and all were afraid. The night before, when the Japanese had arrived and taken charge of the camp, the commandant had declared, "You Americans are merciful, but we Japanese do not know mercy. If anyone attempts to escape, he will be killed. If anyone does escape, we will choose 10 of you at random, and you will be shot. You will be here for a hundred years, so try to make your lives as serene as possible."

Those who had already been in the camp a day showed signs of weariness and anxiety. Some were weeping openly. There were three of us single women who had come in together. We had come without our emergency bags, our bedrolls—with nothing. And we were to make ourselves serene for a hundred years!

In every place we were directed to sleep for the night someone screamed, "No room! We're already all cramped together." Finally an official directed us to the administration building of the school. That building, we found, was being occupied by the Japanese soldiers. We were taken to a classroom bare of any furnishing except for a set of large maps. We had no change of clothes, no toilet articles, no bedding. We tore the maps off the rack to use for bed mats. But we soon found that we had a good friend in town. Miss Wu, our teacher from Shanghai, came later in the evening in a taxi with our emergency bags and our bedrolls. What persuasion or bribery that gentle little woman had resorted to, we shall never know, for she was killed in a bombing raid in the early months of the war.

Late that first evening we heard a commotion in the corridor outside our room, and in came a petite elderly woman wearing a wide garden hat and looking as if she had just come from a garden party. Tossing a bag in the corner she said, "Here I am for goodness knows how long, and all I have in that bag are five formal dresses that my maids packed. The Japanese even took my potty from me. I simply have to have it and, if I don't get it, they will probably use it for a casserole." She was so desperate to retrieve her potty that she defied the whole Japanese army and succeeded.

We were grateful for the potty that night, for earlier in the evening two of us had ventured out to the toilet. When we arrived, accompanied by a soldier prodding us in the back with his bayonet, we found we were sharing the facility with Japanese officers. We resolved that even if it were a hundred years, we would not go out there again.

We stood about uncertainly, wondering whether we should risk lying down on the floor to get some sleep. A young guard patrolling our corridor stopped to speak to one of the girls. In halting English he said, "Do not be afraid, mom. I shall guard you very dearly." And indeed he did guard us dearly; every 15 to 20 minutes he entered the room, flashed a light in each of our faces, and went out, scraping his feet.

Morning came, and we wondered what was happening in the camp. Later, we got a summons to join the others. There had been no breakfast, but there were rumors that our camp cook was preparing a bowl of soup for each of us at noon. Word also came from the commandant that we had to make ready to move to another camp. We could take with us only what we could carry.

It was interesting to see what each of us valued most, and as the long hot march progressed, our sense of values changed greatly. One man offered in vain to trade a new Arrow shirt for a half tin of water. A woman walking beside me had brought a complete set of sterling silver flatware. Exhausted from carrying the heavy burden, she tossed the whole bag of silverware into the roadside ditch, saying, "Of what use is the silver when I'm dying for a drink of water?"

Dusk had already fallen when we reached our new home—Camp John Hay—a plush American military rest camp. But we were put in the crude, empty barracks that the Filipino constabulary had occupied. Most of us were in the main barrack, one large room with an open doorway dividing the two sections. It was late when we arrived, and we were exhausted from the 10-mile march. We welcomed the cup of tea and the cracker we were given. Then everyone scurried about to provide a place on the floor for sleeping.

My two five-foot friends, Esther Olson and Gladys Anderson, had made a bed for the three of us, but when I tried to get my 5'8" frame into it, I found the bed they had made was far too short. We slept in our clothes and hardly dared stir when the guards came in at frequent intervals. But Imperial Japanese Army or not, I had to stretch my legs. Crash! Down came a pile of baggage and whatnots on top of a Swedish man who was bedded down with his Filipino family. A few embarrassed apologies and we settled down again. Sometime during the night my cramped legs rebelled, but this time I extended in the other direction and my head landed on the stomach of an English woman. "Tomorrow," I vowed, "I'm making our bed, and we'll maneuver until we get enough leg room."

There were many little dramas that first night at Camp John Hay. One man woke up in the morning to find he couldn't move his arm. Discovering the cause, he leaned over to the strange woman sleeping next to him and said, "Lady, I'm sorry, but I'm afraid you have pinned your mosquito net to my pajamas."

How did 500 Westerners, mostly Americans, act in such a situation? We began to organize committees, of course—committees for sanitation, for laundry, for food preparation, for garbage, and for recreation. There was considerable vying for leadership.

All the food supplies brought in were put into the common mess hall. Some had brought in great supplies, some very little, and some none at all. The "haves" naturally resented having to live on the same meager rations as the "have-nots." There was some withholding of private supplies. One day a woman who, I'm sure, had seldom raised her voice, banged a young pregnant woman on the head with a washboard because she was munching crackers. She screamed, "You have no business sitting there eating when we are starving!" The executive committee had to come in and settle the fracas and many others like it.

The first three days water was scarce. Before they had retreated, the American army had sabotaged the water system. Ironically, it was we American civilians who were to occupy these barracks without water. We were allowed only one-half cup a day, except for a nursing mother who had a special permit for one whole cup a day. Soon the water mains were repaired, and the supply of water was adequate.

The plumbing system, however, had been damaged and took much longer to restore. Therefore, a privy committee became a priority. The privy had to be built according to Japanese specifications—a long trough with boards along each side for a sort of foothold; it took us a while to understand the arrangement. A low fence or wall gave us a semblance of privacy. It was really quite a chummy arrangement. Mike, the self-appointed town crier, gave the whole project a carnival atmosphere when he banged on a kettle announcing in a loud voice, "Now three ladies may enter."

Instead of chafing under the inconvenience, most people took it with a sense of humor, and there was much laughter and joking in the waiting line. Traffic was light for several days, because we were all suffering from constipation. That report reached the camp doctors, and generous doses of castor oil were administered. This caused quite a traffic jam for a while, and good humor sometimes gave way to outbursts of temper.

When the supply of toilet paper dwindled, another committee was formed to dispense the scarce commodity. The aristocratic wife of a Manila banker lent to this demeaning task a touch of elegance. She would stand at the door of the privy, wearing a lovely lavender gown with lavender chiffon scarf around her silver hair, saying very graciously, "One sheet or two?" She took the job seriously, and if one person requested two sheets too often, she would challenge the request and there would be a whispered consultation.

About a year later, the supply of toilet paper ran out altogether. To cope with this crisis, we subscribed to the *Manila Tribune*, a Japanese propaganda sheet, but sometime during the Camp Holmes days that supply also ceased. Resourceful internees, however, coped again. A tree just outside the latrine began to bloom like a prayer tree at a Shinto shrine, with tiny rags tied to the branches. We each knew our own little rag, and another crisis was resolved.

Now it seems funny, and even then we laughed at ourselves. There was still a bright gleam of hope. "When the Americans come back" was the most frequently heard phrase. Those who didn't believe every fantastic rumor that was circulated knew it would be a long haul.

4

A Day in
Camp John Hay

Baguio, tucked in among the pine-covered mountains of northern Luzon, is a famous scenic resort that attracts many world travelers. As one leaves the scorching heat of the plains and begins to circle up and up the Balatoc mountains, suddenly there is a cool breeze, and as palm trees give way to majestic pines, one enters Mountain Province. Soon the city of Baguio is in sight; then, following a winding, upward trail, one comes to beautiful Camp John Hay, which was a rest camp for the U.S. military before World War II and now is a plush country club with golf course, tennis courts, and lush shrubbery.

Many years after the war, in July 1980, as I sat in the rustic country club dining room overlooking the manicured lawns, memory took me back to another Camp John Hay of about 40 years ago. Then we were not in these fine buildings but across the valley in the barracks of the Filipino constabulary. There our heterogeneous community of 500 human beings had begun a three-year experience in communal living.

I closed my eyes and again could almost feel the noise, the confusion, the hunger, and tensions as we groped for ways to make a meaningful life for ourselves within the confines of the barbed wire. In memory I began to relive one of those days at Camp John Hay.

It could be any day between January 1 and March 1942. It is 7:00 A.M., and the rising gong crashes rudely into the slumbers of the few who are still dreaming of pancakes and bacon and eggs.

As usual a woman named Jennie has already been up for two hours. A consuming thirst for alcohol and aching hunger keep her pacing restlessly every day long before the rest of the camp awakens.

At the guardhouse, just outside the barbed-wire fence, the Japanese guards are going through the morning ritual of saluting the Rising Sun flag.

On the open porch, only two or three yards from the guardhouse, another day is beginning for the 20 women for whom the porch has become home. All are sleeping on the floor but in the far corner Lydia, a frail woman of about 50, sleeps on a camp cot. She has been struggling all night with an attack of asthma and is still fighting for breath.

"Jackie, will you please—bring me—my breakfast? I don't think I can get up today."

"Sure! Bacon and eggs or pancakes and syrup?"

"Either one would be really splendid! Here's my coconut shell for the rice."

Jessica, taking the curlers out of her hair says, "Diane, better get to primping. Your husband will soon be going by for roll call."

Diane, pregnant and uncomfortable, pulls herself up from the hard floor, rubbing her aching back. "This floor gets harder every night."

Jessica, who always has a remedy, says, "I've discovered a good way to control hunger pains. Save out one spoon of rice and eat it just before you go to bed. Put a pillow on your tummy to keep it warm, and you'll sleep like a baby, maybe even have some good dreams."

"Who has an extra pillow?" Jackie, a serious girl in her mid-20s, asks wistfully as she rolls up her bedclothes. "I dreamed last night that I was home. It was Saturday afternoon and I could smell bread baking. A door began opening, and I knew mom was going to enter, carrying a pan of biscuits—but then I woke up. I wish that once I could see mom and taste those biscuits."

Jessica calls, "Here's your sweetie, Diane."

The men are filing past the porch on their way to roll call on the tennis court. The sidewalk along the fence and in front of the women's barracks leads to the double tennis court, the only exercise space for the 500 internees.

A tall, blond Norwegian gives a furtive bird call, and Diane hurries to the edge of the porch.

"Good morning. How's your heartburn, darling?" Jack asks.

"It's not any better. I can't sleep. I feel like I'm choking all the time," Diane answers.

"One of the fellows says charcoal will help heartburn, so I burned some rice crust. Here, perhaps it will help."

Jack has lingered too long, and there is a resounding slap on the ears. Their communication for the day is over.

"I wish we could be together. I'll be alone when our baby comes," Diane says.

"The commandant says no more rushing to the Baguio Hospital for babies," someone says.

"That's because Jane's baby wasn't born until two days after they took her in to the hospital."

Irene enters from the main room. "Have you heard? Louise had her baby last night."

"Here?" a voice asks.

"Yes, under the stairs. They curtained off a shelter for her."

"I wonder what will happen to all of us pregnant girls and our babies," Diane asks.

"What a mistake to think that Baguio was a nice quiet place to have a baby. Twenty-three babies! How in the world will we manage?" someone else mutters.

Diane speaks softly, "There will be a way. I believe God will take care of us. But I do wish Jack could be with me when my time comes."

"Well, this is more civilized than men, women, and children sleeping together in one room as we did in the beginning."

"That's what you think," said Susan, coming out on the porch carrying three-year-old Jamie and baby Ellen in a state of half-dress. "How I'd like a husband to give a little help with the children!"

The children hear a familiar bird whistle, and they squeal with delight as their daddy passes by.

"Hi, honey, how're you doing?"

"Fine."

"Daddy, I caught a butterfly and—"

"Great, Jamie. I love you all." And he passes on.

Grandpa Boyd, slightly bent and with halting arthritic gait but with a sparkle in his eyes, yodels, and out comes grandma as prim as if she were ready for a tea party.

"God bless you, Martha. How are you doing? The Lord is good," Grandpa Boyd says.

"Yes, he is, and his loving-kindness endures forever, and I love you," Grandma Boyd answers.

Sophie, chairman of the ladies' section, appears on the porch. Back in country club days, she was the society leader, always immaculately dressed, with the perfect hairdo, graciously presiding over the Thursday music club. Now in housedress and apron, with arms akimbo, she begins giving orders like a drill sergeant. Her day may include settling a dispute about space in the women's barracks, scrubbing out the latrine, giving work orders, prodding lazy people to do their camp duties, and trying to mollify the few who feel martyred in their assigned tasks. She may even cheer up the gullible with a good rumor.

Peter, a middle-aged nondescript man, pauses on the sidewalk, whistles, waits a moment but no one appears. He sighs and goes on to roll call.

Someone calls into the barracks from the porch, "Audrey, Pete is calling you."

Audrey appears, rouged and beribboned as usual. "Oh, he's already gone. Never mind! Let the old goat wait. I saw him making eyes at Vera last night."

The roving eye of her husband is a bit of fiction she perpetrates in an attempt to make her ordinary husband seem more cavalier in the eyes of the other ladies. She needs to raise her own self-esteem, for she lives in a slough of self-pity. Not only has her marriage been a disaster but all her teeth were extracted just before Pearl Harbor. "One hundred years without teeth," she complains. "Well, there isn't much to chew anyway."

While waiting for the breakfast gong, some of the ladies on the porch are having their morning prayer together. They are Pentecostals, Baptists, Lutherans, Episcopalians, Mennonites, and Christian Scientists. They range in age from 25 to very old. In the group is Olga, a sad-faced, gray-haired lady whose constant smile belies a troubled heart. Her love and her faith have always been expressed under the safety umbrella of the church and the prayer meeting. Love for lost souls, of which she has sung with deep and tender emotion, takes on a different complexion when she must sleep, shower, eat, and work with people of all kinds. It has also been disturbing to her to find that some who profess to have no faith in God have deep wells of inner strength and can cope happily with the most trying situations.

Also in the group is Jessica, a tall, rawboned girl from Wyoming who has come to the Philippines as a Mennonite missionary. In ordinary circumstances she may have been considered plain, but in the prison camp she is not only respected because of her boundless energy and willingness to serve, but her spontaneous humor and droll remarks have endeared her to all.

Morning prayer is cut short by the clang of the breakfast gong. After a breakfast of rice with a spoon of brown sugar and a cup of coffee, if there is some, all tidy up their places in the barracks and go off to perform their camp duties. Of course, there is the bridge-playing gang who will shirk as long as they can.

Behind the barracks are two long tables where the vegetable and rice details are at work, the latter picking weevils and chaff from the rice. The more delicate internees are assigned to this task. Conversation never lags.

"Monica, how's your baby?"

"His stool specimen this morning was normal."

"Mine has been normal for three days."

"I haven't had a b.m. yet today, so I don't know if I can go back to regular food yet."

Jessica, bored with the mundane talk, interposes an uncheery note of her own, "I wonder if they're decorating our graves at home this Memorial Day." There is momentary laughter, but soon minds are back on the mundane.

"My head aches. Didn't sleep a wink last night. Eleanor's snoring is driving me crazy."

"We should do as the men say they did. Harry's snoring was just too much so last night they picked up his bed and carried him outdoors. He was surprised to wake up and find himself sleeping under the stars. He says he'll sleep outside until the rainy season if the guards let him."

"I'm so hungry I could eat this raw rice, and the weevils should be good protein."

"I hear we have vegetable stew with meat in it for supper."

"That makes me sick! When we have good vegetables they mess it up by cooking meat with it. I don't eat meat."

"I'll tell you what. I'll sit beside you and demeat your stew."

At the vegetable table we might hear this conversation:

"Well, the Js can't deprive us of beautiful weather."

"Nor our Filipino squat. It helps when there are no chairs."

"I hear there will be comingling Sunday night. We can actually walk arm in arm with our husbands on the tennis court for a whole hour."

"This conversing with your husband over a 10-foot barrier is no good—no privacy for even a good quarrel."

"Don't complain," Jessica grumbles. "Be thankful you have a husband to walk with even for one hour. We single girls envy you as we watch the parade from the porch. Trouble is, you're all so healthy, there isn't a chance for one of us! Well, maybe I'll just borrow a husband for Sunday night."

"No chance! You have to have a marriage license to join that promenade. Our guards are very moral."

"What was all the commotion at the guardhouse last night?"

"I suppose the guards were drunk again."

"Haven't you read the signs they've put up?"

"No, what?"

"They say Corregidor has fallen and Bataan has surrendered."

"I don't believe it! Corregidor—that pile of rock?"

"I heard a good rumor this morning. U.S. troops are coming in from the north and joining the Filipino guerrillas. It won't be long!"

"Don't believe it! Jack says we'll be here for five years at least."

"I don't think I can stand another five years of this life; I feel like a monkey in a zoo when they bring the school children out to peek through the fence at us."

"That doesn't bother me as much as to see our cameras being used by the Japanese soldiers. One man yesterday had three of our cameras slung over his shoulder."

"Yes, and he had three of our wrist watches on one arm."

"You can imagine how I felt when I saw our new Cadillac on the parade ground yesterday."

"Have they heard anything from the missionaries that were taken to police headquarters?"

"Nothing. It will soon be a month since they were taken out."

"We're having a day and night prayer vigil for the three men; that really helps me to bear the uncertainty," says Marian, the sweet blonde wife of Rufus, one of the men detained.

Sophie strides in. "Girls, hurry with the vegetables. Word has come that a general is coming at noon for inspection of the camp. There will also be inspection of all our baggage."

This last announcement sends everyone into action. One woman in the washroom tries to hide a diamond in her hair. Another writes the numbers of her traveler's checks on the wall of the barracks. A third tries to swallow two precious gems. (Later it took a generous dose of castor oil to restore her jewels!)

At noon the tempo of the camp slows down. The vegetable and rice tables are deserted. The cook and his crew in the kitchen are beginning preparations for the evening meal, which will be served at 4:00.

Many people lie listlessly on the floor. The card players are at the game again. On the tennis court, groups of children listen to women telling stories.

The camp comes alive when the supper gong rings. The women eat first, hurrying to make way for the hungry men. For an hour or two there is lively conversation. There may even be a women's volleyball game, followed by a men's game. Sexes are definitely segregated. For one hour husbands and wives can be on the tennis court together, but there is a 10-foot barrier between sexes, so conversations are hardly satisfying. Children run back and forth between them delivering messages, giving some sense of privacy. A gong rings, and all go back to the barracks.

This is the loneliest time of day, with only the long dark night to look forward to. The few books people brought with them into camp are passed around. On one mat sits a group of ladies, heads close together, listening to a reading from Selma Lagerlöf's *The Ring*. On another mat is a group engaged in Bible study. A few ladies are busy knitting.

This is the hour when rumor mongers swing into action. Women, with heads close together, drink in the incredible stories: "The Japanese are beginning to retreat. There's been a big landing at Leyte. The guerrillas will reinforce them. By the Fourth of July we should be out." It's strange how we like to hear what we want to hear even when we know it isn't true.

At 9:30 there is a steady procession to the privy and washroom. There we stand at the long wash table, our skinny bodies undressed and unadorned. In spite of desperate furtive efforts, wigs, hair dye, glass eyes, and false teeth become exposed to the community.

At 10:00 P.M. lights are turned out. A few sleep soundly. Some toss restlessly on their hard mats. Mothers with babies sleep lightly, for the waking cry of their babies must not disturb others, especially those who are intolerant of small children or the guards who have said, "No crying at night." The exhausted mothers gratefully hand over crying babies to friends who pace with the infants outside the barracks.

The quiet is broken at intervals when a guard passes through the barracks, scraping his feet. One more day to mark off on our calendars.

5

A Day in Camp Holmes

From May 1942, until late December 1944, we were at Camp Holmes, formerly occupied by the Filipino constabulary. The camp was on a plateau with pine-covered mountains in the background, and in the foreground a magnificent view of rice terraces leading like a green staircase to the China Sea, which was faintly visible on a clear day. The gorgeous scenery, the brilliant sunsets, and the fine weather contributed to the physical and mental health of the camp.

At Camp Holmes, 1943 was a relatively pleasant time. Most people had adjusted to camp life. During that year money and food filtered in to individuals. The meals in the mess hall improved; our clever cook made the most of what he had to work with. A camp store was opened, where those who had money could buy limited supplies. There was a relaxed atmosphere, for our commandant, Mr. Tomibe, was always a kind gentleman.

But then came the rainy season. From July until the end of September water poured down and, during the typhoons, it seemed to ooze up from the ground. All our clothes were damp and musty, and there was no place to dry them. We were continually wiping mold off our shoes and books and walls.

On a rainy July 14, 1943, the internees at Camp Holmes awaken to begin their 565th day in captivity. At the Baby House, a small green cottage poised at the edge of a deep valley bordered by green rice terraces, 16 mothers and young babies are crowded together in three tiny rooms. These are the infants that were born shortly before or during our incarceration. There is no need for a rising bell at the Baby House, for those little one-year-olds are eager at dawn to begin another day.

They are living in what their jaded mothers would call chaos. The mothers sleep on beds hanging from the ceiling. Under each bed is a makeshift crib. Four mothers and babies occupy the first room and six and five live in the others. Two of the rooms open up into a tiny kitchen, with a wooden table and a small wood-burning stove as the only furnishings. The fathers have put up some shelves along the wall. Someone is trying to get a fire started with green, damp wood. Soon the house fills with smoke. There is always the musty smell of damp clothes drying and the acrid smell of urine, for soap is scarce and diapers don't get entirely clean. There is a network of ropes in the kitchen for drying diapers and clothes. The mothers have worked out a rotation system so, in turn, each can occupy the front line where things dry more quickly. No longer are there lines of white diapers; even the best are yellow and gray. As diapers have worn thin, resourceful mothers have transformed old dresses and gowns into diapers.

"Mommie, mommie," calls baby Jamie. Nora reluctantly leaves her dream of bacon and eggs and awakens quickly. She knows well that Jamie's gentle "mommie" will soon be a scream, and for the sake of public relations, it's wise to squelch that first call.

"Hush, Jamie. Mommie's here," she answers softly.

She puts a dry diaper on him, leaves some toys in the crib, and shuffles out to the kitchen. There, as always, a row of bottles filled with a green liquid have been prepared by camp workers. When Jamie sees his bottle of bean milk, he squeals with delight.

Soon four other heads hang over their cribs, and an animated conversation of "Ga-ga-da-du" ensues.

Jane leans over the edge of her bed. "Nora, I wonder what concept of the world our children will have."

"Is there really a world outside where families live in houses, drink real milk, and have three meals a day?" Nora asks.

"We'd better hurry up topside or there will be only one meal for us today," Jane replies.

Nora and Jane don what rain gear they own and begin sloshing through the mud to the dining hall at the top of the hill.

As they struggle up the stairs, they meet Jake and Ben, who are bringing breakfast to their wives at the Baby House.

"How did the Baby House stand the typhoon last night?" Jake asks.

"There were a few leaks. I put a pan on my bed to catch the worst of it," Nora replies.

"I hope you remembered the pan."

" 'Fraid I didn't. One reason why I decided to eat topside—I kicked the pan over in my sleep and it landed on Chuck's crib. His mom's not talking to me today."

Jessica comes out of the mess hall. "Hi, great menu at the Ritz today. Rice with a spoon of sugar and 'Submarine 3' (coffee grounds boiled for the fourth time)."

"Wish I could curl up and sleep until the end of the rainy season," Nora says as she enters the mess hall.

Jessica's husband appears, carrying a tin of rice.

"Jessica, I'll watch the baby if you'll cook us a good dinner. I bought some onions, sweet potatoes, and papaya at the store last night. Let's have fried rice. We have enough, don't we?"

"Yes, with what I saved from my ration last night and this morning there's plenty. There's enough cornmeal left for a batch of corn muffins."

Jessica slips and slides happily down to the Baby House to gather up ingredients and utensils. She has to stop at the hospital for stomach pills. The hospital is a two-story structure, a few paces from the Baby House, and poised on the same ledge overlooking the lush rice terraces below.

She approaches the American doctor on duty and asks, "May I have some stomach pills?"

The doctor, with a wry smile, says, "Is this for a single or double recipe?" (These soda pills were the only medications the Japanese provided. We used them for baking. I'm sure the Japanese wondered why we seemed to have so much trouble with our digestion!)

Jessica says thanks for the stomach pills and hurries topside. She passes through the women's barracks, where early morning confusion prevails. Some are dressing; some are making their beds; one woman is trying to mix some kind of casserole with her breakfast rice; a mother and daughter are having a lively debate about how to prepare their two 25-peso eggs. Wet clothes and bedding are draped from bunks and beds.

Jessica goes down a few steps to a small building that has become a community kitchen.

She thought she was going to avoid the rush, but already several irate women are moving pots and pans about on a refractory stove that only emits clouds of smoke.

"Why doesn't someone do something about this stove? It never seems to work."

"I never do any cooking here but, of course, here I am today and the stove isn't even warm!"

"Mrs. Barclay has already made her bacon and eggs. Where do some people get all that food?"

Jessica assesses the situation, goes out, and crawls under the barracks to pick up some dry kindling wood. She returns, replenishes the fire, adjusts the draft, and soon there is a bright fire and a hot stove. The women move in with their pots and are soon joined by a dozen or more other women. Their voices fill the room.

"I never use the stove, but when I do come, the same people are always hogging the space."

"Careful! Don't upset my kettle."

"Listen, I was here first; my kettle goes to the front of the stove."

"I dreamed I was eating steak and kidney pie last night."

"Will the rain never stop? There's no place to dry our clothes."

"I dry them at my bunk but Mrs. Anthony says it's making her asthma worse."

"What do I smell? Something's burning!"

"Oh, it's Bet's pineapple jam. I promised to watch it. Who pushed it to the front?"

"There goes the vegetable gong! To the work table."

"I wish I had a conscience like some of these people."

"I'd like to snuggle into bed with a good book and a cheese sandwich."

"I'd like to go to bed for the duration."

"How long will that be?"

"My husband says two or three years."

"Haven't you heard? The U.S. Army has taken Mindanao, and now there is a big landing on Leyte. It won't be long."

The cozy moment is interrupted by Sophie, who calls, "There are a lot of vegetables today. Everybody get to work and stay until the work is done."

The morning passes quickly. Outside work must cease because of heavy rain. Spirits are low and tempers apt to flare. When camp duties are completed, most people wrap themselves in blankets to try to keep warm. After supper, because of the downpour, there is not even the gorgeous sunset or million-dollar view to raise spirits.

In the evening those who are not trying to keep warm and dry in bed gather in the dining hall for games, reading, eating snacks, or just visiting. Some evenings there will be a lecture or a musical program.

At 9:30 P.M. the procession down the hill to the latrine begins. In the barracks women in different stages of undress are brightening a dull hour with conversation.

"I have always dreamed of living in a dormitory," says one gray-haired woman.

Retorts another, climbing into her bunk, "But I'd never dreamed of a dean with a gun."

Soon most are tucked into their bunks, and Jill, ready to turn out the lights, says, "Everybody ready for lights out?"

From down the barracks, "Wake Stella before you turn out the lights."

By agreement the last one in bed is to awaken Stella, a horrendous snorer. She obligingly sits up and waits until everyone seems asleep before she continues her slumbers. What price peace!

6

Escaping Boredom

No place to go, no radio, the supply of interesting books exhausted, and after three years of conversation, not much left to talk about—we fought against boredom. As time wore on and food became scarce, there was not even the anticipation of a good meal to brighten the fellowship. Hungry people living in crowded conditions and doing only menial tasks do not make for a great society. However, most people met our situation with creativity and unbelievably good humor.

It was not at all unusual to hear someone sobbing into a pillow at night. But the next day that same person might be as chipper as anyone. Each of us at some time retreated into a private slough of despondency, but spirits generally were good. Our high spirits enraged the guards. One day a Japanese officer said, "How can you Americans laugh when your countrymen are dying?"

Life was far from unpleasant, largely because of the kind of people with whom we were incarcerated. There were scientists in the camp who invented machines to grind corn and coffee and to roast the coffee beans. They could extract iron from old rusty plowshares for anemic patients. We single women were a bit envious of the ingenious jewelry carved from water buffalo tusks or coconut shells which women received from their artistic husbands. One of the men even made a set of false teeth out of water buffalo bone and aluminum. Too bad the hapless recipient tried them out on a cup of hot coffee! These same scientists concocted a bean milk which no doubt preserved the health of babies, small children, and the weak. A yeast culture was started, which provided much-needed vitamin B.

In addition to the scientists, there was the corps of carpenters and handymen who contributed generously to our happiness and well-being. They made shelves and tables and even beds. In the barracks the only space allotted to us was that occupied by our bedrolls at night. With many small children and everyone messing around with some private cooking project, the congestion became unbearable. To alleviate this, the carpenters hung some of our beds from the ceiling, about eight feet from the floor. If you were lucky enough to be near a window, you could look out at the stars at night and escape into a free world of fantasy.

The hanging beds did help to alleviate some of the bickering in the women's barracks, but there is something about human nature that can't be satisfied if someone else has a better deal. Floor space had been equitably divided, but when one woman discovered that she had only 12 boards when a neighbor had 15, the conflict was bitter and rancorous. After a screaming encounter with the two irate women, the head of the women's division gave up and appealed to the male executives to settle the argument. All the boards were recounted, an equal number assigned to each, and peace was restored—for a while.

The creativity became almost epidemic as resourceful people began to explore the possibilities of a little private oasis for themselves. I would have been satisfied with our spot on the floor under our hanging bed, but it was not so for Esther, my constant companion. She made life for us free of monotony but was sometimes very exasperating. We were the "movingest" people in camp. There was often a noble motive for a move, but it was the overriding urge for change that moved us from one barracks to another, and even for a while to a cubbyhole under the outside stairway. We made a wall a foot from our double-decker bed with pieces of canvas and wooden boxes, which provided shelves that we filled with tin cans, coconut shells, a homemade frying pan—our whole accumulation of household goods.

We took turns sleeping in the upper bunk. During the second week, when I was to occupy the upper bunk, a crisis occurred. During the night, while answering a summons from my bladder, I swung my legs out of bed, and forgetting I was on the upper bunk, began a precarious descent into space. Clutching at the canvas and cupboard, I landed on Esther's bed with a clatter of tin cans and coconut shells. She sat up in bed rubbing her eyes. "Have the Americans come?"

"Yes," I replied. "One American has landed hard, and she's hurting."

We spent the rest of that night under the stars. Esther soon became bored with this arrangement, and our next project was to dig a space under the barrack. Esther and Marian Grey begged and borrowed boards and cardboard for walls. They pounded and planed while I held up the boards, and Marian even got an electric bulb from the guardhouse. We used this earth house only a few times, but the making of it had kept us happily occupied for a long time. However, when a class in architecture was offered in camp and Esther wanted to enroll, I registered a strong veto.

It was interesting to see how people overcame their boredom. Some played cards. Many copied recipes and menus from the one or two cookbooks in camp. There were two or three women's magazines, and their use was scheduled by a committee. In turn, we sat and driveled over the pictures of food. One woman filled reams of paper with house plans. Perhaps she would never own a piece of real estate, but the activity provided a good escape. The library from Camp John Hay had been brought into camp in 1942, so we had a fair collection of books.

During the days of comparative plenty (late 1942 to late 1943), when food packages came in from friends and one could buy supplies at the camp stores, we did much cooking. Imagine a small wood-burning stove with 65 tins and pans of various shapes and sizes piled on top and a stove that refuses to burn because of raw, damp wood. There you have the ingredients for a fracas—as one woman placed her top pans on the bottom and the next woman indignantly reversed the order. Sometimes when the fire was burning brightly and there would be only about 10 containers on the stove, there was good fellowship. We would huddle around that stove, heads close together, warming our hearts with rumors that our heads told us were impossible. I always went to bed happier if I had just heard a good rumor.

At the same time the Japanese tried to break our morale with rumors that Chicago had been bombed, Colorado had been invaded, and Deanna Durbin had died. We figured that these rumors, lies as even they surely knew, would boost their own sagging morale.

The children coped with boredom by playing war games. There was always controversy over who were to be the Americans, because Americans lost and were put in a camp, while the Japanese won, drove big cars, wore many watches, carried cameras, and were on the outside. After the one shipment from the Red Cross arrived, new impetus and style was given to war games, for each boy had received a wool serge suit, the old knickerbocker style. They must have been found in a warehouse from the early 1920s. But to the boys it was high style, especially because they came in two colors. From then on it was a battle between brown Japanese and blue Americans, with little boys running in suits several sizes too large and hitching up the baggy knickerbocker pants.

We had a style show after the Red Cross supplies came. Some modeled Mother Hubbard nighties of pink crepe with a blue border, or blue crepe with a pink border. Some wore the baggy black gym bloomers that must have been resurrected from a turn-of-the-century storehouse.

Almost every woman received a playsuit (a shirt, top, and shorts) from the Red Cross supplies. They were all exactly alike, but the monotony was relieved by the four different colors. We big women had to settle for the plentiful lavender because the small sizes came in the more limited colors of yellow, green, and pink.

Just as we owed our well-being to the scientists and handymen, no less was the morale of the camp maintained and boosted by the many talented people who entertained us with music and drama of great excellence. We had many happy evenings listening to the beautiful singing of Mary Dyer and Marvin Dirks and his choirs. Winnie Smith's dramatic productions were always excellent. The Christmas pageant and chorus, Easter pageant, the music every Sunday, and the caroling early Christmas morning are unforgettable memories. Even I helped the juniors prepare dramatic bits from Shakespeare, Tarkington, and one Christmas, "The Birds' Christmas Carol." At least while we were preparing these plays we forgot we were hungry.

The most exciting, exhilarating experience for anyone was to take a trip outside the fence. It was my poor teeth that gave me such an opportunity. I needed dental work badly and was given permission to go to town on the vegetable truck. Because the Japanese dentist was absent, they took me to a Filipino dentist who had his office on the first floor of the building in which we had been living before taken prisoner. A guard accompanied us to the waiting room but soon left, and I watched from the window as he crossed the street and entered a tavern. I hoped he would stay there a while, and thinking of the soap and toothpaste and other marvelous things in our apartment, I decided to take a chance and go up and loot our apartment. I spread a sheet on the floor and ran from room to room picking up valuables. Our Polish neighbor came with a bottle of whiskey saying, "You need this."

I was standing in the trunk room with my arms full when I heard the scraping of feet on the stairs and a loud voice calling my name. In came the guard, bayonet in hand, muttering angry words I could not understand. Behind him came the wild-eyed dentist waving one of his dental tools. It was clear that I was to go downstairs. I went, feeling the bayonet on my back. I sat down on one side of the waiting room, arms still full, and the guard stood opposite me, all the time muttering angrily.

Just then two Japanese in plain clothes entered, and one of them greeted me pleasantly in English. Knowing I was already in trouble, I plunged into an explanation. I told them how much we needed soaps and supplies and that I had gone up to our apartment to get things.

One said, "We'll go with you." So the three of us went up, and while they watched, I tied up the four corners of the sheet, and they helped me carry it to the dentist's office. In a few minutes they left, and the dentist called me in. His hand was shaking as he said, "Do you know who those two men were?"

"No, I don't," I replied.

"They are the head of the military police in town, and everyone, even the Japanese officers, are afraid of them."

And I had asked them to help me loot my apartment! For many days after, when I saw a military police truck, I feared that I might be summoned.

There was, however, a sequel to this adventure. There had been an incident of some drinking and rowdiness in camp among some members who were able somehow to smuggle liquor into the camp. The guards were determined to find out who possessed liquor and were threatening severe punishment to the offender.

One day while I was in the schoolroom teaching English class, Esther came running in. "Judy, the guards are searching all the barracks for liquor, and they are angry. Where is your bottle of whiskey?"

It was in my bag under the bunk. I hastily dismissed class, and hurried to our barracks, but it was already too late. The guards and the president of our camp were already in our end of the barrack, only two bunks before mine. I stood there in a panic as they ransacked bags, probed under mattresses, and looked into cupboards. Then they came to my bunk. The guard asked, "Who sleeps here?"

"Oh, just a woman missionary."

They looked at each other with a knowing smile and went on without touching anything at my bunk. That was one day I forgot I was hungry.

Such drama was rare. Mostly our energy was drained by the mundane details of life. But there were channels for escape. The happiest people were those who pursued some study. Languages, science, English, and history classes were all available. On starlit nights there was even a lesson in astronomy. We all shared the knowledge and skills we had brought to the camp. I did some tutoring in history and continued to study Chinese, New Testament Greek, and Norwegian.

For some of us, private and group Bible study made time pass meaningfully. Book studies and theological discussions made many evenings special. I cherish the prayer fellowship with fellow Lutherans and often with Baptist and Pentecostal friends.

We became bored only when we were not involved in some project or planning ahead. Although life was mundane we did not have to succumb to boredom.

During late 1942 and in 1943, as Americans who had been hiding in the mountains were brought in, we realized that we had been fortunate to be in the shelter of an internment camp. As each group was brought in, they told their stories of long walks, narrow escapes, and hardships. One family especially tugged at our heartstrings. The Moules came in with four little children; one had been born during their time as fugitives. They had malaria, dysentery, and head lice. We all admired them for their unswerving faith in God and their cheerfulness. The father, Bill, endured further suffering from a serious attack of polio and torture by the Japanese when two of his friends escaped.

Jack Pearson, who later became a part of our Lutheran family, also had a story to tell of escapes and danger. His wife was a diabetic, and when they realized the supply of insulin was running out, they decided to take the precarious journey to Baguio to get the insulin. If she were to wait for Jack's return, the medicine would come too late, so Jack, wife, and four-year-old Butch began the trip. His wife became so weak Jack had to pull her on a hand wagon. They were soon captured by the Japanese, who would not heed their pleas for insulin. So Jack had to stand helplessly by as his young wife slowly died. After he had buried her, the Japanese took him and Butch to Baguio internment camp. They were actually glad to rest at last within the confinement of the barbed wire.

7

Learning without Books

There were 130 children under 18 years of age. They had little space to play, no TV, no movies, and only a few books. Hungry tummies constantly cried out for food! Children playing war games in the barracks were driving bored and hungry adults to distraction. We had a social problem!

A stopgap solution was to take the children out on the tennis court and tell them stories. We drained our minds of every story from the Bible and Shakespeare to Horatio Alger. When these ran out, we resorted to telling stories of our own childhood.

We knew we had to make some long-range plans for the children. If we were to be there for a hundred years, as the commandant had said, there was not much point in preparing the children for life in the outside world. But to preserve the sanity of the camp, we decided to begin school.

At first we planned for only the first eight grades. Many of the children had brought schoolbooks with them into the camp. These were collected, and the self-appointed school board, administration, and faculty (four women in all) set up a curriculum and organized the school. We held our classes in the camp dining room. Each teacher sat at a long table with her class. By noon of the first day school was humming along very well. This was great! We were preparing for the future. Somehow, the confines of the camp expanded.

But at noon our guards came to collect all our textbooks. They said they would inspect them and return them, but we never saw the books again. New restrictions had been laid on communication with the outside, so chances of smuggling in other books were not good.

We decided we would have school anyway. We gained permission to open school again, with the restriction, "Only reading, writing, and arithmetic."

The curriculum was resumed with a few books gathered from adults, and gradually we smuggled in a few books on the vegetable truck or garbage wagon. I taught one year of junior-high English without a text. Paper and pencils had to be rationed.

Grammar had always been a hobby of mine. I tried to recall all the rules of grammar, organized them, and with more dedication than wisdom we memorized rules and applied them. Those junior-high students learned to diagram sentences—complex and compound; they mastered participles, gerunds, and infinitives. A few years after our release, a girl wrote to her camp teacher that she had been exempted from freshmen English at the university she attended because her tests showed a mastery of English fundamentals.

Only the three Rs were permitted, but soon a few history and geography books were smuggled in. Never have I had such enthusiastic history students. History was a forbidden pleasure, and so American history class became an adventure. Always one student was on duty facing the doorway. If a guard was seen approaching, he'd say, "Here he comes! Sit on the book!" Immediately the book was hidden, and then by agreement we had a spelling lesson.

One day we were having a sentimental lesson about the American flag, which was spread out on the table. So absorbed were we that we didn't notice the entry of a guard until he stood beside the table. It was too late. So, following my lead, the entire class arose and bowed profoundly to the guard. He seemed pleased and left. We were afraid that our illicit activities might be reported and school might be closed again. But nothing happened. School continued for three nine-month terms.

Later, a high school was added. Facilities and books were less than minimal, but intelligent, well-motivated students and excellent, highly trained teachers made it an exceptional high school. On the faculty were several Ph.D.'s in science and the humanities, a bishop, the editor of a city paper, medical doctors, and native speakers of Japanese, Chinese, French, Spanish, German, and Russian.

Three terms of school were held. The seniors were awarded diplomas with a ball and chain. At the graduation ceremony the seniors sang a song which they had composed. The closing lines were:

We hope it won't be long before
There's nothing left of her, our alma mater.

As life dragged on into the third year, the children became too hungry and apathetic for study, and the teachers were needed to care for the sick. So Baguio Internment Camp School was closed.

8

Lonely in a Crowd

No one could escape the stress of living in this human fishbowl. A comparatively young single woman like myself had less to complain about than many, but even I had my low moments. My 30th birthday, June 14, 1942, was such a time. We had been in camp one year, and there had been no news from home. I felt drab and worthless. I was just No. 285 in a concentration camp, a refugee, a burden on the old settlers of Baguio who had brought supplies of food and equipment into the camp. I had tried to compensate by working and contributing what I could. But on that 30th birthday I sat alone beside a tree in a corner of our camp and wept foolish tears of self-pity. Where was Phil, my fiancé? In the bag at my bunk were the white, high-heeled pumps I had bought for my wedding. Would there ever be one?

The drabness and monotony of the camp only augmented the many private tragedies which people had brought into the camp. Mothers disciplined their children completely exposed to the community. There was no place a married couple could unravel their differences in private. The sick had no secrets; every bowel disorder, stomach pain, and headache was apparent to all. The old who felt life could never be the same waited out the duration with little hope. Many of them had known lives of luxury, surrounded by servants. Now they had not only to fend for themselves, but had to do some menial camp task. One man said that every night of his life he had slept in freshly laundered sheets. He began his three-year stint in camp with no sheets. One day an old man was caught trying to go over the fence. He had dressed up in his good clothes, and he carried a bag and bottle cap in his hand, which he said was a ticket to America.

Among the few European Jews in the camp was Herta. She, like the other Jews, had escaped Nazi Germany only to be caught in the Asian conflict. I became aware of Herta at Camp Holmes, where I passed her every day on the way to mess hall. She must have been an early riser, because no matter what time I went to the laundry table or joined the chow line, Herta was already sitting on the bench, watching the world of Camp Holmes go by. She was certainly the loneliest person I had ever seen. She was without friends, with few possessions, a mere onlooker.

She always wore the same green dress with a white collar and little red buttons down the front and a red sweater. The dress was always spotless and neatly pressed. Her hair was piled attractively in a neat bun on top of her head. She was short and stocky, and her most impressive feature was a prominent nose that turned up at an unexpected angle and gave her an air of inquisitiveness. The nose and bright brown eyes suggested not only curiosity but a sardonic view of the world in general. *Who was she?* I wondered. If she were indeed a German citizen, why was she placed in a prison camp by the allies of her own country?

One day I found myself next to Herta in the chow line. There had been much talking and jesting among the internees. Herta had mistaken me for a Norwegian citizen and said, "These Americans are so vulgar and snobbish."

I reacted with a taunt, "And what happens to all of us if we just sit on a bench all day?" The confrontation was momentary. I caught a gleam in her eyes, and we began to laugh.

She hastily apologized, "I'm sorry, I thought you were Norwegian. I have been watching you. You seem busy and happy. I am alone, all alone. I have hated all of you because I thought you were snobbish."

This was the beginning of a close friendship. The next morning I was up very early and met Herta in the washroom. She was coiling her shiny black hair in the usual attractive knot. I washed my face, brushed my teeth, and ran my fingers through my hair. Herta showed amazement at the hair grooming, and I laughingly explained that I had lost my comb. In fact, a crisis had developed in my relationship with Esther, because we had lost "our" comb, and each blamed the other for the loss. Maybe it was a heavier sense of guilt on my part that caused me to skip the combing except for special occasions. We were already sharing a toothbrush, and that was strain enough on our friendship.

Herta was all sympathy. "Judy, you and I will share this, every day we will use it," she said, handing me a small pocket comb.

It was soon discovered that Herta was skillful with the needle, and people began bringing mending to her. Because she was needed, she became much happier. An American flag was under construction, and it was Herta who helped straighten out the stripes and put the stars in place.

One night the two of us were sitting on a mountain ledge just inside the camp enclosure. It was a singularly beautiful night. The mountains sloping down to the China Sea were gleaming in the bright moonlight. We had been sitting silently for some time when Herta spoke, "The mountains are beautiful tonight—beautiful like our mountains in Bavaria." Then she caught her breath as if trying to stifle a sob.

"Herta, please tell me about yourself," I said.

Slowly, reluctantly, she began her story.

"I grew up in the house of my grandfather, a Jewish rabbi. He was a saint and very strict in observance of all Jewish laws. How well I remember the stories he told about Abraham, Isaac, Jacob, and King David. I did not know my father very well. He came to see me only a few times. One of these times, when I was a little over 20 years of age, he found a husband for me, a German businessman from Munich who was much older than I."

"Did you love him?"

"I neither liked him nor disliked him. Love him? No, I don't think so. We were married, and I went to live in Munich. Two years later our son was born, and he became my whole world. How I loved him! He was beautiful and very smart.

"My husband joined the Nazi party. More and more he seemed afraid to have me meet his friends. I became alarmed by all the political talk I heard. When Hitler spoke on the radio, I trembled and refused to listen. My husband urged me to become active in women's Nazi meetings. I went a few times, but was frightened. So far I had been sheltered by my husband's name and position, but how long would that last? Already ladies were calling me to ask why I had discontinued attending the Nazi meetings. Did they suspect I was Jewish? If the ax fell on me, it would surely fall on my son also. That thought struck terror in my heart. I had to drop out of their lives in such a way that my husband and son could know nothing of my purpose or my plans.

"The day of my departure was like any ordinary day. I prepared breakfast for my husband and son. When he went off to work, I said good-bye to my husband as usual. Then I took my son to his middle school. His thoughts were full of school and the ball game of that day. I just casually said good-bye to him at the door of the school and watched him disappear down the corridor, knowing I would never see him again. I longed to throw my arms around him, to tell him I loved him, and to warn him against the evil which was threatening to destroy us all. But I just turned and walked away.

"Then I took a train to Italy, where I withdrew money from our account. To what country could I go where a Jew would not be hunted out like a rat? There was a ship ready to sail for the Philippine Islands, so I boarded it, wanting to get away from Europe as quickly as possible, to a place that seemed quiet and safe."

This was the only time that Herta spoke freely of her former life. She had put it behind her and lived only in the present. She was very outspoken, and some of her observations on people and situations were entertaining. She was curious about everything. Her many questions about my faith led us into a study of the New Testament.

She brought a wealth of Old Testament knowledge to the study. We forgot hunger and boredom as we discussed the covenant and the Old Testament prophecies. The Jesus she met in the gospel of John at once had a strong appeal. *But really, who was this Jesus of Nazareth?* she wondered. Often with finger on the text and her head tilted upward she would say, "Jesus was a good man. But how could he say he was God? Was he lying? But he was a good man." She felt drawn to believe in Jesus Christ but held back because it would seem like a betrayal of her grandfather.

One day when I was in school with my seventh graders, a friend came running in with the message, "Herta has been called to the guardhouse, and they are taking her away in the police truck." I hastily dismissed my class and ran to the guardhouse, but the truck was already leaving. I had only a brief glimpse of Herta as she leaned out of the window waving and calling, "Good-bye, Judy." That was the last I saw or heard of my friend.

9

No Word from Home

From December 1941 until February 1945, we really lived outside of the normal world, in a sphere all our own. It was like being suspended in space. Time stood still, for all our plans and normal activities had come to a halt. Inside the camp we reckoned time B.C., C.C., and A.C. (Before Concentration, Concentration Camp, After Concentration.) Favorite gifts for birthdays and Christmas were homemade calendars.

We tried to guess at the progress of the war by the attitude and actions of the guards. If there were extra rations, we guessed that they were preparing for the day when the tables would be turned and they would be behind barbed wire. Or perhaps it meant that the course of the war was overwhelmingly in their favor so they could afford to be magnanimous. Our interpretation depended on whether we were inclined to be optimistic or pessimistic.

There were men in the camp who kept a radio hidden in parts. But they had to be careful not to divulge news which might bring a noticeable reaction, for the Japanese must not become suspicious. We had to be content with the propaganda broadcasts of Tokyo Rose, which for a time we were allowed to listen to every night at the guardhouse. When that source of information was cut off, we concluded that the news was so bad for the Japanese that even Tokyo Rose could not gloss over it.

The lack of communication was no fault of our government agencies. On our return to the United States, I found this letter from "Relief for Americans in Philippines" (Special Bulletin #25):

> Serious obstacles have prevented anything but greatly delayed communication with civilian internees and prisoners of war in the Philippines . . . every effort will be made to place them [messages from the United States] in the hands of civilian internees and prisoners of war upon their liberation.
>
> At long last the invasion is under way and the day of liberation at hand for the Philippine Islands. Soon all our people in internment and prison camps should be free. Let us constantly keep before our minds that for those brave and gallant people over there the sound of battle will be music in their ears. After long years of internment fraught with bitterness and dismay together with the deadly monotony of their lives, lack of decent food and clothing, this nearness of freedom will surely transcend all trials and hazards which they must temporarily face until the fight is won.

We heard rumors that the Red Cross had been trying to send us letters as well as supplies, but none of it reached us. People had even seen empty Red Cross boxes at the guardhouse during the second year, so we realized that the efforts of the Red Cross had been frustrated.

Finally in December 1943, a shipment of food, clothes, and medicine was delivered. This time a representative from the Swiss Red Cross personally supervised the unloading of the material. A representative from our camp was allowed to go down to a central dispatching station and help with the reloading and transfer to our camp so that this shipment would reach its intended destination.

When our representative came back, there was a general assembly of the camp, and for two hours we sat spellbound and with watering mouths discussed those boxes. The ques-

tions went on and on. "How big were the boxes? What was
in each one?" We went back to our bunks that night and
dreamed of cheese and milk and goodies. One night about
a week later the dream came true. We were in bed when
we heard a truck coming up the hill to the guardhouse. The
Red Cross supplies had come! Everyone rushed out to the
parade ground. It's too bad no one had a camera. We
laughed to see ourselves out in our night attire, which for
many had become very makeshift.

It was too dark for clear vision but we could read the
print on the boxes: "For American Prisoners of War. American Red Cross." We dwelt on every letter. We were not
forgotten! Our country had reached out with her bounty.
We feasted on the words. We sniffed at the boxes to get a
whiff of home. Then the commandant announced that they
would all be taken down to a storehouse at the foot of the
hill for inspection—lest we get some illegal propaganda or
news from home.

The inspection took several days. A few people from our
camp were chosen to go down to the storehouse to aid with
the inspection. Every box had to be opened and the V for
victory label had to be removed from every package of cigarettes because it might have been too much of a morale
booster! But while our people removed the V for victory
labels, they also smuggled paper used for packing inside
the boxes. Those papers were bits from the *New York
Times*. They were carefully pieced together, and one day
there appeared a notice on the bulletin board: "Come to
the dining room tonight to read a letter from home." No
one was absent. We were all fascinated with the news
gleaned from the paper. There were not only bits of war
news, but styles, and special sales. The one item I remember clearly even after 35 years was a story about a GI who
had been arrested for speeding on his way to a baseball
game. When the police learned he was soon bound for the
war front, they dismissed him, wishing him God's blessings.
It all seemed so normal in a crazy world. Americans were

still playing baseball, and even GIs could take time off for a game.

When those wonderful boxes finally arrived on Christmas Day 1943, we felt like millionaires. We took each item out— cheese, butter, canned meats and fish, powdered milk, crackers, cigarettes. We smelled them, felt them, discussed how we should use them, and for days were arranging and rearranging them.

Others reacted differently. One boy took the package of cheese and ate it all while walking down to the barracks. One lady used up her whole boxful in two or three parties; that was the way she could enjoy it best. We nonsmokers bartered cigarettes for food. Of course, we appreciated the food, but even more our hearts were warmed and encouraged by being remembered by folks at home. It also gave us a certainty that our country was moving on to victory.

Three times during captivity mail came in. I stood in line each time, my heart pounding, waiting for my name. It was never called. After liberation, mail came in several times but still my name was not called. There was something wrong! Even if Phil, my fiancé, had forgotten me, surely some relative was still alive who would remember.

After the battle of Manila, I gained permission to go to the military post office at Santo Tomas. I insisted that not all the mail had been sent to Old Bilibid Prison. The sergeant in charge became annoyed but finally granted me permission to come in and look at the files myself. As I was looking around, I saw a large box in a corner wrapped and tied, labeled "For the Deceased." The sergeant informed me that those were letters that had come for prisoners who had died. I was granted permission to open the box, and there I found seven letters for myself, as well as letters for other people who were in Old Bilibid. Apparently my name, Judith Beatrice Skogerboe, was too much for them to handle, so they had relegated me and my name to the deceased file.

10

Unexpected Friends

During the three years we came to realize that our Japanese captors were a variety of human beings, just as we inside the camp were. Among them were brutes whose humanity had been tarnished. Yet there were others who were gentlemen and humanitarians of high order.

With thankfulness we remember a young guard whose name is unknown. During the first three days we were allowed only one-half cup of drinking water a day. Our only wash water was a basin of strong Lysol solution placed at the entrance to the dining hall and another at the door to our improvised latrine.

One morning three of us were seated by a tree near a corner of the barbed wire enclosure, reading our Bibles. Three-week-old Maren Hinderlie was being passed from one to the other as we tried to soothe the hungry baby. Even though Mary, her mother, had received a special permit to have one whole cup of drinking water per day, her breasts were drying up.

We were reading Psalm 27, "The Lord is my light and my salvation, whom shall I fear?" But we were afraid. We had a sickening fear that the baby would die of malnutrition. We were afraid of the soldiers who came and went, staring at us, demanding our watches, blankets—whatever caught their fancy.

As we were reading, we became aware of one soldier pacing outside the fence with gun and fixed bayonet. We sensed he was slowly coming closer and closer, until he was standing directly behind us. We were apprehensive, wondering what to expect.

He smiled, pointed to our open Bibles, and in halting English said, "I am sorry. I am a Christian, too."

We returned his smile. Here was a brother in Jesus Christ on the other side of the barbed wire! God had spoken words of encouragement through a Japanese soldier that day.

Mr. Tomibe was a Japanese officer whom the Baguio internees remember with respect and gratitude. Mr. Tomibe was the camp commandant for more than one year; that time was the most pleasant period of our internment. He was a man of integrity, educated at an Episcopal mission school. During his command we were given freedom to roam the hillside above the camp, food was more plentiful, and food packages from the outside were allowed in. At that time everyone relaxed; there was laughter, partying, and entertainment.

This period came to an abrupt end when two of the internees escaped. Mr. Tomibe was transferred, and the day he left was a sad one for all of us. We soon realized that the new commandant was a very different kind of man, and we surmised that he had been given to us as a punishment for the escape.

The day Mr. Tomibe said farewell at roll call, he wished us "as serene a life as possible under the circumstances" and expressed the hope that we might meet again in a happier life.

That hope was realized for me a few years later in Kyoto, Japan. My husband and I had come to Kyoto for a mission conference. I knew Mr. Tomibe was in Kyoto, but when I encountered four or five pages of Tomibes in the telephone directory, I almost gave up trying to contact him. The first try failed, but on the second a woman said, "I think you want to speak to my uncle," and she gave me his number. Before I could call, he called me, and in a few minutes he was at our hotel. He took us to his home, where we had a good visit with him and his lovely family.

Mr. Kawagiri is another Japanese man whose memory we cherish. We had been in the camp about a month when one morning at 8:00 A.M. roll call, the commandant announced that all missionaries were to leave the camp in two hours. No explanations were made. What did it mean? Release? Repatriation? The next two hours were a bustle of activity as we picked up all our possessions, which now had been augmented by coconut shells and cans made into usable eating equipment. There was a new value on cans, safety pins, and string.

At 10:00 A.M., wearing what we could not squeeze into our bags, we assembled on the tennis court and began loading into two trucks. The 300 other internees were frankly jubilant at our departure. For them it meant twice as much space, more food, and no more Bible reading, praying missionaries to cast a pall on frolic and fun. They would celebrate with a dance that night!

We boarded the truck, hoping for the best, but fearing the worst. Because three missionaries from our camp were being held in the city jail, we already knew that the suspicions of the Japanese were directed particularly at the missionary group. They could not believe that we were in the Orient only to propagate a faith. They were sure we had an ulterior motive, and they suspected we were agents of the U.S. government.

So it was with mingled apprehension and anticipation that we rode out of barbed-wire confinement into the free world.

But the world was no longer free. The happy, singing Filipinos were silent. Those whom we passed dared not wave or smile.

We were promptly brought to military police headquarters, where we were ordered to get off the truck and enter the building. Then began a long day of answering questions, filling out endless forms, and waiting, waiting. The questioning went on all day, until about 1:00 A.M., when we were ushered into a large room where at a long table sat about 20 intelligence officers. Then began the tedious process of passing along the table, stopping in front of each officer for further questioning, and having our forms checked.

By 2:00 A.M., extremely weary and weak from the daylong fast, we were mechanically answering questions. I had just handed my forms to a handsome young officer and was surprised to see him run a finger under my statement of occupation, "Lutheran missionary." Putting his finger on the "Lutheran," he said in a scarcely audible whisper, "I'm a Lutheran, too—a Lutheran pastor."

Soon the processing of us single women was completed, and we were told that we could return to our homes. Our homes! Most of them had been looted and were now occupied by the Japanese military. Which of our homes would be safe? As we peered down dark Session Road, we were fearful. As we stood in the doorway, undecided, Mr. Kawagiri, the intelligence officer who had identified himself as a Lutheran pastor, came to us and asked us where our homes were. When he heard that some of us lived in the Lopez Apartment on Session Road, he said, "That is good; because of the Polish family living there, your apartment is unoccupied and has not been looted. There is a military seal of protection on the door. You will be safe there. But if you have trouble with the army, call me." And he gave us his telephone number.

On another occasion several people from the camp had been arbitrarily released for a short time, and Mr. Kawagiri was reading the rules that were to restrict their lives. When he had completed the reading, he folded the paper, saying, "What you have heard is the spirit of the Imperial Japanese Army. It is not the spirit of Jesus Christ."

We were released to our apartment, but our return to camp followed very soon. We had barely gone to bed that morning after we had returned to our apartment when we heard the stomping of boots on our stairway and three Japanese soldiers walked in. They had come to tell us that we had to be at police headquarters at 8:00 A.M.

We asked, "What does this mean? Shall we bring our bags?"

"No," they said. "You will be asked some more questions and then you can return to your homes."

We took their word for it and went off in the morning without any belongings. The questioning lasted all day. Late in the afternoon they lined us up by twos on the road and said, "Now you will walk back to Camp John Hay."

Back to the camp, empty-handed, just at suppertime, back to the miners and others who had been so glad to see us go.

We were soon picked up in trucks and arrived in camp just as the others were about to eat supper. To our amazement, the mining families welcomed us with open arms and made us sit down first to eat. They said, "After you left we realized you had been doing most of the dirty chores in camp, and you had kept our children occupied. While you were gone, the children have been driving us crazy." This was the beginning of a new relationship. The missionary/miner barrier was broken down, and we began to respect and love one another as fellow human beings.

The suspicions of the Japanese resulted in other groups of missionaries being taken to police headquarters for interrogation. Some were not as lucky as we had been. Three missionaries—Rufus Gray, Roland Flory, and Herbert Loddigs—didn't return to the camp after interrogation. The night before Herb Loddigs was taken out, Carroll Hinderlie, a fellow Lutheran, had been severely beaten during the questioning at police headquarters. His only offense seemed to be that his address was the same as that of Herb Loddigs. Needless to say, Herb faced his ordeal for the next day with well-founded fear. Earnest prayer was offered for Herb, as well as for Rufus and Roland, who had not returned to the camp. Weeks passed and there was no word from the three who were supposedly in the jail. In the women's barracks we had day and night prayer vigil for them. The quiet courage of the wives—Edna, Marian, and Josephine—gained the admiration and respect of the whole camp. They went quietly about their camp duties without complaining.

One evening, after two months, a truck came into the camp carrying Roland Flory and Herb Loddigs. While Roland was gone, his wife Josephine had given birth to a baby boy. Roland was the quiet, strong, heroic type who took the torture stoically. This was the wrong psychology, for his stoicism only aroused the ire of the Japanese, and they had heaped on fierce torture—even giving him the dreaded water cure.

Herb, on the other hand, had read a book on Japanese torture and knew how to react. He had delivered a lecture on Japanese torture one night at our dinner table in Baguio before the war. He said that we must remember if we should ever be tortured to scream and cry as if we were being killed. That would lead to milder treatment. At that time we had laughed and said, "Don't spoil our dinner. Whoever expects to be tortured?"

Herb ordinarily had a loud voice, but it was a very quiet, subdued Herb who returned to camp. In a barely audible voice he spoke of his weeks in a jail cell shared with 15 Filipinos who had been convicted of criminal offenses.

While he was in prison, Herb had had a brief encounter with our friend, Mr. Kawagiri. One day he saw Mr. Kawagiri pass by his cell, and shortly thereafter Herb was released and sent back to camp. We can only guess at the part Kawagiri played in his release.

It was not until the summer of 1943 that we were informed of the death of Rufus Gray. He had apparently died the first night after he had been taken out. Brutal beating and the water cure had ended his life. Marian, his wife, was a valiant woman with deep faith in God. She cared for her infant son Billy, and in spite of the illness of both of them, she was always cheerful and calm.

As for our friend Mr. Kawagiri, his death in Santiago Prison shortly before the end of the war is veiled in mystery. Was he put to death for some misdemeanor of his own, or for his Christian witness and for befriending American missionaries? Or, as some say, did he die of disease? Whatever the end of his story might have been, we remember Mr. Kawagiri with deep gratitude.

11

Setting Priorities

Standing on the bridge of the *S.S. Coolidge* on our way to the Philippines, we 10 Lutherans had sung:

Let goods and kindred go
This mortal life also . . .
His kingdom is forever.

When I had squeezed all my worldly possessions into one trunk, a footlocker, and a few suitcases and had set out to proclaim the gospel in China for $59 a month, I thought I had turned my back on the world and its ambitions. Equipped with an Aladdin lamp, hiking boots, lots of warm underwear, and winter clothing, I had felt ready for a life of austerity in China.

Instead of seven years in China, we had found ourselves in Baguio, Philippine Islands, a delightful resort where the climate is nearly perfect the year around, an ideal place for language study. Sometimes as we walked into town, people from the gold mines would pass us in their chauffeured limousines. Maybe we envied them a bit; at least, we were curious about these people, who seemed to have everything. Little did we realize then that we'd be sleeping, eating, and working with them in close proximity for three years. We all were to realize that nothing is more precious than life and freedom.

December 27, 1941, had brought a sudden halt to our well-ordered lives. Limousines, mansions, bank accounts, cameras, art collections—all had been left behind. Diamonds and precious jewels had been put away, if possible. For those who had had time to think and plan, a few things were salvaged, but for others, the clothes on their backs had become their only possessions. Professional and business people, who were used to giving orders and making plans, were given a number and had to line up for the latrine, for a shower, and for food. Our lives and our possessions had passed out of our control.

We experienced the truth of Diogenes' words, "I have learned that there are many things God has made that we can do without." Fine china was replaced by coconut shells and tin cans. Jobs were assigned irrespective of one's training or accomplishments. There was much vying for choice positions. Number one was kitchen duty, for that placed one near the food. Next was the garbage detail, for the garbage crew could go outside the gate once a day with the garbage wagon. This gave them opportunities to barter and make deals with the Filipinos.

Attachment to things had seemed to me to be the peculiar malady of the rich. I had grown up in a parsonage, where worldly possessions were scarce and where accumulating more and more things was not one of the prime goals in life. Poverty and freedom from grasping materialism had always been linked together in my mind. To my dismay, I found that the less I had the more grabby and things-centered I became. Lack of material goods did not make me more spiritual. When one is hungry, it is not easy to concentrate on spiritual matters. The craving for food interfered with prayer life. How many times at night I would begin to pray—only to waken in the morning realizing that my mind had drifted off into a fantasy of bacon and eggs and pancakes.

Esther and I would pray the Psalms aloud to aid our concentration. Often we would wait until after the 10:00 patrol of the guard to slip outside the barracks. There, on a ledge with a gorgeous view of rice paddies bordered by majestic pine trees, we would voice our prayers. Those nightly prayer times were precious and offered an escape from our confinement. Our prayers went out for our country, our church, and for dear ones in the homeland, from whom we had heard nothing. One night we were very hungry, and as we gazed over the Baguio mountainside, we were reminded that now was the time for the peanut harvest.

Esther said, "Let's ask God for peanuts." We began to voice the prayer that some of those peanuts would come our way. The thought was all right, but when we heard the words, they seemed ridiculous. We began to laugh, the heartiest laugh we had enjoyed in weeks. Here we were, two single missionaries, in the middle of a global war, when generals and admirals were calling on the Almighty for guidance and victory, and we were saying, "Please, God, you know how hungry we are. Give us some peanuts, please." The laughter was good therapy. But God who watches the fall of a single sparrow and who has promised to supply our every need heard our foolish prayer. The next day we had a chance to exchange a watch for three pounds of peanuts. The question for us was, "Whose watch?" Mine had great sentimental value because it was a confirmation gift from my grandmother, so Esther's gold watch was sacrificed.

It was not unusual to see people searching the garbage cans for bits of edibles. I remember one woman, a member of one of the wealthiest families in the United States, who daily scrounged through the garbage cans. One day a sign appeared above the garbage cans, "Save something for the pigs. They're hungry, too." The keeper of the pigs obviously had his problems too!

Before internment, our group of 500 had represented almost every economic level of society. There were, of course, those whose whole lives had centered about the accumulation of material possessions—automobiles, jewels, houses, sugar plantations, even gold mines. The camp uncovered the materialism in all of us. How tenaciously we had clung to our possessions, whether coconut shells or diamond rings. When we had been moved from Baguio down to Manila, all clung to their pathetic possessions. Some had a collection of tin cans and homemade cookware. Some had hoarded boards and filled a trunk with them. There were women who didn't trust expensive fur coats or jewelry to the trucks, so they wore the fur coats and heavy jewelry on the trip into the sweltering heat of Manila.

Later, the months of slow starvation in Bilibid Prison had radically altered our attitude toward possessions. We were all united in one common passion—to preserve and prolong life until the day of freedom. That day came and with it inexpressible joy!

When after a brief removal to U.S. Army headquarters (described in Chapter 17) we were returned to Bilibid Prison, we found the place completely ransacked and looted. Our possessions were gone, but we lay down on the cement floor in a dark prison and there was scarcely a murmur. We had learned during the three years of internment that all that really matters is life and freedom.

12

Recipes from a Concentration Camp Cookbook

The few cookbooks which had found their way into the camp were avidly studied. They were much in demand, and there was always a waiting list to use them. We copied the recipes and with drooling mouths discussed them with friends. We skipped over such gourmet dishes as Lobster Thermidor or Scallopine Farcite, but our eyes became riveted on a peasant concoction like Indian Pudding, the ingredients of which seemed to be within reach. Talk of food rarely dwelt on steak and lobster, but the thought of ham or cheese sandwiches or eggs or doughnuts and coffee made the saliva run. A father said, "My dream is to sit down to a plate of six eggs." His son commented, "My dream is to have one egg today and to know there will be one egg tomorrow and one the next day."

These are some of the concentration camp delicacies which resourceful people concocted:

CORN MEAL MUFFINS

2 cups corn meal (coarsely ground)

1 cup bean milk
2 Japanese stomach pills (soda)
Dark sugar, 1 or 2 tbls. as available
Shortening—1 tbls. coconut oil, lard,
   margarine, or albolene (an odorless cold cream included
   in our Red Cross boxes)
Bake 20 min.—longer if the wood is raw or if someone forgot
to stoke the stove, or until a more urgent concoction is
brought to be baked

COFFEE

A strong brew made of good mountain coffee beans out of
Baguio Mountains
Submarine 1—second dunking
Submarine 2—third dunking
Submarine 3—fourth dunking
Submarine 4—fifth dunking
Submarine 5—by this time it took a bit of imagination to
   identify the yellow liquid as coffee.

And when even this failed:

CORN COFFEE

Burn carefully hard kernels of corn. Cool. Dunk in kettle of
boiling water. The grayish fluid resembles real coffee more
closely in appearance than in taste or smell.

BEAN MILK

Greens, mango beans, coconut milk, rice, flour, sugar, and
vegetable water. (Babies cry for it!)

HEAD CHEESE

(A Norwegian delicacy served at Christmas)

Butcher a pig. Render the lard. Distribute the cracklings to
about 500 people who will chew them with delight. Collect
the hard rind that was not chewable (as many as you can
rescue before they go into the garbage). Cook these rinds

slowly, for as many hours as 60 other women will let you take room on the stove. As the rinds begin to soften, add salt, pepper, onions, garlic (if you are lucky enough to have some) and grated ginger (we found a few ginger roots in the pigpen, which we were converting into a garden). When you have occupied the stove to the limit of everyone's patience, pour the mess into a pan. When it has congealed, slice and eat with your rice.

RANDY COX'S SPECIAL

1 sparrow (defeathered and cleaned)
Spread albolene (cold cream received from Red Cross) on pan.
Sprinkle with salt.
Fry as long as fire lasts.
Eat (with little relish).

13

Spiritual Hunger

For over three years 200 missionaries lived closely together with 300 people from various secular walks of life. Here were the ingredients for a great spiritual revival. But as far as I know, there was no pronounced spiritual movement. There were some who found new meaning for life, but only a few. It seemed that unbelievers were only confirmed in their unbelief, and the cynical found new fuel for their cynicism. Instead of learning from one another, each religious group, of which there were about 21, became more confirmed in its particular form of dogma or religious practice. Maybe too many of us were religious people by vocation. Or perhaps life was too easy and we didn't really have to suffer!

Yet there were some spiritual highlights. The first Easter service in 1942 on the John Hay tennis court was the most memorable. It was our first assembly of any kind since our incarceration in December 1941. No speaking was allowed, only the reading of Scripture, prayer, and hymns. It was God who spoke to us—and with compelling power. People who had not attended church since childhood were deeply moved. Hearts were tender, and we were all open to hearing God's voice.

The Christmas and Easter pageants, sacred concerts, church services, and open-forum discussions also had an impact on the camp.

Later, as we were given freedom to assemble and conduct the meetings as we wished, the strident voices of people were too often heard above the voice of God. There were many debates over doctrine. They were not only incomprehensible, but offensive to many. People outside the church or on the periphery are not very much interested in the truth value of what is said. Their concern is, "How does this faith work in daily life? What is there in Christian faith that would improve the quality of my life and make me a happier, better person?" What a chance we had to demonstrate this with no conventional props—literally undressed, chafing under lack of privacy, with no chance to shout out our frustration and no corner in which to hide our selfishness and depression! Sometimes I wished I could follow the example of one woman who often crawled under a sheet in the afternoon and sucked her thumb until she could tolerate all her "low class" neighbors again.

Those who professed Christianity were on stage all the time. People outside or on the periphery of the church had a right to scrutinize our lives. If faith is genuine, it can stand scrutiny.

There were those who were much annoyed by Christian activities in the camp. Bible study and prayer groups were very offensive to some.

I am deeply grateful for our close-knit family of Lutheran missionaries. We were a group of rugged individuals, and even within our family there were frequent religious debates, sometimes acrimonious. We studied together; most of us studied Greek under the tutelage of our pastors. We read and discussed various theological books.

Our three pastors, Carroll, Herb, and Herman Larsen kept us intellectually stimulated. It was refreshing to meet one of them on a drab morning when all the talk had been only about lab specimens, food, and trivia, and without any preliminaries we'd delve into a theological discussion.

Our Lutheran family was sorely tried by illness. Mary Hinderlie and little Maren, a beautiful blue-eyed girl, had a three-year long struggle with dysentery, and Carroll nearly died from a bleeding ulcer. God heard our prayers and brought him back from the brink of death. I shall never forget his first sermon after he had made a partial recovery. There was an outpouring of faith, refined and strengthened by fiery trial.

Herb, truly an aggressive proclaimer of the gospel, was spinning out new ideas every day from his active mind. But I especially cherish the memory of Herb Loddigs, not only as a stimulating theological thinker, but as a cheerful servant who stayed at his menial job as dishwasher to the end. During the first year of internment there was much vying for a job in the kitchen; even dishwashing was a prize, for then one could scrape the kettles. But as time went on, food became scarce, and even the scrapings from the rice kettle were so much in demand that they were rationed out by a committee; by that time no one wanted to wash dishes. But faithful Herb and Brother Antonio stayed with that unpleasant job to the end. Passing the kitchen any day one could hear, above the clatter of pots and pans, the Reformation battle going on between Lutheran Herb and Roman Catholic Brother Antonio.

I can't speak for the camp in general, nor do I venture to speak of what was happening to any one person. I must speak from my own point of view. The story of what was happening in my own journey of faith may strike responsive chords in the hearts of other ex-internees.

During our internment, the grace of God became a practical reality, and the strong emphasis on the gospel by our pastors made God's grace very real and precious. I had grown up in a parsonage, in a very pious, legalistic environment, where the question was not so much, "What does God say?" but "What will these other Christians say?" I remember the prayer meeting back in Erskine, Minnesota, when Mrs. H. prayed for 15 minutes with tears and sighs, asking God to forgive the worldly pastor's family (my family) for having traveled 70 miles to Grand Forks for a Barnum and Bailey-Ringling Brothers circus.

So I grew up not feeling free to be myself for fear I might upset the precarious balance in the congregation. I knew Jesus had forgiven my sins and I knew I was a child of God. However, my feelings were up and down. Under proper inspiration, and when I had reason to feel I was a somewhat "good" person, I was on a high plane of joy and assurance. But when annoyed with others and with my own inclination to think and say what was wrong, my feelings plummeted.

I had thought the decision to become a missionary would change my nature. It didn't. In fact, in Baguio Concentration Camp my faults were augmented many times over. I would wake up in the morning only to have a woman in the next bunk complain, "You certainly were restless last night." Then the smell of bacon and eggs and coffee—someone was cheating and feasting from his little private cache while we were to dine on rice and syrup and corn coffee! Before I had my clothes on, I was already out of sorts with the world. The prospect of three hours in school and two hours of slushing through deep mud, trying to convert an old pigpen into a garden, did not enhance my zest for living. I had to force myself to read the Bible. I'd rather lie down with a novel, especially if it mentioned food.

So I decided to take myself in hand and impose a little discipline. I resolved to get up very early, between 5:00 and 6:00, and have an hour alone with God before the camp began to stir. That helped. There were times when God seemed very close. But one day as I was climbing the hill, with blanket and Bible, returning from my private chapel,

I met a friend who said, "Well, Judy, I suppose you think you are holier than the rest of us."

No, far from it. I loathed myself. That morning the sun had been shining directly in my face, giving me a headache. That made me sleepy, so I had drifted off to sleep while I was trying to pray. Camp annoyances had warred with thoughts of God—and now this taunt! Maybe I *was* trying to earn merit by my early-morning vigil.

Then something happened that brought my doubts and frustrations to a climax. For a long time in a bunk near us was Lydia, who was suffering from asthma. She was a believer in Christian Science, and sometimes she sought solace by reading the Mary Baker Eddy lessons with fellow Christian Scientists. She also frequently joined our little group in Bible study and prayer sessions. Often at night when she was having difficulty with breathing she would call, "Judy, please come and pray for me." I would hold her hand and pray until she felt more comfortable. She would also ask me to read from the Bible. At those times she always requested a story of one of Jesus' miracles from the Gospels.

Early in the third year of internment, she became so ill that she was moved to the hospital. We saw her often there. One night Esther went to the hospital with her Bible, and Lydia again asked her to read the story of a miracle. Esther refused. She said, "Tonight I want to read the story of the cross."

"I don't want to hear that gory tale," Lydia said, turning her face to the wall. Esther spoke of our need for this redemption won on the cross, but there was no response. So Esther left.

Two or three nights later Lydia died in her sleep. Her body was prepared, a box was made, and we had a burial service on the hill above the camp. I should have been crushed by this experience. We had been close friends in camp, and our last encounter had been a dismal failure. But something had happened to my emotions. My heart was stony cold. My head told me this was tragic and this leave-taking with Lydia was sad, but my heart did not respond.

After the burial, as we were descending the hills, a friend came running to meet us with the news, "Judy, we just got a lump of sugar." This was a raw, unrefined sugar which could be cooked up into a candy. The anticipation of having this candy brought tears of joy. Tears over a lump of sugar, but none for a friend who had died so alone! Suddenly I was revolted by what I had become. I hated myself, and I was sure God could no longer love me either.

I went out to a ledge in a corner near the fence, and there I wept bitterly. I told God, "I am no longer your child, much less a missionary. I don't even care anymore. I find the Bible boring. I can't sense your presence when I pray, and it all seems like delusion."

Then God spoke to me, clearly, unmistakably. The ledge on which I was sitting overlooked the lush green rice paddies like a green staircase down to the China Sea, shining faintly in the distance. All around were the magnificent Baguio Mountains. God was there! He came to me with words of a song learned from childhood:

Wide, wide as the ocean
High as the Heavens above
Deep, deep as the deepest sea
Is my Savior's love.

I, though so unworthy,
Still I'm a child of his care
For his Word teaches me
That his love reaches me—everywhere.

It seemed to me as if God's love came bounding out of the China Sea, up those gleaming rice paddies to the ledge where I sat. The towering mountains, the blue sky above, the shining sea below, all spoke of God's unlimited, unconditional love. His love had reached me!

I had no scrap of virtue with which to earn his love. "Nothing—no nothing in my hand could I bring." Then I remembered my Baptism. When I was a helpless bit of human flesh, prone to disobedience and unbelief, God had made me his own, called me by name, given me all the gifts of his grace—eternal life, forgiveness, security, hope. That was a glimpse into the mystery of God's grace. I had spoken the phrases before and at times I had been deeply stirred, but also at times doubts and my own willfulness had robbed me of assurance and joy. Now I was overwhelmed by the grace of God and raised to new life. That was the beginning of a new walk in grace.

14

Entry into
Old Bilibid Prison

The days, marked off on our homemade calendars, had passed by in monotonous succession since December 1941. Hope of imminent release may have waned at times, but was never completely lost. Always the next Fourth of July, the next Thanksgiving, Christmas, or Easter was the target of our hope. When one holiday came and went with nothing happening, we pinned our hopes on the next holiday.

As Christmas 1944 approached, there was little means for celebration. Except for the first Christmas in 1941 when there had been a great deal of uncertainty and fear, the succeeding holidays in captivity were rather pleasant. In 1943, as the exciting climax of a plentiful holiday celebration, the wonderful Red Cross boxes had arrived, but the Christmas season of 1944 had roused little anticipation. Offerings from the camp kitchen had become very meager, and private supplies for most of us had dwindled to nothing.

That good old Christmas spirit of cheer and goodwill, however, just couldn't be suppressed. Nor could we disappoint the children. As Christmas was approaching, there was much secret activity as scraps of material became pot-holders, aprons, children's clothes; sweaters were ripped and fashioned into gifts; down at the shop the men were making trinkets and gadgets out of coconut shells, water buffalo teeth, and scrap metal. Evergreen trees on the parade ground were decorated, and the dining hall was given a festive appearance with boughs from the pine trees.

Christmas Eve, after a supper of rice with a mushy sweet-potato gravy, we gathered down in the natural amphitheater below the barracks for the Christmas pageant. The singing, the angels, shepherds, and Wise Men carried us away to that night long ago on the plains of Bethlehem. Memories of home often brought tears—a white frame house, lights in the window, the family gathered at the table, the reading of the Christmas gospel, mother, father, brothers—yes, where were they this Christmas Eve?

Hail the heaven-born Prince of Peace . . .
Born that man no more may die.

The words echoed over the hills that were soon to be the scene of great bloodshed and suffering.

The most poignant memory of that evening was the group of Japanese guards, silhouetted on the rim of the hollow, listening intently. How wistful and lonely they looked compared with the internees sitting in a cozy circle on the hillside singing the Christmas carols. The guards, too, were lonely and homesick.

Christmas morning we were awakened by the singing of the Christmas carolers. It was a beautiful day, and the jolly holiday spirit dispelled all gloom. One of the men, dressed in a makeshift Santa Claus suit, came riding into the parade ground in a cart drawn by a recalcitrant horse. The children were delighted. Coconut candy and coffee had been brought in that morning, so each child received a piece of candy and a banana, and the adults each had a strong cup of aromatic coffee.

Christmas dinner was served at tables set up on the parade ground. We had a feast of hamburgers, sweet potatoes, and two cookies apiece.

The morning of December 26, we all suffered a severe letdown. Christmas with its special cheer was over, and we faced the monotony of another year in captivity. Suddenly an order came from the guardhouse that we must break camp and be ready to leave in two days. Where were we going? Rumors ran wild. "There was a repatriation ship in Manila harbor!" someone declared. Spirits soared. The water buffalo, pigs, and chickens that had been kept against that day were slaughtered, and the camp went on a wild spree of feasting. Such laughing and talking as we sorted out our pathetic possessions! Books, string, safety pins, and good tins had priority. Carefully we each packed the one bag that each person was allowed.

Baggage was piled high on the waiting trucks, and at dawn we happy prisoners took our precarious places on the top of the baggage. What a ridiculous picture we would have made! Some of us were dressed in the scantiest and most worn attire, while others, fearing to lose valuable possessions, were decked out in fur coats and capes, hats, heavy clothing, and jewelry for the dusty trip down to the hot, humid lowlands.

There were not enough trucks for all, so about half our group had to wait until the next day. What fun we had the night after the others had left, going through the barracks looting what had been left behind! My shoes had worn out, so when I found a pair that seemed to fit me, I discarded my own. During the journey to Manila the looted shoes caused painful blisters, so I threw them away and entered the new chapter of internment without any shoes.

We had begun the day with a wild surge of joy, buoyed up by marvelous rumors. As the day wore on, however, we began to have some apprehensions. Three times that day we halted, were ordered to unload the trucks, and after a wait were ordered to load again. The third time, we were told to begin walking. As we walked, it began to rain, so we took refuge in a coconut grove, where we sat down to rest. Soon an order was given, "All able-bodied people line up by twos; you will walk back to the *bodega* (the storehouse where our baggage had been unloaded)." The men on our truck were sick, so Esther, my petite friend, and I were the "able-bodied" who had to load our truck. As it had to be done quickly, we were not able to pile the baggage in efficiently. This pile of baggage, loosely loaded and extending above the sides of the truck, became a real hazard to us passengers. To prevent any of us from slipping off, we bound ourselves together with a rope.

By evening the rich diet of the last two days began taking its toll. We begged often for relief stops, which our guards granted but with the stipulation that we must not go out of sight. No matter! Modesty was a luxury we had given up long before. I was not even greatly embarrassed when I found myself sharing a small bush with an Anglican priest.

It was a beautiful night with a nearly full moon. With mingled apprehension and joy we noted signs of recent bombings along the way: joy, because it was a sign of American advance; apprehension, because we would be a perfect target on this road. Our apprehension increased as, mile after mile, we met the Japanese army retreating to the north. Did the American military have any idea that not only Japanese troops but American prisoners were moving on the Kennon Road that night?

Later we learned that every night for two weeks the Kennon Road had been bombed. The night we were on the road was clear and lighted by a full moon. We would have been a perfect target, but there was not a bomb those two nights our camp was being moved. Several years later I was visiting in the home of a U.S. Air Force pilot who had been in on the bombing operations from Linguyan Gulf. He said that during the two-week bombardment of Kennon Road there were four nights when the planes could not go up because needed fuel supplies had not arrived. Two of these nights we were traveling on the road. Happenstance? No.

It was a long, rough ride, and only the danger of falling off the truck kept us awake. The guard on our truck was often overcome by sleep; his gun would slip out of his hands as he nodded. Suddenly he would wake, grab his gun, and begin counting his prisoners. Toward morning we were all very sleepy, and our driver must have fallen asleep, for the truck began careening crazily from side to side and was making toward the edge of a bridge and a steep precipice. We screamed and pounded on the roof of the cab. The driver got the truck under control in the nick of time. He stopped, smoked a cigarette, did some calisthenics and we were on our way again. Captors and captives, we were one in a desperate desire for survival.

On that night ride down Kennon Road, I came to a new awareness of the Japanese. These long lines of silent, dejected soldiers, moving quietly in the dark, were a sorry contrast to the arrogant army and navy officers, dressed in immaculate uniforms, who had frequently visited our camps. They were nearing the end of a course to which they had given their fanatic loyalty. Our hearts went out to this army in threadbare uniforms, many barefoot. We could hear only their heavy breathing as they pushed their handcarts of ammunition up the mountain. Often our bare feet hanging over the edge of the truck brushed their camouflage as they passed by. We prayed that night, audibly, together, for the people of Japan.

The night passed without any bombing, and gray dawn found us approaching the city of Manila. Were we heading for the harbor and repatriation? No, that hope was dashed, for we were going directly toward the Pasig River and the center of Manila. Another prison camp? The question was soon answered. We drew up to a forbidding pile of gray rock and read the inscription: "Bilibid, Bureau of Prisons, Philippines." Bilibid was an old Spanish prison that had been condemned before the war.

A great iron gate swung open. We passed through a narrow courtyard, and another gate was locked and barred, then another, and we were in the inner prison. Three gates were locked and barred behind us. Before us stood the uninviting two-story stone structure that was to be our home. With deep foreboding we viewed the iron gratings over paneless windows. A little to the right were two double rows of cell blocks. Over the wall and in the next compound were the military prisoners, the skeletal survivors of Bataan and Corregidor.

Morale had reached its low point. We stumbled off the truck. Herb Loddigs fell in a heap and was carried off to the hospital cell blocks, unconscious. We had hardly any heart to try to make a place for ourselves on the dirty cement floor. There was no soap, so we had to try to clean out our space as well as we could with cold water. When I was told that the truck which carried all my possessions had overturned somewhere in the mountains and no attempt had been made to pick anything up, I felt such a bleak sense of loss that I threw up. The dress I had worn on the trip had been patched several times by using the sleeves for patches, and on the trip it had torn over the shoulder. A kind person had lent me a safety pin that had kept the dress on me. Now I had no clothes, no shoes. The only link with the past was my Bible and an old housecoat.

Esther restored my interest in life, however, when she made shorts for me out of some material we had wrapped around our rice. One of the men gave me his white shorts and shirt, so I was ready to go again.

Two rows of cell blocks were prepared for the sick, whose numbers were growing daily. Only those with dysentery or some other contagious disease could be cared for in the hospital. Food was scarce. The corn detail was too weak to work, so we ate weevils with our corn mush. Hardly anyone was escaping some stage of beriberi. Our pleas for protein were answered by the appearance of one pig's head! When our cook saw the bloody, hairy mess, he dumped it as it was into a cauldron of water. It all went into the gravy for our corn mush, along with generous amounts of hair. The flies were such a pestilence that we usually ate under our mosquito nets, where it was too dark to see either hair or weevils anyway.

Laughter had nearly vanished, but 500 Americans couldn't all lose their sense of humor all the time. Our battle over some green Japanese army mosquito nets was grim, but also had its humorous side.

As soon as we had arrived at Bilibid Prison, we became concerned about the sanitary conditions. The place was filthy. We had to sleep on the dirty cement floor with rats and mice running about. Of course, mosquitoes and flies and bedbugs were ever present. The latrine was a more serious problem. A trough had been dug, with a slanting drain board inserted so when necessary we could flush it by overturning a bucket of water down the trough. Planks were nailed in on either side of the trough, so we straddled them, squatting butt to butt. Not a very genteel description, but neither was this a very genteel or private arrangement.

Our problem was more serious than merely maintaining modesty. There was a dysentery epidemic in our camp, and across the wall, among the military prisoners, there was not only dysentery but cholera. With flies and mosquitos freely crisscrossing the two compounds, how could we shield our camp? The green Japanese mosquito nets were the answer. Someone had found them in a vacant building, and clever people constructed a tent over the latrine with a trap door that would keep flies from entering or leaving.

The camp relaxed. But not for very long. When our commandant came on a tour of inspection, he was furious. "Have you no respect for the Imperial Japanese Army? It is an outrage to desecrate these Imperial Japanese Army nets by using them to cover your latrine!"

Our camp officials adamantly refused to remove them. They said the life of the camp depended on them. A petition to retain the nets was sent to the guardhouse.

The answer came. "These are Japanese nets. It does not show proper respect to the Japanese Army." The commandant ordered them down by sundown.

The battle went on. In the afternoon this unintelligible message came from the commandant:

> Next, I stress the importance of strict salutation. It is advisable to get good fame by little effort, also with inner inclination.

Who could interpret that message? How should we respond? Nellie McKim, our resourceful liaison, said, "It might refer to bowing. When the commandant comes to our camp this afternoon, maybe several of you would please stroll by and bow very profoundly to him." We agreed. When it was rumored that the commandant was in the camp, we casually walked by him bowing low. It worked.

About 5:00 P.M. there was a communique from the commandant:

> You have used old nets with mending. We didn't give you new ones for special "billet use," did we? Differences of opinion is due to misunderstanding of appearance.

The message was slightly ambiguous, but the dignity of the Imperial Japanese Army had been preserved and we could keep the green nets.

And so life settled down to a daily struggle with bedbugs, flies, hunger, and monotony.

15

A Day in
Old Bilibid Prison

Morning and night come quickly in the tropics, without
the gentle interim of dawn and twilight. One moment night
seems to hang like a damp, murky blanket over the city.
Suddenly the blanket is lifted, and a blazing sun mocks the
earth with its relentless heat.

The morning sun comes with no friendly glow, but as a
fierce, hostile intrusion into Bilibid Prison. The pebbled
courtyard soon burns through thinning soles and cardboard
slippers. The sun reveals the prison building standing like
an evil fortress beside the double row of cell blocks.

Clang! Clang! The rising gong calls us to begin the 1124th
day of captivity.

About 500 inert forms, lying on the cement floor, begin
to stir, bodies damp and limp. In the courtyard in front of
the open shack which serves as kitchen, a few shabby men
are standing in line holding their tins or coconut shells.
They have been standing there since long before dawn.
When sleep escapes, what else is there to do?

Awaking, Jessica rolls over on her mat and, still half asleep, bumps into the Reverend Mr. Scott. "I'm sorry!" she says.

"I'm sorry, too. We're not even civilized," he grumbles as he begins to shed his pajamas and help his wife dress the children.

Soon the large building is a scene of much activity. Some people, hanging on to their prudishness, dress under their mosquito nets. Some dress in the aisles and greet the others as they walk past on their way for breakfast rations. As she struggles into her girdle in full view of the passersby, one woman mutters, "It's dreadful how we women have lost all our modesty here in the camp."

A man passing by says cheerily, "Never mind, ma'am. We men have lost all our curiosity too."

There is a sign on the wall, "If you want privacy, shut your eyes."

Soon all have received their corn mush, which is eaten merely as a means of survival.

One woman slips up to the balcony where she can get an occasional glimpse of the gaunt skeletons across the wall, the military survivors from Bataan and Corregidor. We are forbidden to go out on this balcony, but she hopes for a glimpse of her husband.

As she returns downstairs, someone asks, "Any sign of your husband?"

"No, none. But they are digging a new grave again this morning."

"We got a note in the bean curd basket yesterday. It said, 'We couldn't sleep the night you came in. When a baby cried we cried, too; it was music. God help us! We can't hold out much longer!' "

Sophie appears in worn dress and apron. The snap is out of her commands as she says, "Try to clean up your spots and the aisle in front of your area."

Some are already out with pail and mops, trying to clean with cold water and no soap. These chores over, most lie idle. Children no longer run boisterously up and down the aisle. They walk, and no one has any inclination for war games.

A few heroic souls are still studying Greek or Japanese or science. But for the most part, study books and heavy reading have been laid aside. In a slightly recessed alcove some nuns are lying on their bunks, the warm, uncomfortable garbs wrapped about their thin bodies, reading pulp fiction and mysteries. Two women sit at a bunk poring over a magazine. A bishop and a doctor are taking a slow stroll in the courtyard and seem to be in deep conversation. Is it about theology or science? I get a snatch of the conversation as I pass: "Well, I'd settle for a cheese sandwich when the Americans return."

"I dream of coffee and doughnuts."

Even the old bridge-playing gang has lost some of their zeal. Conversation lags. There is not even a new budding romance to make tongues wag. After three years, what more is there to say?

"I think we're trapped in here. If there is an American invasion, how could we be saved?"

"There's a lot of noise outside the wall at night."

"My husband says they're fortifying the city. Thousands of troops are being moved in."

"The guards seem to be more and more jittery."

"Yes, that crazy roll call at 2:00 this morning!"

"What in the world was the reason for that?"

"John says a bird must have alighted on the electric wire inside the wall and set off an alarm at the guardhouse."

"Who would be so crazy as to try to escape from here?"

"I hear there are five new dysentery cases."

"No room in the cell blocks for more sick."

"I know. Those with beriberi or something not contagious have to stay at their bunks."

The day drags on. Cold showers offer relief from the heat as well as the boredom. There are always a few men and women at the washstand washing out their clothes in a red fire bucket.

Supper of corn mush and maybe some green tops of the sweet potato plant is over by 5:00 P.M., and the internees gather out on the stone steps of the prison building to wait for the relief from the heat that evening brings.

"I wonder how rats fried in albolene would taste," says Jessica.

"Two of the boys shot a sparrow yesterday and fried it in albolene. By the time it was ready, they had lost their appetites."

Two men who have been strolling in the courtyard return to the prison. "Guess I'll have a ham sandwich and turn in," says Joe.

Dim lights are burning and several groups are gathered under mosquito nets. Some are playing cards, some are reading their Bibles and praying, and others are indulging in idle talk. At 9:30 all the lights are out, and camp settles down for another hot, restless night.

16

Liberation

The camp had settled down to a dreary battle with rats, dysentery, beriberi, hunger, and boredom. Most of the books had been read. We had nothing interesting to say to each other anymore. Almost any conversation began and ended with a discussion of ham sandwiches, doughnuts, eggs, or milk.

Even rumors had come to a stop. There was no news. At night there seemed to be much movement and activity in the city, so we surmised that the city was being fortified and prepared for something. How helpless we felt! The number of very sick patients crowding the hospital cell blocks was increasing rapidly. Across the stone wall new graves were being dug each day, and time was running out. Three walls, each with a gate locked and barred and a charged electric wire around the inner wall, and armed guards pacing the wall day and night were the barriers to freedom. Even if the Americans should invade, how could we be saved in the center of this heavily fortified city?

On the night of February 3, 1945, Manila was dark, hot, and strangely silent. No flickering stars shone. There were no lighted windows, for Manila was under a heavy blackout. Two of us were on duty at the hospital cell blocks. A dysentery epidemic had broken out, and there had been emergency surgery that day. The patients were in pain—hungry and uncomfortable. There was so little we could do for them. We might have been tempted to doze were it not for myriads of savage mosquitoes that kept up a continuous bombardment. The only solace was in closing the eyes and dreaming of a stack of pancakes with syrup and butter dripping over the edges.

The night finally was over. We went back to our bunks and began our 1135th day in captivity. Little did we dream that this was to be one of the greatest days of our lives. It was Saturday night, February 4, about 7:00, when we heard an unusual noise outside. From a tiny window in the second story of the building we could get a glimpse of MacArthur Boulevard, the main road into the city of Manila. There was much shoving and pushing to get near the window. We saw what looked like big houses rolling down the boulevard.

"It's the Americans. They're back!" said the women, always on the optimistic side.

"It can't be the Americans, but something is going on," replied the men.

One man ran out to a back gate where a single wall separated the prison from the outside. Through a crack in the gate he saw the first tank stop and heard a voice call out, "Should we go on, or should we go back the way we came?"

Then he heard a voice from the third tank back reply in a beautiful southern drawl, "Let's go on and give 'em the works, Haa-vy." Beautiful American voices! Those really were American tanks. The news spread quickly. We reacted with excitement, joy—hysterical joy!

The next hours were a blur of shell fire, bursting of bombs, and fireworks. We were on the front line of one of the big battles of World War II. Later we learned that the

American tanks had gone directly to Santo Tomas University, the large internment camp, about six blocks from Bilibid, had crashed the gate, subdued the guards, and had set the prisoners free.

Did the American military know that we were in the Bilibid Prison? The American tanks had moved just beyond us when the Japanese opened fire from the Far Eastern University, a few blocks in front of Bilibid. So by a miracle, we were behind the American defense line. Later we learned that General MacArthur had held the city that night with a very small force and sheer bluff. One of the GIs told us later that General MacArthur would not let them rest after they landed at Linguayan Gulf. MacArthur had urged, "Drop your unnecessary weights. Run. We must take the city by surprise. If we don't, there won't be a prisoner alive." Thanks to MacArthur's genius, they did take the city by surprise.

Just a moment before the arrival of the tanks, Nellie McKim, our interpreter, had been talking with one of the Japanese officers from the guardhouse. She was saying, "Oki-san, can't you tell us something about what is happening on the outside?"

"Well," he said, "there has been an American troop landing at Linguayan Gulf, but the Americans are being pushed back."

Just then pandemonium had broken loose and Nellie said, "They are saying the Americans are here now." At that point she ran off to find out what was going on, and as she left she saw the gallant Mr. Oki sitting on her bunk with a pillow over his head.

Fear could not dampen the ecstacy of joy in our hearts. There was real cause for fear, to be sure. The prison was rocking with shellfire. What would our guards do? Shortly after the arrival of the tanks our guards filed through the barracks carrying machine guns and tins of gasoline and climbed to the roof of the building, where they remained all night. Later we learned that the American military did not know whether Bilibid housed a Japanese garrison or American prisoners. Tanks were placed at entrances and a wait-and-see policy was adopted.

There was no sleep that night. We sat on the floor, not knowing what to expect. We opened our last can of Red Cross Spam, saved for that special time.

Sometime during the night we became aware of an unusual commotion. Several men seemed to be carefully carrying some heavy object: we guessed this was a wounded person on a stretcher. We learned it was not a stretcher but the autoclave from the hospital, ordinarily used for sterilizing instruments and equipment. There were resourceful people in camp who always seemed to be one step ahead of emergencies. Now they knew we couldn't continue to live on joy alone. Our empty stomachs were crying for food. So they had brought over a sack of soybeans our friendly Taiwanese guards had stolen for us. There was no electricity, but a fire was kindled to heat the autoclave. At that point no one asked where the wood had come from. All night we took turns feeding and fanning the fire.

The next morning when I counted 18 cooked soybeans on my plate I said, "Thank you, God, for this feast, for life, for hope." I sat on the floor savoring each soybean slowly. Never had anything tasted so good. It was flavored with the sweet hope of freedom.

What do you do in a crazy world of bursting shellfire? There was a life-and-death battle going on outside our prison walls, but there was nothing we could do to help. Others were fighting the battle for us. Boys from home were shedding their blood that we might live again.

It was Sunday, February 4. Early in the forenoon our guards came down from the roof and walked out of the barracks. Our hearts went out to them. They looked so forlorn. We wished we had had tea or some food to give them. As the last left the great truth dawned on us: there were no longer guards. We must be free! The chairman of our camp, Carl Eschback, promptly arrived with a note from the guardhouse: "We are now leaving. You are free."

Free! We couldn't comprehend it. Someone ran upstairs and took the American flag we had made out of its hiding place. Each of the stars had been sewed on by a native of that state. Esther and I had sewed on the star for North Dakota. As we sewed we had prayed that we could again see the Stars and Stripes waving over the wheatfields of North Dakota.

As the flag was unfurled we tried to sing "The Star Spangled Banner" but the high notes and emotion were too much. It ended with a sob. Even the men were weeping openly. After a few moments we did better with "God Bless America."

Still we had had no communication with the outside. It was Sunday morning, so as usual we gathered in one of the cell blocks for a worship service. Dr. Mather, a veteran China missionary, rose from his sickbed to address us. The noise of battle was so great we could not hear him, so we decided to sing instead, and Dr. Mather suggested "Peace, Perfect Peace."

Peace, perfect peace, in this dark world of sin?
The blood of Jesus whispers peace within.
Peace, perfect peace, with sorrows surging round?
On Jesus' bosom nought but calm is found.

A strange setting for this song!

The day wore on, and still no word from the outside. Some of our men were posted at the outer gate all day, and late in the afternoon they saw some GIs walking along with two Japanese prisoners. They called out, "Hey, we're Americans in here."

The wary GI replied, "You're lying!"

"We *are* American prisoners."

"You can't be prisoners. We're here." And they passed on.

The encounter must have been reported, because about 10:00 that night an officer called in at the gate: "Who are you in there?"

"We're American civilian and military prisoners."

"I'm going to send some of the GIs in to see you," he responded.

The word spread quickly, and soon we were all gathered in the prison courtyard, which one moment would be pitch dark and the next bright as day. Five or six GIs entered quietly. We could say nothing. This was the moment we had dreamed of for three years, and now that it had come we were dumb. A woman broke the silence, "May I touch you?"

Then a GI said, "Is there anything we can do for you? Is there something you would like to know?"

"Yes, who is president of the United States?" a man asked. This was the beginning of our reentry into the world.

17

Rage and Fire

We were free, but the city was by no means safely in American hands yet. The American troops had arrived Saturday night, and all day Monday constant shellfire reminded us of the fierce struggle going on. No food had come in, and we were hungry. Toward dusk we realized a new danger. The heat within the prison was not only from the tropical sun but from great fires which seemed to be coming closer and closer to our prison. From an upstairs balcony we could see the fire. The Japanese were burning the city of Manila and were reportedly advancing toward our prison. Not only was there intense heat from the fire, but cinders and ashes were falling on our compound.

An American officer entered our compound and quietly announced, "We will soon be under attack. Everyone who is able, stand up and begin walking out the door as we direct you. Don't stop to get anything. We will carry out the sick."

There was scarcely a murmur as we filed out of the prison. GIs were everywhere. "Take it easy!" they said. These quiet, soft-spoken men were a contrast to the scraping feet and loud, harsh voices we had become accustomed to. We got our first close glimpse of the military prisoners next door. It is a sight that haunts me yet. It was almost as if there had been a heavy snowfall, for the ground was covered with sheet-draped litters. These were the survivors of the military prisoners from Bataan and Corregidor. There were reportedly only 800 left of the thousands who had been taken prisoner, and 600 had to be carried out on litters that night.

As we walked down the road flanked by GIs and Filipinos, we heard many say, "God bless you. Where are you from?"

Filipinos came with their offerings of water and shells of coconut milk.

I found myself walking alongside a military prisoner who said, "Please say something to me. I haven't heard a woman's voice for three and a half years."

A truck carried the sick to Ang Tibay (a shoe factory which had been converted into the headquarters for the 37th Ohio Infantry Division) and then returned for us who were walking. We were suddenly catapulted from a dark prison to the headquarters of advance military operations. We were told that Bilibid prison had been attacked about 15 minutes after our departure.

The next morning we had our first American breakfast—oatmeal with milk and white sugar, cocoa, crackers, and jam. The sergeant who was dishing up the oatmeal went back to the kitchen and wept. He couldn't believe Americans could be so happy and grateful for a bowl of oatmeal.

During the morning Esther and I were on duty with the sick from our camp. They had been put in improvised hospital quarters together with the sick military prisoners from Bilibid. I felt a fierce anger at what we saw—men blind because of malnutrition and abuse, a large enclosure of those who had become mentally ill. I remember one man who lay on a sort of board with wheels, body and mind immobile, a living corpse. They said he had been a strapping six-footer when he entered the prison, but had been beaten almost to a pulp. They all bore evidence of years of inhuman torture and abuse.

The military doctors said that there were 40 at the point of death that night. One died during the night. The doctors were trying to revive one young man who had given up. They said, "If we can only make him realize he is free, he will live." One of his buddies knelt by his bed, saying "Jim, listen to me! We're free. It's all over. The Americans are here and we're going home."

But he turned his face to the wall saying, "I can't stand it any longer. Let me die." And he died. The message of freedom had come too late to penetrate his tortured mind.

The day at U.S. Army headquarters was spent in talking with GIs and the military prisoners, whom until then we had only been seeing from across the wall. Late in the afternoon an officer announced, "This place will soon be under attack so we must move you back to Bilibid Prison. You will find none of your possessions there, because the place was thoroughly looted after you left."

We were taken back to Bilibid on trucks. The place really had been ransacked. Scarcely anything was left, and the electricity was off, but we lay down on the cement floor and slept. We were alive and free. That was all that mattered.

The morning after our return to Bilibid we went through the vacated barracks of the military prisoners who by then had been evacuated to an American hospital. There was a calendar on one wall with the days marked off until January 15, and there the marks stopped. It was likely the story behind one of the graves that had been dug those last days before our release.

There were many scribblings on the wall. Two stood side by side in sharp contrast: "Damn the U.S. Army. Damn the U.S. Navy. Damn the U.S. Marines." On the same wall was another writing: "Breathes there a man with soul so dead, who never to himself has said, 'This is my own, my native land!' " And another, beside the calendar which ended on January 15, 1945: "Words cannot describe, nor the mind conceive the trials, hardships, and tortures which we have experienced here. We are men broken physically, mentally, and spiritually, at the hands of this nation of perverts."

My rage mounted when I saw the pile of sulfa drugs which had been sent by the American Red Cross and had never been given to our men. They were now swept up in a pile at the guardhouse. For the first time I knew hatred toward the Japanese.

As we walked out into the courtyard, we passed the cell blocks that had been improvised by the U.S. Army as a hospital for the sick Japanese prisoners. I couldn't believe what I saw. They were giving plasma to a Japanese soldier. That was blood sent by Americans to save life. *It's not right!* I thought. Suddenly, with great revulsion, I asked myself, "What's happened to me? How can I decide who is worthy of the plasma which has been given to save life?"

I remembered a day back in the camp hospital in Baguio. An old man was dying. In fact, he had been declared dead by the camp doctor, and I had been delegated to wash the body and prepare it for burial. His friends were outside pounding a box together to serve as a coffin. I was washing his toes when he sat up and said, "What are you doing?" I fled in terror to the operating room.

A while later Dr. Cunningham was preparing a bottle of plasma for this same patient. Another doctor entering the room said, "Who's that for?"

"For Mr. Gruble."

"Are you crazy? Are you going to waste this precious bottle of plasma on that old man? Save it for someone more worthwhile."

Dr. Cunningham replied quietly, "This blood was sent to save life. Who am I to decide whose life is worth saving?"

The ugliness of war is that it distorts our moral judgments and impairs our vision. Feelings prevail over reason and right thinking. In any conflict, no side is totally evil and the other completely good. There was a massive misunderstanding that had brought our two nations into a bloody, costly war. We and the Japanese had had a long history of being friends, so we should never have become enemies.

18

Homecoming

Now the weeks passed quickly, and we were impatient to be on our way home. Because there was still war in the Pacific, we had to wait for a repatriation ship. Our release came on February 4, but we did not arrive in the United States until May 8. During that interim we remained in the prison camps, but we were free, as free as possible in a combat area.

As our section of the city came under the control of the U.S. military, we were permitted to go out on the streets of Manila. The first day that we had ventured a few blocks from the prison, I heard running steps behind me and someone calling "Judy, Judy." It was Helmer Hauge, a boy from my home community in northern Minnesota. He had manned the tank placed at the entrance to Bilibid Prison the night MacArthur's troops had entered Manila.

Every day GIs came to our camp, and there were many happy reunions with old friends. One day as a tall young man in combat attire approached us, Gladys Anderson said, "Why, you look like my brother. Oh, you *are* my brother!"

Every morning we filled a can of coffee from the army supply, and with sugar and chocolate given by GIs we made fudge. So as GIs came to visit we would serve coffee and fudge. One day a soldier looked around our living quarters and said, "You people don't live this way, do you?"

Those servicemen gave us a valuable reorientation to American life. We had left America during the Great Depression, and now with everyone employed at wages higher than we had ever dreamed of, it was a transformed world. From the GIs we learned that Americans had money and good clothes. It seemed as if everyone could plan on higher education and good jobs.

This was a pleasant interim, but also very unreal. We became restless for a return home to a normal life. Early in March all the married couples were told that they were to be taken out by plane. The day they departed, we who were left behind were envious and sad. This was the end of a long, intimate fellowship with many whom I have not seen since. In our last glimpse of them, they were sitting on the ground with their bundles of belongings, truly a group of refugees—skinny, suntanned bodies dressed in what was left of their wardrobes, supplemented with ill-fitting GI donations. We said our good-byes as if in a trance, without any emotion. Carroll, Mary, and little Maren Hinderlie had eaten breakfast with us that morning at our bunk. As we closed our last meal together with prayer, we were deeply moved. We had been through so much together, and those three in spite of serious illnesses had never wavered in their faith or in their sense of humor.

When the married couples had cleared out of the prison, we single women picked up our belongings and walked over to Santa Tomas University, where we were to stay until repatriation. Our departure from Bilibid was void of feeling. I can't even remember any of the details. There was no rapture at leaving the confinement of the stone walls, nor any sentimental looking back to reflect on our communal life of the past three years. I can only recall a certain fearful holding back as we walked toward Santa Tomas and new experiences. I was afraid of new places and reluctant to meet new people.

We remained in Santa Tomas a month. There we were fed by the American military. We had a little more space, although our room was shared by about 30 other women. The atmosphere in this camp was quite different from that of Bilibid. There we had been a close-knit community, sharing food and our skills. The Santa Tomas internees seemed jaded and bitter, each one grabbing for herself. The military who were trying to serve us reacted to the complaining attitude with impatience and resentment.

Finally on Easter Sunday afternoon the announcement came that the *U.S. Eberlie* was in Manila Harbor, and we would be on our way home the next day. I told myself that I was hilariously happy, but I wasn't. Deep inside, I was afraid to leave the unreal life of the past three and a half years that had become my consuming reality. I sensed an involuntary cringing from resuming normal life in America.

We were carried away from Santa Tomas on army trucks, and that ended our life as guests of the Imperial Japanese Army. There was no sentimental looking back, but there was also no joyful anticipation. We went through it all as if we were sleepwalking.

The passage on the *Eberlie* was not altogether pleasant. It was a Coast Guard ship with several thousand passengers. Space was at a premium. We would get up at 5:00 in the morning to reserve a spot on the deck. It wasn't difficult to leave our beds early, for we were in the hold, sleeping on hammocks swung in four tiers and allowing scarcely any room between bunks. Many of the passengers were seasick, so the atmosphere was very unpleasant. To add to the discomfort, an enemy plane had destroyed the air-conditioning system, so the hold became unbearably hot. Tempers flared, and there was much complaining.

But there was always a song in our hearts, "We are on our way home." The night before we reached Los Angeles, we were all too excited to sleep. Early dawn found us on deck straining for that first glimpse of home. When finally we disembarked, I felt like following the example of the GI in front of me, who knelt and kissed the ground.

At the foot of the gangplank a sweet-faced Red Cross lady put her arm around me and said kindly, "My dear, you look tired. Would you like some coffee and a doughnut?" Then the dam of emotion broke. Coffee and doughnuts! We had daydreamed about it, and it had been in our daily conversations. And now to actually hold coffee and doughnuts in my hands—and even more to receive the kindness and sympathy—was too much. At best, we had hoped to slip back into our homes without any recriminations for having been captured and having been a burden on our country. Many of us had had a recurring dream of being home beginning to tell about our prison experiences, only to have people walk away.

Buses took us to a repatriation center where we were given a lavish meal, served with love and kindness. We looked at the menu in amazement, unable to make any decisions. The serving ladies assured us that we could have everything on the menu. The sounds of eating and clatter of dishes were temporarily silenced when a father sitting at the table with his four children bowed his head and in a ringing voice thanked God for food and freedom and asked a blessing on America. There was scarcely a dry eye at the amen.

The processing took a long time. As we stood in the line at the repatriation center, one of our friends became hysterical, and we learned later that she had to go through a period of therapy. An old man clung stubbornly to his tin cans in spite of assurances that in America he would not need them.

Esther, Marian Gray, her three-year-old son Billy, and I spent the first night at the home of Pastor O.H. Egertson, a good friend of Esther. As we entered their home, Billy said, "And now let's go find daddy." His father, a Southern

Baptist missionary, had been tortured and killed at Police Headquarters during our first month of internment.

"But, Billy," Marian replied. "Your daddy is in heaven."

"Yes, but this is heaven, isn't it?"

Not only to Billy, but to all of us it truly seemed like heaven. Our first bath in a tub, sleeping on a soft bed—it was all beyond belief.

Later Marian found Billy in the bathroom with his fingers in his ears, "I can't hear, mommie." It was the first time in his three years of life that he had been in a quiet place.

America's open, welcoming arms overwhelmed us. We were given gift certificates to Los Angeles department stores, where we could buy clothes for our homecoming. I entered Bullock's Department Store just as a group of Federated Women's Club members were assembling at the front entrance. Someone shouted, "Make way. This is a repatriate from the Philippines." Immediately a wide path was made for me, and I took a long walk to the elevator, painfully aware of my stringy hair, leathery complexion, my size 10-C army shoes, a WAC jacket too small, and WAC skirt too large.

In retrospect I know that shopping trip was premature. I couldn't tear myself away from anything the eager sales lady came with. I emerged with a shocking pink dress and a bright blue coat—looking like a clown!

Those days in Los Angeles were not only a time of joy and anticipation, but also of unexpected sadness. The time had come to say good-bye to those with whom we had lived so intensely during the years of internment. The four of us—Esther, Marian, Billy, and I—had become very close in the camp, and we had traveled together from Manila. After we had eaten lunch, we began walking to the trains which would take us to our homes—Esther and me to Minneapolis, and Marian and Billy to South Carolina. After two blocks Esther and I were to turn right, and Marian and Billy were to go straight on to their train. As we approached the place of parting, Marian pleaded, "Let's not say good-bye or anything. Please just turn the corner and don't look back. Billy and I will just go on."

That was the last I was to see of Marian. Several years later, as my husband and I were returning from Japan on furlough, I heard that Marian was dying of cancer in a San Francisco hospital. I planned to go directly from the ship to the hospital, but she had died before we arrived. Marian had met terminal cancer with the same brave trust in our Savior that we had seen in the camp. She also had kept on studying theology at a seminary until almost the end.

Our train took us to Minneapolis, and as we came nearer and nearer home, a strange feeling of apprehension took hold of me. I longed to see my family, and at the same time I was afraid. At last the conductor announced Minneapolis. There was no one on the platform, for that was forbidden during the war. We were directed to elevators that brought us up to the main lobby of the Great Northern station. The moment was too great. Phil, the fiancé who had been faith-fully waiting for me, mother, father, the little brother who had become a man, other brothers, sisters, friends, all with tears streaming down their faces, were singing "Now thank we all our God." A foretaste of the great homecoming in glory! I went through it all, however, as if it were happening to someone else. But now after 40 years I cannot speak of that homecoming without tears.

19

A New Beginning

What lives on in the present from those three years in the shadow of the Rising Sun?

There is a deeper love of country and a constant prayer, "God bless America!" I love the Stars and Stripes, a symbol of freedom, and I pray we may never see it go down again because of weakness and unpreparedness.

There is also a constant prayer for the people of Japan, whom we have come to love and appreciate.

It is true the brutal atrocities of the war have not been exaggerated. It is difficult to reconcile the brutality of the Japanese military with the gentle, polite, loving Japanese we have come to know. The Japanese soldiers of World War II were trained and conditioned by militarists who knew no mercy.

Often during these ensuing years in Tokyo as I have awakened early in the morning to hear the scraping of feet of the vendors on the street below, I have felt myself back in Baguio, with guards shuffling through the barracks. We soon learned not to fear them; for though they could be brutal out at the guardhouse during the day, at night when a guard saw a child uncovered he would lift up the mosquito net with his bayonet and gently cover the sleeping child. One night a mother was trying to soothe a crying baby when a guard was passing through. He held out his arms for the infant and carried it back and forth outside the barrack, crooning Japanese lullabies until the baby went to sleep.

There is a new generation of Japanese youth, far different from the ragged, silent columns of young men whom we met in the retreating army on the mountain road of Luzon in 1945. These well-dressed young people, pressing on for higher degrees, forging ahead of the Western powers in technology and science, know nothing of economic depression or war. They are enjoying the good things in life. But there is emptiness in the center of their lives. The majority of students who attended our student center in Tokyo said, "There is no meaning in our lives." A doctor at Tokyo University said, "Now I have reached the height of my profession. I have everything I have been struggling for, but I'm not happy. I don't know why I'm living."

Modern affluent Japan has no faith to give life meaning. There is no God to thank, no God to turn to in time of need. "I am my own God," a student will say. In this world there is little meaning, for life is a meaningless circle of birth, life, a fierce struggle to get ahead, then retirement and trying to fill up the time until the end. Around this circle is a dark band as foreboding as any prison walls—the band of death. No one can avoid this reality. It circumscribes all human life. Death is the inevitable conclusion. Jean-Paul Sarte said, "Death robs life of all meaning." So we have a picture of a huge cauldron of humanity held prisoner by their own mortality.

Our prison camp was a microcosm of this assembly of human beings. The barbed wire surrounding us was a constant reminder of our helplessness. We could pretend to live a normal life within the enclosure, but the ultimate conclusion was beyond our control. Within the confines of the camp the little details of life, struggles for food, for space, for dignity became important to the point of distortion.

At Bilibid the stone walls with the charged electric wire inside were a grim reminder that life and death were out of our control. Humanly speaking, there was no way out. As more and more people took to their beds and as we saw new graves being dug every day in the military compound, we realized that time was running out.

Then early one January morning I was crossing the prison courtyard on my way to the washtable, carrying a red fire bucket, when we heard a plane overhead. We paid scarcely any attention, for there were single planes now and then. But this time there was a barrage of antiaircraft fire. This was a plane from America! Our country was back in the Philippines. We were wild with joy, hugging and kissing anyone near. But our ecstacy soon turned to horror, for the plane was hit and immediately became a ball of fire. The pilot tried to jump, but his parachute was immediately enveloped in flames. Yes, how much we wanted to be free, to live again! But no amount of wealth, no amount of wishing, hoping, or striving could open those iron gates—there was only one way—the shedding of blood. That was a boy from home who had given his life that we might live. There was hope!

Life is not a meaningless circle. There is a point, and at that point is a cross. There Christ fought a life-and-death battle with Satan, who held us in the bondage of the fear of death. As it is written in the Letter to the Hebrews 2:14-15: "He too shared in [our] humanity so that by his death he might destroy him who holds the power of death—that is, the devil—and free those who all their lives were held in slavery by their fear of death."

He won the battle. He cried out, "It is finished." And now whoever wants life, eternal life in Christ can walk out the gate which he has opened. God's Son has set us free—free, indeed!

We were not only freed from captivity, but we were released to begin a new life. How could we spend the years bought at so great a price? Our new freedom meant new responsibilities. Life in a prison camp is in some ways easy—no significant decisions to make, just drifting along in a timeless sphere, concerned primarily with survival.

An incident during the battle of Manila awakened me to a renewed call from God. Our camp had been under American control for several days, but because of the battle going on, we were kept within Bilibid prison for safety.

One day during that time, an American officer came to the gate and said, "This section of the city is now under our control. We'll open the gates so the prisoners can come out for a few minutes and breathe free air." It was a great experience to walk through those three gateways and step out into a free world—but it was a desolate world! When we had entered the prison, Manila was a beautiful, modern city. Now we saw only ruins—the charred remains of buildings, a heap of ashes.

As we were returning to the prison, we noted a pile of rubbish heaped up against a wall of our building. We began poking around in that heap hoping to find some of the things that had been looted. I was poking about with a stick when I felt something solid and pulled it out of the pile. It was my Bible. It was like finding an old friend. I was holding something that can never be destroyed. The book was a little water-damaged and burnt around the edge, but it had survived.

God had placed in my hands a book much more powerful than the dive bombers that had been bombarding the city day after day, much more powerful than the great Navy guns that had been blasting away at the walled city. They had succeeded only in leaving a heap of ruins and a great deal of bitterness. But in this book is the story of a God who has broken the bonds of death and has set us free. This is the message that gives meaning to life.

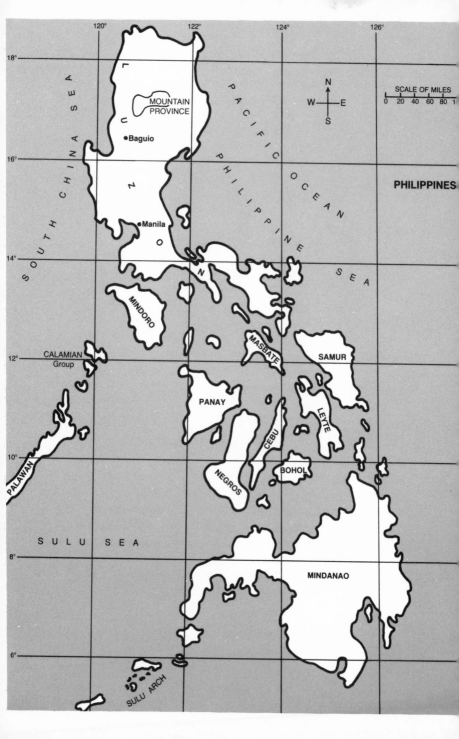

PHILIPPINES

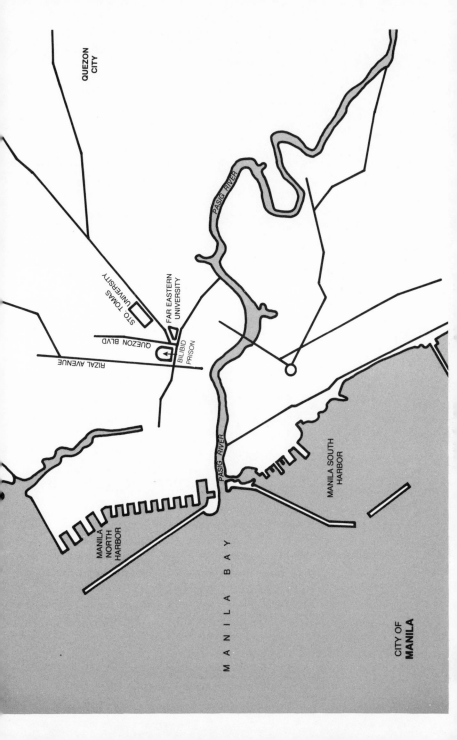

arboreal desert (because of the cactus, shrub and tree forests). Most people call it cactus country.

The Sonoran Desert by now has been divided, bisected and sub-divided many times, not only by the cities of Phoenix, Tucson, Yuma, Nogales, Hermosillo, but also by an evergrowing complex of highways, superhighways, corporate factory farms, open-pit copper mines, power lines, dams, bombing and gunnery ranges and huge tracts of real estate. We must accommodate ourselves to the fact that the unspoiled desert no longer exists as a single integrated unit. The fragments that remain, however, comprise some of the most interesting wilderness areas on the North American continent.

I have looked into most of them and have a few things I want to say, beginning with the Superstition Mountains, working out from there to Organ Pipe Cactus National Monument and the peak and range of Baboquivari, going farther yet to the Kofa Mountains, and finishing up with two of the remotest and wildest areas left in the big cactus coun-try, both south of the border in Mexico: the gulf coast of Sonora and the volcanic region called Pinacate.

I am not a naturalist; what I hope to evoke through words here is the way things *feel* on stormy desert afternoons, the exact shade of color in shadows on the warm rock, the brightness of October, the rust and si-lence and echoes of human history along dusty desert roads, the fragrance of burning mesquite, and a few other simple, ordinary, in-explicable things like that.

I saw the cactus country first in my student days, ranging out far from Albuquerque. Descending from the highlands of New Mexico and north-ern Arizona after 200 miles of nothing but grassland crawling with bald-faced cows and yellow pine forest creeping with smoke and fire, I glided into this new, unknown region of grotesque plant forms: bear grass in giant hummocks rearing from the rock; sotol, a 10-foot stalk rising from a nest of sawtooth leaves and topped with a plumelike cluster of creamy flowers; agave, the century plant, that floral monster, a 15-foot shaft sur-mounted by efflorescing blossoms of brassy gold, the structure based upon a rosette of swordlike blades with barbed edges and needle-tipped points. After that, descending still farther, I encountered varied cacti: cholla (in Spanish the word means head or skull), teddy bear, chain fruit, buckhorn, and cow's tongue prickly pear, clock-face prickly pear, Englemann's prickly pear. Then came the realm of the many-armed flame-flowered ocotillo, 10 to 20 feet high, looking something like a squid or octopus buried head downward in the sand; and fat leaning barrel cactus, fishhook cactus, pincushion cactus—empires of spine and thorn, needle and hair, hook and point and knife and dagger—to the crowning glory of America's Arizona rock garden, the saguaro cactus. Supreme symbol of the Southwest, the saguaro is a giant among cacti, a 20- to 50-foot-high fluted column of chlorophylled plant flesh that comes in as many different shapes and sizes as human beings do. Like planted people, no two alike, individual and idiosyncratic, each saguaro has its own form, its own character, its own personality. Or so it seemed to me then; and now, 25 years later, it still does. When nobody else is around, I talk to them. On simple subjects, of course.

Down from the hills, into the richest and liveliest of American deserts, a land dominated by the big cactus but home also of wild pigs called javelinas; reptiles like the coral snake, coon-tailed rattlesnake and Gila monster; eccentric arachnids—the scorpion, the centipede, the tarantula, the eight-eyed wolf spider. The big birds live here too: baldheaded redheaded turkey vultures, kin to the condor, king of all soaring things; hawks, in over a dozen varieties; golden eagles; the roadrunner, cousin to cuckoos. And little birds: the lively gray rock wren; the canyon wren, a sweet and lyrical singer; the cactus wren, builder of nests in the midst of cactus branches, a small bird with a big mouth and a song like the sound of a rusty adding machine. And others: ravens croaking in the stillness; tiny elf owls nesting in holes in the saguaro, great horned owls adorning telephone poles at night; the black crested *Phainopepla,* the only bird of its kind in the United States, whose name, translated, means glossy robe. There is a nice variety of mammals: mountain lion, bobcat, bighorn sheep, pronghorn antelope, mule deer and Mexican wanderers like the jaguar and wolf. The big cactus desert is blessed with many beasts, some venomous, some weird, but all—in their way—beautiful.

On that first trip, so long ago, I drove my old Chevy among the rocky hills and into the sunny southern reaches of Arizona through Tucson —still a small city then—and across the Papago Indian Reservation under a sapphire sky. I was bound for Organ Pipe Cactus National Monument, named for the tall plant that dominates the place. Why? Because it seemed about as remote a place as you could find.

Off in the distance, as everywhere in this desert land, rose the arid mountains, all rock and angles sparsely grown with brush, floating under cloud shadows, dappled with sunlight, colored by superstition and

CACTUS COUNTRY

THE AMERICAN WILDERNESS/TIME-LIFE BOOKS/NEW YORK

BY EDWARD ABBEY
AND THE EDITORS OF TIME-LIFE BOOKS

THE AMERICAN WILDERNESS

SERIES EDITOR: Charles Osborne
Editorial Staff for *Cactus Country:*
Text Editor: Harvey B. Loomis
Picture Editor: Mary Y. Steinbauer
Designer: Charles Mikolaycak
Staff Writer: Gerald Simons
Chief Researcher: Martha T. Goolrick
Researchers: Joan Chambers, Angela Dews,
Barbara Ensrud, Rhea Finkelstein,
Helen M. Hinkle, Beatrice Hsia,
Gillian McManus
Design Assistant: Mervyn Clay

Editorial Production
Production Editor: Douglas B. Graham
Quality Director: Robert L. Young
Assistant: James J. Cox
Copy Staff: Rosalind Stubenberg,
Eleanore W. Karsten, Florence Keith
Picture Department: Dolores A. Littles,
Joan Lynch

Valuable assistance was given by the following
departments and individuals of Time Inc.:
Editorial Production, Norman Airey, Nicholas
Costino Jr.; Library, Peter Draz; Picture
Collection, Doris O'Neil; Photographic
Laboratory, George Karas; TIME-LIFE News
Service, Murray J. Gart; Correspondents Margot
Hapgood (London), Marilyn Drago (Tucson),
Earl Zarbin (Phoenix).

The Author: Edward Abbey, a self-proclaimed desert rat, has written in *Desert Solitaire* of his experiences as a park ranger in Utah. He is also the author of four novels.

The Consultant: Mervin W. Larson is the Director of the Arizona-Sonora Desert Museum near Tucson. He has collaborated with his wife, Peggy, on four books dealing with deserts and the behavior of social insects.

The Cover: Giant saguaros, the largest species of cactus in Arizona, stand in silhouette against a desert sunset east of the Baboquivari Mountains.

Contents

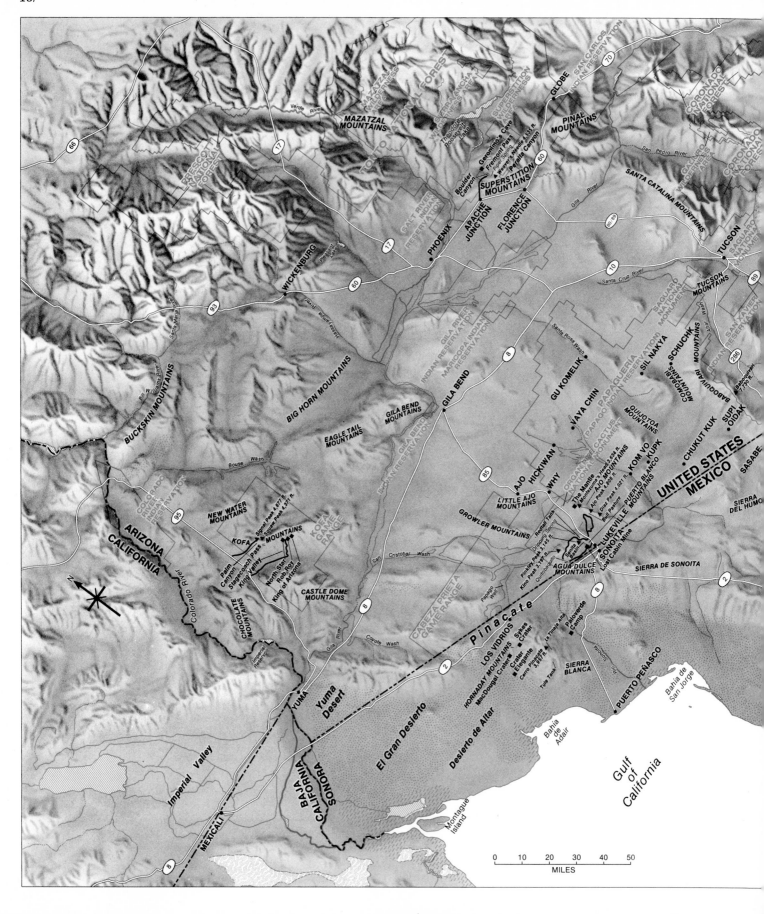

MAZATZAL MOUNTAINS

SUPERSTITION MOUNTAINS

GLOBE

PINAL MOUNTAINS

SANTA CATALINA MOUNTAINS

PHOENIX

APACHE JUNCTION

FLORENCE JUNCTION

TUCSON

WICKENBURG

PRESCOTT NATIONAL FOREST

BUCKSKIN MOUNTAINS

BIG HORN MOUNTAINS

GILA BEND MOUNTAINS

EAGLE TAIL MOUNTAINS

GILA BEND

TUCSON MOUNTAINS

SAGUARO NATIONAL MONUMENT

GU KOMELIK

SCHUCHK

SIL NAKYA

KOMOBABI MOUNTAINS

BABOQUIVARI MOUNTAINS

VAYA CHIN

QUIJOTOA MOUNTAINS

SUPI OIDAK

CHUKUT KUK

NEW WATER MOUNTAINS

Signal Peak 4,877 ft.
Squaw Peak 4,571 ft.

KOFA

KOFA MOUNTAINS

KOFA GAME RANGE

AJO

HICKIWAN

WHY

ORGAN PIPE CACTUS NATIONAL MONUMENT

AJO MOUNTAINS

LITTLE AJO MOUNTAINS

GROWLER MOUNTAINS

KOM VO

KUPK

PUERTO BLANCO MOUNTAINS

UNITED STATES
MEXICO

SASABE

SIERRA DEL HUMO

ARIZONA
CALIFORNIA

Palm Canyon
Stagecoach Pass
King Valley
North Star
Rob Roy
King of Arizona

CASTLE DOME MOUNTAINS

San Cristobal Wash

The Mantle
Montezuma's Head 3,634 ft.
Ajo Peak 4,808 ft.
Diaz Peak 4,021 ft.
Bull Pasture

Redtail Tank

Dripping Spring

LUKEVILLE
SONOYTA

Lost Cabin Mine

SIERRA DE SONOITA

CHOCOLATE MOUNTAINS

Colorado River

Pinkley Peak 3,145 ft.
Kino Peak 3,197 ft.
Quitobaquito

AGUA DULCE MOUNTAINS

Papago Well

CABEZA PRIETA GAME RANGE

Gila River

Coyote Wash

Pinacate

YUMA

Yuma Desert

LOS VIDRIOS

HORNADAY MOUNTAINS

Sykes Crater

MacDougal Crater
Elegante Crater
Cerro Pinacate 3,957 ft.

La Tinaja Alta

Tule Tank

Papago Camp

SIERRA BLANCA

PUERTO PENASCO

Bahia de San Jorge

Imperial Reservoir

Imperial Valley

BAJA CALIFORNIA
SONORA

El Gran Desierto

Desierto de Altar

Bahia de Adair

Gulf of California

MEXICALI

Montague Island

0 10 20 30 40 50
MILES

SAGUAROS AND CHOLLAS AT SUNSET IN THE SANTA CATALINAS

BRITTLEBUSH AND BARREL CACTI IN THE PINACATE REGION

LUPINE EDGED BY BRITTLEBRUSH IN THE MAZATZAL MOUNTAINS

SAGUARO NATIONAL MONUMENT UNDER A RARE SNOW BLANKET

THE PALOVERDE, ARIZONA'S STATE TREE

EL GRAN DESIERTO OF MEXICO UNDER A LOWERING SKY

LIFE WORLD LIBRARY
LIFE NATURE LIBRARY
TIME READING PROGRAM
THE LIFE HISTORY OF THE UNITED STATES
LIFE SCIENCE LIBRARY
GREAT AGES OF MAN
TIME-LIFE LIBRARY OF ART
TIME-LIFE LIBRARY OF AMERICA
FOODS OF THE WORLD
THIS FABULOUS CENTURY
LIFE LIBRARY OF PHOTOGRAPHY
THE TIME-LIFE ENCYCLOPEDIA OF GARDENING
THE AMERICAN WILDERNESS
THE EMERGENCE OF MAN
THE OLD WEST
FAMILY LIBRARY
   THE TIME-LIFE BOOK OF FAMILY FINANCE
   THE TIME-LIFE FAMILY LEGAL GUIDE

A Dry Corner of the Continent

The arid wilderness explored in this book covers some 69,000 square miles of southern Arizona and northern Mexico (tinted rectangle above) and represents about half of the vast Sonoran Desert. The region, shown in tan on the detailed relief map at left, has a terrain both rugged and varied. Many mountain ranges break it up into broad plains and rough-sloped valleys. High peaks, indicated by black triangles, overlook jagged foothills with abandoned gold and silver mines and natural tanks—rocky depressions that conserve the spring rains for much of the year. The intermittent streams and gravelly dry washes, marked by broken blue lines, are the result of runoff from rare desert rains; they are found throughout the region, though they scarcely penetrate several great tracts of sandy wasteland, indicated on the map by red stippling.

Though harsh, and hostile to many plants, the region offers ideal conditions for the bizarre members of the water-storing cactus family, which thrive here in more than 140 species from pincushion cacti two inches tall to ponderous saguaros and cardons that reach heights of 50 feet and more.

1/ The Real Desert

The real desert? Yes, but which one? I sit here on the terrace of this old stone house above Tucson in the foothills of Arizona's Santa Catalina Mountains and think about the deserts I have known. And the ones I've only imagined.

The city glitters softly, 10 miles down and away, under its tender veil of smog. Airplanes like fireflies circle slowly through the twilight. From this distance the city remains as inaudible as it is lovely. Moonrise over the Rincon Mountains, beyond a shore of clouds. Great gory sunset in the west, behind the jagged pinnacles of the Tucson Mountains. The clouds over that way, underlit by the sun, resemble boiled salmon—pink gold against the velvet purple sky. Such skies are common during the summer stormy season in the Southwest; I've seen them over the canyon lands of Utah, the burned iron hills of Death Valley, old lost adobe missions in Chihuahua, the white sands of New Mexico, the dunes of El Gran Desierto in northwestern Mexico. Which desert did I love the most?

Which lady did I love the most? I loved them all. But one was lovelier than any other. One was richer, more complicated, most various. For all its harshness, loneliness, cruelty and cunning, one desert haunted me like a vision of paradise. Still does, though now I live here. I mean that mountain-studded portion of southern Arizona and Mexican Sonora that geographers call the Sonoran Desert and botanists call the legend. I imagined them full of lost gold mines, sun-bleached skeletons of men and horses, antique rusty weapons, hidden springs, crumbling cabins, wandering trails, the abandoned hulks of mining machinery, 1922 Maxwells, gin bottles turning blue under the ferocious sun, all things old, worthless and wonderful.

I saw the Papago villages along the highway; stone and adobe huts, wooden ramadas for summer living in the shade, many children all brown as acorns, many horses, many goats, many cattle, many cannibalized automobiles resting upside down among the junk and garbage, chickens scratching in the bare, dusty yards. Occasionally I'd see a wagon, an old man under his sombrero on the seat and a team of horses, eight legs trudging along the highway, hauling hay, cattle feed, water, women, children, sometimes nothing. Over all, soaring without visible effort against the sky, drifted the hungry, arrogant, wide-winged buzzards, waiting for something somewhere soon to die. The patience and complacency of the scavenger, whose business never fails, whose customers always come.

Death and life usually appear close together, sometimes side by side, in the desert. Perhaps that is the secret of the desert's fascination: all lies naked, out in the open in this all too vulnerable land. Wherever we look we are reminded of death—by the glimmering wastes of alkali flats; by the burned-out volcanic hills; by a mesquite tree under a lethal burden of parasitic mistletoe, a plant as distinct from the Christmas sprig as stealing is from giving, delivering its kiss of death to the tree by means of suckerlike roots; by the occasional little white crosses along the roadways, marking the sites of fatal accidents on the heat-shimmering straightaways, by the remains of a maggot-swarming, dehydrated cow; by the hulk of a rotting saguaro, whose sloughing skin seems to present decay and decomposition in its most vivid form: nothing, not even the waiting vulture in the sky, looks more deathly than a dying giant cactus.

All, even these, are aspects of the desert: and with me it was love at first sight. Across the Papago Reservation I drove, across the solemn desert hills where the ranks and squads of saguaros towered over the rock, over the mesquite trees, over the bur sage and brittlebush. This was good saguaro country. They grew along the skyline of the hills, on the stony slopes, in the little meandering canyons creasing the hills, on the fans of rock debris that spread out toward the basins separating each range of mountains from the next.

I camped at night far out in the middle of the reservation, pulling off the main road and driving for maybe three or four miles into the desert on a winding wagon track. I built a fire of mesquite wood and cooked my supper in the evening gloom.

Autumn in the Sonoran Desert. The great horned owls lulled me to sleep, as I lay in my cheap Sears Roebuck amateur-outdoorsman sleeping bag in the middle of a sandy wash, across a cattle path. A flash flood could have washed me into the Gulf of California, but I didn't know any better. I slept well too, except that around midnight I was awakened by the distant sound of drumming and chanting. Off in the wasteland, out in the bush, some Papago were having a sing. The music came my way on small waves of wind, from a considerable distance, now here, now gone. I was not alarmed. Indians are no longer dangerous except when tooling their pickup trucks, loaded with sheep, wives and kids, down the white man's asphalt trails.

I opened my eyes in the lavender twilight of dawn to see a tarantula, big as my hand (standard size) and furry brown as a muskrat, walking across the sand toward my face. Walking, I say, not crawling, not creeping; a tarantula stands up on its eight long black hairy legs and *walks* where it wants to go, like a man.

The tarantula's poison is not dangerous, the desert guidebooks assure us, despite its ancient reputation as an aggressive killer, and although the bite itself can be painful. Still, the tarantula looks much bigger than a spider should look, especially when viewed from ground level at a range of 30 inches. I rolled hastily aside, still zipped up in my Dacron sack, and watched him—her—it—walk on by in a straight line across the wash. Whatever the creature was hunting it was not me. Mostly the nearsighted tarantula eats insects and sometimes small lizards and mice. The tarantula in turn is the prey of a wasp known as the tarantula hawk. Also of cowboys with six-guns.

One time driving through western Texas I saw a car parked off the road and a group of tourists watching a tarantula stroll across the highway. I stopped to watch too. A moment later a pickup truck screeched to a halt close by and a large red-nosed man in cowboy costume rolled out and came up to us waving a revolver. "Stand back, folks," he said, "y'all stand back now." He aimed his piece at the tarantula and blasted away from a cautious range of six feet. One, two, three, four explosions, asphalt and gravel flying in all directions, before he succeeded in gunning down the terrified tarantula; on the fourth shot it vanished in a splatter of dust, lead, hair and fragmented chitinous tissue. "That there's a dangerous animal, folks," the cowboy said, lowering his weap-

Perhaps spurred by the mating urge, a male tarantula—usually a nocturnal prowler—takes a walk in the sun in the Sonoran Desert. These huge hairy spiders, with an average body length of two inches and legspans of five inches, are less menacing than they look. They bite only if teased, and their venom is not deadly to human beings.

on. What animal? We contemplated the bleared impact area on the edge of the pavement.

I don't fool with tarantulas myself. I drove on across the Papago Reservation to a fork in the road, with gas station, café and post office, called Why. Why, Arizona; named for the "Y" formed here by the junction. Ten miles down the road to the west lay the old mining town of Ajo (meaning garlic), occupied by the Phelps Dodge Corporation, site of one of the biggest open-pit copper mines in the world. A dirty smudge across the sky, waste from the plant smokestacks, provided plain evidence that the mill was in operation.

I took the south fork and soon reached the entrance to Organ Pipe Cactus National Monument. I didn't know it then but this was the place where I would later work for three winters as a seasonal ranger for the National Park Service.

More desert country; all about grew the gray-green shrub called creosote bush, most common of all low desert plants, with mesquite, paloverde and saguaro on the hillsides, and mountains, mountains, always more mountains in the background. And the vast quiet sky, with clouds and buzzards, as always. On the left, to the east, I could see the towering shape of Montezuma's Head, a 1,400-foot-high structure of volcanic materials, the sides as vertical as the walls of a building. But not unscalable, as I would learn one day, 20 years later.

I drove all the way to monument headquarters, 16 miles, without seeing a single organ pipe cactus. When I finally stopped I figured out why: all of the organ pipes grow on south-facing slopes; I had come from the north, not looking back.

The organ pipe cactus is a conspicuous plant, though perhaps not so impressive as the saguaro. At most the organ pipe grows to 10 or 15 feet, only about half the saguaro's height. Instead of a single main column the organ pipe, as the name implies, produces a cluster of branches from a single base. Though common in northwest Mexico, this cactus grows nowhere in the United States except in this part of Arizona, which is the primary reason the area was set aside by Presidential proclamation in 1937 as a national monument.

Near the sun-baked village of Lukeville, on the Mexican border, I turned west to follow a dirt road through the cactus "forest" to an oasis called Quitobaquito. On the way I saw my first Gila monster.

There it was, a fat, beaded bag of nonchalance, ambling across the road in front of me. I stopped the car and got out to inspect it, not getting too close, for this is one of the two lizards in North America with a venomous bite. (The other is a Mexican cousin.) My monster neither stopped nor turned but continued its leisurely crawl across the stony floor of the desert beside the road. I followed it with much more interest in it than it had in me. Finally, as my interest became too persistent, the big lizard took refuge under the low branches of a creosote bush. I squatted on my heels to study it for a while.

It was about 20 inches long, including the fat, heavy tail, and entirely enclosed in a scaly skin that resembled Indian beadwork, salmon pink and black. The legs seemed much too stubby for such a long and broad body, and in this respect the Gila monster reminded me of its distant kin the alligator. I poked it, gently, with a stick, and it whipped its massive head around and hissed at me; I had a glimpse of a pink-lined mouth and rows of small white teeth.

The Gila monster is supposedly quick and agile when seriously molested, but has no fangs and in any case its neck is so short that it cannot lunge and strike like a snake. The poison, secreted by glands in the mouth, is worked into the flesh of a victim by prolonged gripping and chewing. One of the legends concerning this lizard is that once it gets its teeth sunk in your flesh and the jaws clamped shut, it never lets go. I did not experiment. Another story has it that the Gila monster has no anus, and cannot eliminate wastes. False. Actually, the creature is defenseless against humans armed with anything more than their bare hands. Famous and hideous, protected by law as one of Arizona's natural tourist attractions, it nevertheless suffers much persecution from the ignorant, and may already be an endangered species.

Leaving the Gila monster in its natural habitat unharmed and only slightly alarmed, I went on with my journey through the dusty hinterlands of Organ Pipe. After a day and night at Quitobaquito, an uninhabited oasis of sweet, cool water and green cottonwood trees that I would come to know better some years later, I headed north, following a different road.

Somewhere out in the open desert of west central Organ Pipe I came to a fork in the road, with signboards. One sign said, "Park Hdqtrs 21 Mi"; the other something like "Primitive Road, Not Patrolled." Naturally I took the latter, which looked more interesting and led in the direction I wanted to go.

The old road took me through more miles of creosote flats, the creosote bush being the only plant of any size that grows in that wide arid basin between the desert mountain ranges. Jack rabbits in astonishing number sprang away from the road at my approach, seeming to swarm across the land like a plague of grasshoppers. Not enough coyotes to keep them in check.

As I rounded a knoll and headed down a long straightaway, five sleek pronghorn antelope leapt from the shade of some paloverde trees and raced along ahead of me, paralleling the road. I followed through the dust from 20 pounding hoofs, watching the white rumps bounce across the rough, brushy terrain. Glancing at the speedometer I clocked the pronghorns' pace at 26 miles per hour before they finally veered from the road and faded away into the flat, vast, dust-green emptiness of what the maps call Growler Valley. I thought of Africa. I thought of original America.

Another 40 miles of primitive road brought me to the town of Ajo and the highway. I headed the old Chevrolet homeward to Albuquerque through Gila Bend and Phoenix and what seemed like a thousand miles of cotton farms, feed lots, hayfields, used-car lots, power plants, housing plantations, barbed-wire fences and telephone lines—the fat rich commercial gut of Arizona.

The familiar dreariness did not dim my sense of the desert still waiting out there. I would not forget the rocky hills studded with giant cactus, the secret canyons winding into unknown places, the purple, shadowed mountains on the horizon, the rich complex of animal life, bird life, plant life, all that strange, sometimes bitter magic of the natural world. I knew that I would be back, many times.

NATURE WALK **/ To a Foothills Canyon**

TEXT AND PHOTOGRAPHS BY DAVID CAVAGNARO

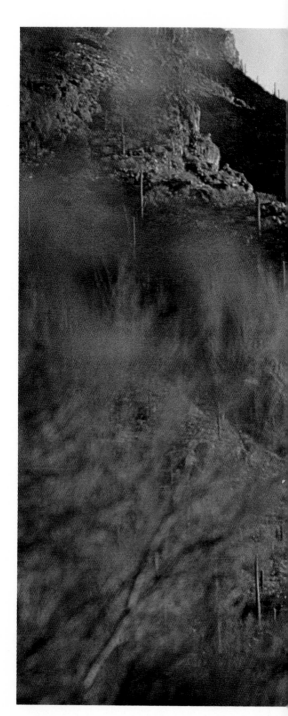

The time was April. I was visiting Edward Abbey for a few days, and I was also visiting the part of the Sonoran Desert he lives in and with, the ancient cactus and shrub desert of Arizona. Behind Ed's old stone house loom the steep, deeply eroded Santa Catalina Mountains; below lies a great sweeping plain through which the distant Santa Ritas and Tucson Mountains protrude like islands in a dry sea.

The desert's day shift was about to come on. The songs of wrens, flickers, doves and Gila woodpeckers mingled with the fading cries of coyotes; clouds of droning insects, emerged from their nighttime hiding places, surrounded blossoming mesquites. The sun peered over the eastern end of the Santa Catalinas, its low-angled rays gliding along the rugged range. Impatient to get out and explore, I downed a final cup of coffee, picked up my camera and struck off toward the forests of juniper and fir in the highlands.

My destination, one of the many deep canyons that cleave these hills, was only about three quarters of a mile from Ed's place. But as I headed toward it my pace slowed. The plain I was crossing—part of an enormous alluvial fan that extends for miles and miles—was fascinating in its own right.

Beneath my feet and all around me lay the stony rubble of millennia, much of it carved from the mountains during wetter times produced by the distant breath of glaciers far to the north. The boulders and rocks and gravel have lent a wild, unsettled look to the landscape; time and again they have been washed across the skirt of alluvium by torrential floods that occasionally, even now, relieve the desert of drought.

This year, however, the winter rains had not come. The many washes, large and small, were dry. The huge saguaros that thrive in this rocky realm looked shrunken, their accordion pleats deeply folded because of the lack of moisture. Had the rains been right, vast carpets of verbena, owl clover and gold poppies would have been blooming on this April day. But here and there a stunted plant had blossomed quickly and set a few seeds. The rest, tough little capsules, lay dormant in the sand, waiting.

An unusual midwinter snowfall had brought a bit of moisture to the lower slopes of the Santa Catalinas. Wherever the meltwater had accumulated, flowers—zinnias, daisies,

A STAND OF SAGUAROS AT THE ENTRANCE TO AN ARROYO

penstemon—were now slightly taller and more numerous, and the graceful paloverdes were solid gold with blossoms. But on the higher, drier ground other paloverdes were bare of leaves, forced to rely entirely upon their green stems and branches for photosynthesis. Only a few blossoms testified to the life that persisted within these sturdy desert trees; they, too, like the dormant flower seeds, awaited rain.

On the large climatic scale of geologic time, the southwestern United States and northern Mexico are in the grip of a dry phase. Forests of pine and fir and the oak woods that fringe them have retreated to the tops of the highest, coolest mountains. Strange cacti, thorny shrubs and delicate little desert annuals have advanced out of the southern desert highlands. For example, seedling saguaros will gain a foothold, over a period of years, a few yards farther up the rocky slopes of a range or progress a small distance farther north around its flanks. But the expansion of the desert—or its contraction during a wet phase —takes place over an immensity of time; in this larger climatic rhythm, a year is only a tiny vibration. And so there will be wet years and drought years for the paloverdes, saguaros and seed capsules I saw in this corner of the desert. For whatever hardships come, every living thing here is superbly prepared.

As I walked on, the sun's rays streamed down through the saguaro groves. Spiny pads of Engelmann's prickly-pear cactus, laden with buds and blooms in spite of the drought, were haloed by bright morning light, and the heat was strong and palpable; sunlight was reflected too from the brilliant silver leaves of the brittlebush. The dawn bird chorus had dwindled to periodic calls.

I settled for a while on a rock-strewn flat between two washes. Beneath a stone I found black darkling beetles, and a striped-tail scorpion scurried nervously to and fro, disturbed by the sudden intrusion of sunlight. A species common in the Tucson area, this scorpion is a fierce predator, active at night: it uses leglike pincers to catch insects, subduing them, if necessary, with a sting from its upturned tail. Although its

A STRIPED-TAILED SCORPION

sting is painful, the striped-tail is harmless to man.

The ground was littered with old prickly-pear pads. The weather and the attacks of insects had reduced them to skeletons of woody lace. Some pads still bore a coat of masonry constructed by termites from mud and their own droppings. When the ground is moist, termites surface from subterranean passageways

ENGELMANN'S PRICKLY PEAR

and feed on fallen organic debris.

A tiny earthstar nearby, less than an inch across, was also a relic from the last rain. Mummified by the sun, its dry outer covering folded back against the ground, this strange relative of the puffball fungus contains a round central packet of microscopic spores that are eventually released into the wind.

The desert ground is a quiet place during the heat of the day, but close examination reveals a host of signs of nighttime activity. Within one small area I spotted the tracks of darkling beetles and Gambel's quail, a small pile of dry rabbit pellets, and a ring of seed chaff surrounding the nest entrance of harvester ants.

A black hole about three quarters of an inch wide and lined with spider webbing indicated the presence of a wolf spider somewhere deep within the cool recesses of the earth. These weird hairy spiders—with no fewer than eight eyes—emerge at night to hunt their prey on the move rather than trap them in a web. When mature, wolf spiders measure about two inches in leg span; in spite of their fearsome appearance, they are altogether harmless to humans, though their bite—inflicted only if they are provoked—is mildly toxic.

Shade at Noon

The morning was just about gone. The increasing oppressiveness of the heat finally drove me from the exposed plain in search of shade. I found it, not far from the deep canyon that was my ultimate goal, in the main arroyo that drains the canyon. Nurtured by abundant ground water,

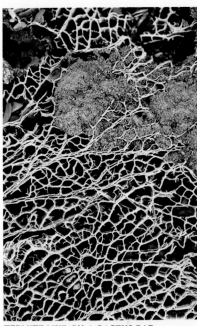
TERMITE MUD ON A CACTUS PAD

AN EARTHSTAR PUFFBALL

A WOLF SPIDER'S BURROW

trees and shrubs grow larger in this gully, and their branches afforded welcome protection as I walked.

I soon found that I was not alone. From a honey mesquite directly over my head came a sudden explosion of feathers, and a white-winged dove settled several yards away in a paloverde and eyed me suspiciously. I had come upon it in nesting season, and it was instantly on guard. But I climbed up through the mesquite's stiff branches for a closer look at the nest. It was of simple design, a loose bowl of sticks set far out among the twigs, and within it were two elegant white eggs.

Other birds, too, had found haven in the dense growth of the arroyo. Gilded flickers and Gila woodpeckers flew in and out of holes they had carved high in the saguaros. I caught a brief glimpse of a cardinal among paloverde blossoms, and recurrently

A MOURNING DOVE (LEFT) AND ITS WHITE-WINGED KIN IN A PALOVERDE

A WHITE-WINGED-DOVE NEST IN HONEY MESQUITE

A CACTUS WREN AND ITS NEST IN JUMPING CHOLLA

I heard the strange rasping call of the cactus wren.

The largest wren found in the United States, this spotted brown bird chooses the most densely armed cacti for nesting sites. Nearly every teddy bear, staghorn and jumping cholla in the area contained at least one nest, either old or freshly built. Each one was a neatly fashioned envelope of grass, tucked securely among the spiny joints of cholla, and each had a single, tube-shaped entrance hole.

A Good Place to Nest

The cactus wren is not the only bird that nests in cholla. The curve-billed thrasher is also a frequent occupant, and in one gnarled jumping cholla I found a mourning dove with two pinfeathered young. Relying upon protective coloration, adaptive stillness and the armor of the cactus itself, the dove allowed me to approach within two feet of the nest with no more reaction than the indifferent blink of an eye.

I paid a small price in exercising my curiosity, however, for as I stepped back from the nest my heel flipped up a loose joint of jumping cholla and it lodged firmly in the back of my calf. A few painful moments drove home the point that the dove had chosen its nest site wisely. The ground was littered with spiny cholla segments, some of which had taken root as new plants. The pendulous arms of the cactus were heavy with long strings of knobby green fruit, which may persist for many seasons—even years—before falling. Some of these would even-

A MOURNING DOVE AND YOUNG IN JUMPING CHOLLA

tually generate new cactus plants.

Inspecting another cholla, this time with greater respect, I detected a jet-black cactus beetle hiding from the sun between the branches. A full inch in length, this peculiar insect, which feeds upon the succulent tissues of the cactus, belongs to the family of long-horned wood borers;

A CACTUS BEETLE

A CACTUS FLY ON BARREL CACTUS

A CACTUS BUG NYMPH

but it differs most markedly from nearly all its relatives in being entirely flightless.

What a strange landscape of enormous daggers this beetle inhabits; and yet, as I watched, it scrambled expertly among the spines, clinging firmly to them with sharp claws and strong legs, its tough exoskeleton immune to the pricking of the sharp points. And so this insect has penetrated perhaps the best line of defense in the desert. At the same time the spines help protect it from birds, rodents and skunks.

Another insect that has done well in a cactus habitat is the cactus bug, young nymphs of which I saw dotting the pads of Engelmann's prickly pear. Equipped with long, piercing mouthparts with which they suck

SYRPHID-FLY EGGS ON A BARREL CACTUS

plant juices, these insects, when numerous, may inflict quite noticeable wounds on the cactus pads.

An Army of Insects

Healthy cacti effectively fend off the hungry hordes of desert creatures that would relish their juicy flesh. But as soon as a plant is injured or dies of old age, a host of insects attack it. Along the arroyo bank was a fishhook barrel cactus, lately dislodged from its rocky perch. Though its tissues were still very much alive, tiny cactus flies were laying their eggs among the spines, and large syrphid flies hovered around it, droning incessantly in the midday heat, occasionally landing for a drink of exuding sap.

When I moved in for a closer look, I discovered that many of the long fishhook spines bore clusters of oval white eggs deposited by a species of syrphid fly. When the eggs hatch, the larvae of this insect burrow into the cactus, where they feed on the larvae of other insects.

Farther along the arroyo a pair of saguaros had died but had not yet fallen. Their flesh had long since been consumed by insects. Spines and slabs of dried skin lay at their base in a heap, home now for several funnel-web spiders. One 15-foot saguaro skeleton still stood erect, but the woody ribs of the other one arched like a sculpted fountain of water, bending toward the earth, to which their entire substance would eventually return.

As I walked on through the arroyo toward the mouth of the canyon, an early-afternoon breeze whispered

SAGUARO SKELETONS

A TARANTULA HAWK WASP

A DAINTY SULPHUR BUTTERFLY

A WILD HONEYBEE

A QUEEN BUTTERFLY

A SNOUT BUTTERFLY

A MARINE BLUE BUTTERFLY

A LYCID BEETLE ON CATCLAW ACACIA

along the dusty wash from the hot plain behind me.

Honeybees gathering pollen rummaged through the golden anthers of prickly-pear blossoms. Most of the gatherers seemed lazy with excess, but here and there I glimpsed a solitary bee flying the same mission with far greater speed. Green lynx spiders —predators that spin no webs—occupied some of the flowers, pouncing on the bees themselves or, more often, on small beetles, which are easier to catch.

In open places where the glare from white sand was intense, small silver clumps of wild zinnias attracted dainty sulphur and marine blue butterflies. They flitted from one blossom to another, sipping nectar while quaking in the breeze like tiny banners. I saw a few strange long-beaked snout butterflies land in twiggy bushes, and in their stillness they seemed suddenly transmuted into dead leaves.

The Butterflies' Colorful Warning

A large reddish queen butterfly, southern relative of the monarch, soared up the canyon on the breeze and settled near several scarlet lycid beetles among the puffy pale yellow acacia flowers. These netwinged beetles, like the queen and the monarch butterflies, are unpleasant tasting to predators, and they advertise the fact through their conspicuous coloration.

Enormous tarantula hawk wasps rattled slowly through the air on their way between acacias, their wings a brilliant orange blur against the sky. These wasps are nectar feeders themselves, but each female, in order to provide food for her larvae, must seek out and paralyze a tarantula with her powerful sting. She then finds an unoccupied underground burrow, drags in the helpless spider, lays a single egg upon it and seals the burrow entrance. When the egg hatches, the larva food is right there—in the form of a paralyzed tarantula. The female wasp may repeat the process many times before her own short life has ended.

Like the lycid beetle and queen

A BLISTER BEETLE

and monarch butterflies, the tarantula hawk's bright color warns potential predators. In this case, however, the warning does not concern unpleasant taste but potent sting. An animal that tangles once with this insect is not likely to try again.

In a thistle plant beneath the acacias, I saw another insect that predators may well beware because of its unpalatability: the orange blister beetle. Some species of this insect can also cause trouble for people; its secretions can cause nasty skin sores. I watched from a prudent distance as several of these beetles probed the blossoms with long, strawlike mouthparts, sipping nectar from the thistle's tubular disk flowers. While some were feeding, others were mating and laying eggs underneath young buds. The eggs hatch just about as the buds open, and when a bee comes for pollen some of the larvae may manage to attach themselves to its hairs and be carried back to the bee's nest. Once the bee provisions and seals the cell in which it has laid its egg, the blister beetle larvae remain behind, destroy the egg and consume the carefully stored pollen themselves.

A Sound of Water

Beyond the acacias, the Santa Catalinas rise like a great convoluted wall. Ridges line the canyon I had come to explore, and as I entered it I heard the sound of falling water. It was only a trickle, a mere suggestion of the torrents that must pour from the mountains during a good storm. Now the flow was gentle, spilling over algae-draped rocks, slipping into quiet pools dotted with hundreds of tiny whirligig beetles and fringed with yellow monkey flowers —so called because the blossom resembles a monkey's face.

A stream on the canyon floor proved cool and refreshing, the sound of the water almost as much as its taste. As I drank, so did dozens of honeybees, butterflies and wasps, quenching their thirst along the wet sandy shore.

In this narrow stream-bottom oasis, broad-leaved trees largely re-

SYCAMORE TREES FRAMING THE CANYON WALLS

place the desert trees and shrubs common in the arroyo below. The first trees I encountered were small, twisted western hackberries, whose dark green leaves nourish caterpillars of the snout butterfly. Farther along, I came to an ancient Arizona oak, the only one in the lower reaches of the canyon. The cool shade beneath its spreading canopy invited a rest from the afternoon heat.

But the oak also marked the end of easy walking for me. Above it, the canyon narrows and ascends more steeply. Vertical cliffs of weathered gray gneiss faced each other closely, casting the boulder-strewn cleft in shadow. Confined by this funnel of rock, the wind blew like a gale, roaring through the leaves of huge sycamore and Arizona walnut trees and rattling the slender daggers of sotol leaves as though a ritual dance

ASH LEAVES

were in progress. One of the desert's most beautiful lilies, the white-flowering sotol was once prized by the Pima Indians of this area for the strong fibers in its elongated leaves, which they used for weaving.

Here and there, as the sun slipped behind the west ridge, its last rays of light glowed upon a high rock face and illuminated the leaves of ash trees. Dusk had come early, and canyon tree frogs, a perfect color complement to the waterworn gneiss upon which they huddled, began to croak. Nearby, on a sheer face of rock, protected from above by an overhang and from below by a deep reflecting pool, a pair of black phoebes had built a half-cup mud and straw nest. As I watched, one of the birds returned from its insect hunting and settled to incubate the eggs.

There was activity, too, in a fallen

A SOTOL PLANT

A POOL AT THE CANYON MOUTH

sycamore log where honeybees had taken up residence. In the fading light bees flew home, one by one, entering through a hollow knot. The log hummed faintly as the workers ventilated the hive with their wings. Raccoon tracks in the soft sand and mud near the pool reminded me that soon the night creatures would be out and it would be time for dinner back at Ed Abbey's stone cabin.

I found a precarious route up a dry side gully and scrambled toward the crest of the ridge on the canyon's eastern flank. On the way I noticed that the harvester ants, having by now come out of the underground nests they occupy during the heat of the day, were foraging across the steep slope in search of seeds, their favorite food. A heap of spiny cactus joints was almost hidden in a

A LACY CACTUS SKELETON

crevice, dragged there from a nearby stand of teddy bear cholla by pack rats, which collect the cactus as a kind of barricade for their nests.

On the driest face of the ridge there were tiny woolly lipferns, growing where overhanging rocks protect them from the worst heat. It is an unlikely place for ferns, yet their fuzzy leaves and their ability

to remain dormant for long periods between rains enable them to survive where nearly all other ferns would quickly perish.

The wind faded to a breeze as I left the confinement of the canyon, perspiring from the exertion of my climb. Rewards come in strange packages, however; one little discovery made scaling the canyon wall seems especially worthwhile. As I neared the top of the east ridge I broke at last into the sun, warm now more from its yellow glow than from the heat of its rays. In a small rock crack I saw something bright and stopped for a close look.

A Spiny Carcass

Pinned between the rocks was a piece of lace less than an inch across, part of the shell of spines that once covered a fishhook pincushion cactus. The cactus had died and rotted away, leaving behind its more resistant spines like a miniature skeleton of white bones. In time they, too, would add their substance to the scarce soil accumulating slowly in this rocky place.

The sun was dipping toward the distant horizon. I descended an easy slope on the far side of the ridge and stepped once again onto the sweeping fan of alluvium that skirts the base of the range. The sun set behind tall saguaros, and the sky blazed. It was a warm evening. The wind had died entirely. The time had come for the daytime creatures to rest. I headed back for the cabin, hungry for dinner, no longer pausing to look and marvel, replete with the discoveries of the day.

WOOLLY LIPFERNS

A SUNSET OVER THE CANYON RIDGE

2/ The Mountains of Superstition

*The glittering treasure you are hunting for day
and night lies buried on the other side of that hill yonder.*

B. TRAVEN/ *THE TREASURE OF THE SIERRA MADRE*

One brutally hot day in mid-April my friend Douglas Peacock and I decided to go for a walk in the Superstition Mountains, a rugged but relatively accessible desert range some 30 miles east of Phoenix. It was
too hot for hiking; we went anyhow, knowing the weather wasn't likely to cool off any for the next six months.

Driving north from Tucson to Florence Junction, then west halfway
to Apache Junction, we reached a dirt road heading north over the desert through thickets of cholla and sparse stands of giant saguaro. Ten
miles away through the haze loomed the rock ramparts of the Superstition Mountains. The western end of the range rises vertically from
the desert floor, naked cliffs a thousand feet high surmounted by terraces, talus slopes, and farther, higher tiers of cliffs that merge with the
main body of the range extending eastward toward the town of Globe.
On the summit are boulder battlements, pinnacles, knobs and domes of
bare rock, with a stubble of brush and trees here and there. A much
eroded remnant of old volcanic structures, this range looks something
like an antique Assyrian fortification, a mirage in the desert, a specter
of olden times, abandoned by mankind.

Nobody seems to know the origin of the name Superstition for these
mountains, but probably it is derived from the recurring, ineradicable,
incurable belief held by so many over the past 150 years that somewhere in this giant rock pile lies an elusive treasure of gold—Apache

gold, Spanish gold and, most elusive of all, the Lost Dutchman Mine.

We drove for five miles toward a pass in the mountains, bound for the end of the road and the Weaver's Needle trail head. Somewhere in the foothills, however, we missed a fork in the road and were soon stopped by a locked gate. A man was loafing nearby, apparently camped there, for we saw a pickup truck, tent and saddle horse with canvas water bags hung from the mesquite trees, their contents slowly evaporating—and thereby cooling—in the heat. The man wore a revolver strapped to his hip.

Characteristic of the area. The Superstition Mountains are full of gun-happy cranks, touchy old prospectors, truculent treasure hunters from faraway cities, all sorts of eccentric, unreliable freaks, misfits and odd-balls attracted by the fame of the name of the place, coming here to live out their childhood fantasies of the Wild West. Little wonder that a few people get shot or mysteriously disappear from time to time in the Superstitions.

This particular gun nut was tolerably sociable, however; he lounged against the shady side of his truck looking tough and mean, but when we asked him to kindly direct us to the Weaver's Needle trail head he was willing to oblige. We got the information we needed and pulled out of there. I wasn't alarmed but Doug was annoyed: veteran of Vietnam, ex-Green Beret, he hates guns, hates gunfire, hates the mess a bullet makes in our all-too-vulnerable human flesh.

End of the road, head of the trail. We climbed out of the car and looked around. Bloody hot afternoon—the glare of the sun, the op-pression of the heat became quickly apparent. Springtime in the Sonoran Desert. But the bees buzzing in the new-blooming mesquite and paloverde trees were happy. Big jojobas, large shrubs with tiny green leaves, grew among the cacti and trees; in season the jojoba bears a thin-shelled nut like an acorn, which it much resembles both in ap-pearance and flavor. Some of the cactus was in bloom—the barrel with its purple blossom, the scarlet hedgehog and the brilliant yellow cups of the prickly pear.

Flowers; also garbage: we were only 40 miles from the great met-ropolitan miasma of Phoenix. Looking westward we could see, against the light, the 50-mile-wide pall across the sky. Is it possible that Phoe-nix may someday rise from her ashes? She lives in soot and smoke, dust and confusion and crime, half pickled in sulphuric acid, a city dying from too much gluttonous success.

Well, dammit, we were out to leave all that behind for a night and a

couple of days. We stuffed our packs with supermarket dried foods, dehydrated spaghetti dinners, that sort of thing, plenty of jerky, chocolate,
peanuts and cheese, and six quarts of water each; a heavy load but we
knew we could need it. We might or might not find much free water in
that burned-out wasteland behind yonder hills.

We started off.

The trail is dusty, steep, rocky and well beaten. Generations have
trodden here, hoping to find an easy pot or two of that rare metal Au,
hoping to reap, as Thoreau said, where they had never planted. Is not
all gold fools' gold? And yet who can quite honestly completely resist
the allure of hidden treasure? Not I. Not Douglas Peacock. Perhaps all
truly good things come as gifts, unearned, unearnable. Or put the other
way, anything you have to work, sweat and scrabble for is not worth
having. Who knows? Ask the butterflies, flittering about among the barrel cactus, bright wings in the sunlight, free as leaves dancing on the
wind. How many hours a day of honest labor do they put in?

We tramped upgrade through the sweltering heat, the pale glare of afternoon. Above us towered the walls of the main range, fretted on the
summit with goblin rocks and hoodoo boulders. Nothing much alive
was stirring except fools like us, and the ants and a few lizards here
and there, dashing from shade to patch of shade, bush to rock and
back; and of course, far up in the blue, a big soaring bird: cousin buz-
zard, indolent watcher of desert scenes.

In the shadows under the rock rattlesnakes watched us pass. We
didn't always see them, but we knew that they were there, watching
us. It was their kind of country.

What to do if a snake bit? In 20 years of wandering, mostly in the
American Southwest, I have yet to be bitten by a rattlesnake nor has a
companion been bitten. Not that I'm complaining.

God knows we've seen them often enough. Or not often enough. A
couple of times, striding along in daydreaming euphoria, I have walked
right over a sluggish, dozing rattler without seeing it—the friend behind has called my attention to what I almost stepped on. The point is
that the rattlesnake cannot always be relied on to give the traditional audible warning; cold-blooded beasts, their body temperature determined
by air temperature, they tend to be comatose, inert, when the air is too
hot or too cold for them. Thus it is possible to get very close to a rattlesnake without rousing it, unless of course you are unlucky enough actually to step on it. That should always provoke the lightning strike.

The light of the setting sun accentuates the stark outlines and austere grandeur of the west wall of the Superstition Mountains.

What then? I am no doctor, but having given it some thought and talked to a few experts, I feel free to advise:

First make certain it is a rattlesnake that got you. If possible, kill the snake; your life or limb might depend upon proper identification. One good look and a rattlesnake cannot be mistaken for anything else: the spade-shaped head, typical of pit vipers, and of course the unique rattle on the tip of the tail make certain evidence. Also, the potency of the venom varies among the different varieties of rattlesnake; correct treatment may require exact identification.

Anyway, you've established that it was indeed a rattlesnake that bit you, you're sitting on a comfortable rock near the scene of the encounter staring at the blood oozing from the fang marks on your calf, or forearm, let us say, and rolling a cigarette and deciding maybe it would have been better, after all, to have stayed at home this weekend, and you're wondering what to do, what to do.

Traditional first aid calls for the cut-and-suck treatment. Most desert hikers carry something like the Cutter snakebite kit, which includes a razor blade, a suction cup and a tourniquet. The tourniquet, improperly applied, is more dangerous than most rattlesnakes and should rarely be used, according to current first-aid theory. The razor blade should be used only if you have a steady hand—or a friend has—and if you are too far from professional medical help. How far is too far? No one knows precisely; it depends on your state of mind—and body. But if your motor vehicle is close and a doctor's office not more than 30 minutes' drive away, you might best leave your skin alone, keep you hands off knife or razor blade, and head at once for town. If you did kill the snake, take it with you; the doctor will want to see it.

If you are truly out in the wilderness, however, it is necessary to operate. Otherwise you might lose an arm or leg, possibly even your life.

Exactly how dangerous is a rattlesnake bite? Again, no exact answers are available, only approximations. According to Laurence Klauber, one authority on the subject, about one thousand people a year in the United States get bitten by rattlesnakes; among these thousand cases 30 are fatal. Chances of survival therefore are excellent.

If you are far from aid and you wish to maximize your chances and minimize injury, it is certainly best to make a few shallow incisions right away, at the site of the fang marks, and suck out as much of the poison as possible before it is picked up by the blood and carried through leg or arm. I do not know from my own experience any cases in which death resulted from rattlesnake bite; I do know of one case in which a young man suffered an amputation because of a rattlesnake bite and lack of adequate and immediate first aid. Hiking alone in the Panamint Mountains west of Death Valley, he was bitten on the hand, attempted no first aid, walked for four hours back to his car and drove for three hours more to the nearest hospital. He lived, but lost an arm.

In the Sonoran Desert or big cactus country we have four major species of rattlesnake: the western diamondback, which is the largest (averaging five to six feet in length) though perhaps not the most potent; the tiger rattler, smaller but meaner; the blacktail rattler, rare; and the Mojave, or ringtail, rattler, which is common, wide-ranging and considered highly dangerous. We have as well several different varieties of sidewinder rattlesnake, much smaller and thereby generally less poisonous than the others. In neither size nor menace do we have rattlesnakes that can equal the magnificent seven-foot diamondbacks of such places as the swamps and hammocks of the Everglades.

This cursory review of rattlesnakes is not meant to exaggerate their danger to hikers and campers. In the first place, though common, they are easily avoided: all you have to do is watch where you put your hands and feet. And in the second place, even if you are foolish and careless enough to get bitten by a rattler, your chance of survival is in the area of 97 per cent.

Besides, though it won't ease the pain, remember that rattlesnakes, like all other living things in the natural world, fill a useful, perhaps essential, function in the stability of the ecosystem, helping for example to keep the population of rodents, their principal prey, within wholesome limits. This land is their land as well as ours; they were here before the Daughters of the American Revolution, before Coronado, even before the ancestors of Cochise and Geronimo made their way across the Bering Strait. They are elegant, cool, quiet creatures and quite simply, they *belong*.

So we tramped up Peralta Canyon, the creek bed dry and brittle as old bone, the rock and brush and trees all pale and dust-colored in the hot hazy light. A sycamore, a willow, a cottonwood—roots clutching the stone, searching out the last of the winter moisture. Looking for history, we took a brief side trip to a place called Geronimo's Cave, a shallow grotto under an overhanging bluff. But we found only bits and shards of Phoenix civilization, e.g., tinfoil, gum wrappers, aluminum cans, plastic sacks and Styrofoam baskets glittering in the sunlight.

Why keep carping about a little garbage? After all, we have to put it somewhere. Two hundred years of strenuous effort, hard work, sober sweat and careful planning went into this, grossest of all national products, to create on the North American continent the highest standard of consumption and the biggest pile of junk known to man or woman in all of human history.

Geronimo's Cave, this alcove in the rock littered with trash, has more mythic than historic significance. Here, according to legend, Apache warriors hid their gold, which modern-day treasure seekers, armed with revolvers and metal detectors, still scour the hills in hopes of finding. But there was never any treasure here except what the sun and the stillness, the desert breeze, the canyon pools, the birds and buzzards and barrel cactus have to offer.

A little beyond the cave, following the main trail, we came to Fremont Pass and our first view of fabled Weaver's Needle. Here if anywhere is the locus of the search for Superstition treasure, for here supposedly was the hideaway of Jacob Waltz the Dutchman and his hidden cache of gold.

Who was Waltz? Or Walz? Or Walts? The name has always had several spellings. And what is the Needle?

The latter can be said to resemble a needle only from certain points of view. Seen end-on, it does appear as a tall and slender spire, a dark pinnacle with perpendicular walls and a sloping, gently rounded summit. Seen from the sides, though, the Needle is longer than it is high. Rising 1,500 feet, it is made entirely of volcanic rock, mostly basalt, and according to geologists is actually the eroded remnant of a volcanic neck or plug—solidified magma that once closed the throat of a dead volcano. The original volcano having long since been completely eroded out of existence, the more resistant igneous material still remains.

The slender spire known as Weaver's Needle (center) has long served as a beacon for treasure hunters in the Superstition Mountains. According to local legend, it is supposed to have been named by a dying prospector as a principal clue to the location of precious deposits of gold ore.

Jacob Waltz the Dutchman, really a German, from Deutschland, apparently arrived in the Phoenix area around 1862 and died there in 1891. These dates have been well established, supported by still existing newspaper records. During the 30 years he lived in the Phoenix area the Dutchman achieved local fame by disappearing eastward from time to time, in the direction of the Superstition Mountains, and coming back with his saddlebags full of gold. According to the legend Waltz cashed in, over the years, some $254,000 worth of gold ore, a fantastic sum of money for that period. According to available evidence, however, as spelled out by journalist Curt Gentry in his book *The Killer Mountains*, there is no proof that Waltz ever sold more than $20,000 worth—a much more likely figure. All that is known for certain is that Waltz had found a little gold somewhere—where, no one knows. So it remains quite possible that the Dutchman's mine never existed at all except as fantasy in the minds of generations of treasure seekers—although mere lack of evidence was never enough and never will be enough to shake the faith of the devout. As with the devotees of any other cult, the more improbable the story the more tenacious is the gold seekers' belief.

The connection between the Needle and the Lost Dutchman Mine is this: as in most lost-gold tales, Waltz waited until his dying hour to reveal the location of his mine. In delirium on his deathbed, according to Gentry, he told his mistress, one Julia Thomas, and a boy named Reiney, "There's a great stone face looking up at my mine. If you pass three red hills you've gone too far. The rays of the setting sun shine on my gold. Climb above the mine and you can see Weaver's Needle."

Thus Julia Thomas became the first of many to spend her final years in a fruitless search for the Dutchman's Mine. In the 80 years since Waltz's death hundreds of people, possibly thousands, have tramped around in the bleak and barren hills trying to make sense of a dead man's elusive clues. Weaver's Needle, a striking landmark in itself, has quite naturally been the focal point of these many expeditions. The hills are pocked with prospect holes and littered with abandoned campsites, spent cartridge shells and—they say—missing persons.

Quite naturally this most famous of all lost-gold-mine legends has attracted crackpots, treasure fanatics and easy-money freaks from all over the country. And most of them, venturing for the first time into desert mountains, overawed by the tradition of rattlesnakes, ghosts, Apache warriors and outlaw gunslingers, come stumbling in here with revolver strapped to nervous paleskin hip, with high-powered scope-sighted rifle slung on palsied shoulder. It's worse than opening day of deer season. No wonder there have been 36 verified deaths and disappearances in the area (according to Gentry) since that old joker Waltz croaked out his final words in a sleazy pad on skid row in Phoenix.

One final twist: the geologists assure us that gold will never be found in the Superstitions, unless it was carried here from somewhere else and cached. These contorted hills are composed mostly of igneous materials such as tuff and andesite—the dust and ashes of ancient volcanic convulsions—that are rarely if ever found in the presence of gold. Chemically impossible. Gold is where you find it? No doubt. But you won't find it here, the experts say.

Well, Douglas and I found no gold, no human skeletons in pictur-
esque disarray, but we did see, although it had been a dry winter, a few
spring flowers. Near Piper's Spring below Weaver's Needle we came
upon the flamboyant little orange blooms of globe mallow, woolly gold-
en desert marigold, violet phacelia and the delicate, slender blue flower
with the name of bluedick. These are annuals that can grow anywhere
in the desert when moisture conditions are favorable. In good years
they may cover entire hillsides with masses of color.

But Piper's Spring was dry that season. Good thing we had plenty of
water in our packs. We left the trail and wandered down the dry stream
bed of what the maps call Boulder Canyon, below the Needle. There
was not the slightest trace of water anywhere on the surface of the canyon floor. We kept going, shuffling through the arid sand, picking a way
among and over the boulders. The canyon sank into bedrock, forming a
narrow gorge, and here we discovered a series of lovely natural tanks
in the solid rock—holes drilled in the stream bed by pebble power during eons of flash floods. Some of the holes were partly filled with month-
old water from the most recent rain.

We stopped to admire. Douglas went for a dip in the biggest of the
potholes, waist deep. Although the water in the pools was old and stagnant, much condensed from long evaporation, it still contained plentiful
aquatic life. Tadpoles, mosquito larvae, and water bugs known locally
as "boatmen" swam indolently about among the soft green strands of
algae. A microscope would certainly have revealed a far denser world.

Some of the smaller pools contained no life at all that was visible to
the unaided eye. In these isolated aquaria the processes of reproduction and decomposition, aggravated by water loss through evaporation,
had terminated in a micro-habitat hostile to life. The metabolism of the
little community had passed through the anabolic into the catabolic
phase—that is, from growth to overgrowth and death. Total catastrophe for this miniature world within worlds: the banquet of life became
a feast of fools, a teeming culture bouillon, then finally a quiet little disaster area picked over by transparent scavengers from the bacterial
realm, swarming through the clear but toxic soup.

Merely an episode, of course, in the endless biodrama of a peaceful
desert hidden place. The next flood to come down the canyon would
flush the pools of their poisonous residue and refill them with fresh material and a reinvigorated medium, providing new opportunities, new
catastrophes, ever-new returns.

Twilight filled the canyon, saturated the clear air in which we, like the smaller creatures in their fluid spheres, stirred ourselves. The sky became rosy, the silent evening took on a lavender tint, the storm-carved basaltic rock, scoured and polished by 10,000 roaring floods, changed in tone from sober gray to a somber, surrealistic purple blue.

We made camp on a long slick rock ledge beside one of the longest and clearest of the pools. We built a little squaw fire of mesquite and cooked our supper: beef stroganoff out of a box from the Safeway supermarket; cocoa and cookies for dessert. Among the rocks above our campsite we found a deposit of cartridge brass: .38s, .44s, .45s, .30-30s, .22s. Who had been potting whom from here and why?

Old Weaver's Needle rose against the evening sky, wrinkled with wear, wrapped in shadows, resting on its pedestal of stratified volcanic tuff, surrounded by clusters of goblin rocks—dumbbells, gargoyles, drunken soldiers, porphyritic phalluses, pregnant goddesses, Easter Island stone faces, petrified tyrannosaurs.

Javelina sign—tracks and droppings—around the waterholes indicated that these animals had stopped there recently. Also coyote, skunk and badger; we could probably expect a few visitors sometime during the night. We heard a canyon wren, a thrasher, a flock of quail somewhere out in the cactus and creosote brush.

Douglas banked our fire with sand, not to put it out but to make charcoal. In the morning we would use the charcoal to filter the pothole water, trying to purify it, since we had used most of the canteen water we had packed in. Nevertheless, on the next day, despite our precautions, we both got slightly ill on the long trek around the Needle on the eastern side. From the water? Perhaps; perhaps we hadn't purified it enough. Or maybe it was the heat. Or then again, as legend would have it, maybe it was a bit of the Dutchman's Curse.

Nobody gets in and out of the Superstition Mountains *completely* untouched. Even the most hexproof infidels cannot escape the power of such a magic name, the glamor of that sinister reputation, the occult touch of all those bored and restless haunts, the spirits of the place.

The Anatomy of a Colossus

PHOTOGRAPHS BY WOLF VON DEM BUSSCHE

Although it is the mightiest of all of Arizona's desert plants, the saguaro has no secret weapon or unique armament with which to combat the drought and heat of its environment. Less formidable members of the cactus family also employ its protective mechanisms, some of which are shown on the following pages in pictures taken at the Saguaro National Monument near Tucson. What sets the saguaro apart from other cacti is its sheer size, and everything else about it is correspondingly spectacular in scale.

The saguaro's root system, shallow but spread wide to absorb maximum rainfall in the thin, quick-draining desert soil, may cover an area as big as 100 feet in diameter. Aided by an expansible, bellowslike skin, the saguaro may increase its girth by 50 per cent or more as its spongy interior sops up one summer's rainfall. After a relatively wet desert summer, a large saguaro may weigh as much as seven tons, of which water constitutes 75 per cent or more. By making only sparing use of its stored-up moisture, a plant can live for a year or two without another drop of rain.

In the course of a century of bearing fruit, a mature saguaro may produce as many as 40 million seeds. But only three or four seeds out of that total produce plants that survive to maturity, according to one botanist's estimate. This high mortality rate is due both to the general hardships of survival in the desert and the particular passion of white-winged doves, ground squirrels, coyotes and other creatures for the saguaro's sweet, succulent fruit.

Even under conditions ideal for the species, the saguaro's growth rate is ponderously slow. A seedling that does survive usually takes nine years to grow six inches tall, and a plant that reaches the age of 40 will be no more than eight to 10 feet tall. Yet a number of saguaros have lived to roughly 200 years, and attained a height of 50 feet—the height of a five-story building.

To the nonscientist, standing in a saguaro forest, statistics matter less than the sense of awe that engulfs him in the presence of these splendid desert colossi. Puny as he feels, however, he can enjoy a stir of pride as well. For the saguaros grow nowhere else on earth other than the Sonoran Desert. They are, as the naturalist Paul Griswold Howes has put it, "something purely and wonderfully American."

Having defied the astronomical odds against its survival, this saguaro has reached the stage of magnificent maturity—over 130 years old and 30 feet tall. Its branches emerge about one third of the way up its trunk.

A mere adolescent, probably between 40 and 50 years old and about 13 feet tall, this saguaro betrays its immaturity by its branchlessness. The slow-growing species rarely produces arms before the age of 75, and a saguaro growing in a poor site may remain branchless throughout its long life.

Cottonlike blobs and supple spines identify a youthful saguaro or recent growth on an older plant. The blobs, which dry as the tissue beneath matures, provide shade for the soft young skin. The spines, which stiffen with age, ward off would-be nibblers and help temper desiccating winds.

This majestic saguaro, probably 150 years old, shows its age in several ways. It soars nearly 35 feet from a base about two feet in diameter —dimensions rare in plants less than 130 years old. Its glistening skin, whose waxy surface reduces moisture loss through evaporation, is mottled with brown, and many spines on its lower trunk have atrophied and fallen off.

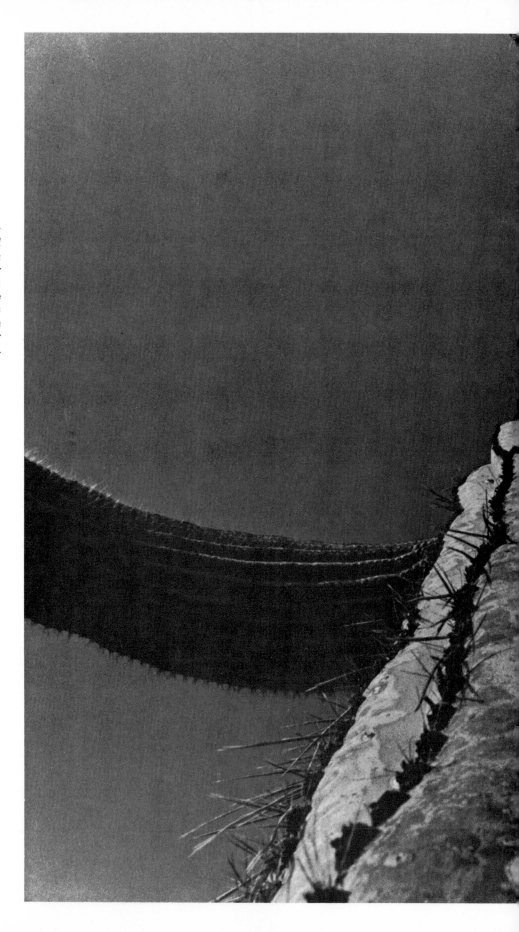

A long-dead saguaro (left) has
dwindled to a skeleton of woody ribs,
with the pith that once filled its rib
cage now reduced to a dried-out pile.
Saguaro trunks have eight to 15 ribs,
depending on the individual plant's age
and size. The ribs, strong enough to
dull a knife blade yet flexible as
whalebone, also provide a skeletal
structure for both trunk and arms.

A wide gash in a saguaro's trunk
reveals the thickness of the expansible
water-storing tissue that lies between
the plant's skin and its supporting ribs.
The two knobs below the wound are
budding branches whose growth may
have been triggered by the injury itself.

A saguaro forest covers a bajada, or rocky slope. The giant cacti grow best on such slopes; rugged hills above provide them with the runoff of infrequent rains and protect them from strong winds. As the slope levels out (background), the saguaros give way to ironwood and mesquite, plants better adapted to the drier, sandier flats.

3/ Winters in Organ Pipe

The desert...is made like an old-fashioned museum. Each object is an individual specimen, standing on its own solitary pedestal. WILLIAM T. HORNADAY/ *CAMPFIRES ON DESERT AND LAVA*

A man or woman could hardly ask for a better way to make a living than as a seasonal ranger or naturalist for the National Park Service. The pay is modest but the atmosphere is good. Some of the routine might become irksome but the scenery is always nicely assembled. In what other occupation can you be paid an honest wage for doing what most people would regard as a vacation? The boss is usually far away in Washington and your companions are usually amiable; there's something about the Park Service that attracts good men and women.

True, you have to wear a semimilitary uniform and keep your hair trimmed back; but this indignity is a small sacrifice in return for all the fresh air you can breathe, more stars than you can count, more constellations than you can learn to name, more bugs and bees and bears and birds and bats than you can find in any field guide yet written.

Finally, there is this to be said for seasonal work of any kind. Whenever the hours tend to drag, the customers become tiresome, you have that most wonderful event of all to look forward to and comfort yourself with: termination day. End of the season. Out of work again at last and free to starve or thrive, as you make it, in your own style.

What I started to say is that back in 1968 I was offered a job as a seasonal park ranger at Organ Pipe Cactus National Monument. Organ Pipe, or ORPI for short, is a unit of our national park system, an area of some 510 square miles of desert and desert mountains on the Mexican border beginning 100 miles west of Tucson. Square in the middle of the Sonoran Desert, Organ Pipe has a tourist season that begins in November and ends in May, the remainder of the year being much too hot for pleasure. Only the most dedicated of desert aficionados venture forth during the 100°-to-115° days of June, July and August.

My job began in early December and ended in the middle of April. I lived in the south half of an old military Quonset hut, vintage World War II, that had been relocated there in the early development days of this park. The north half of the hut was occupied by Bill Hoy, ranger-naturalist and desert rat first class. I spent one or two working days each week tending the public campground, and that was the least interesting part of my job. In this role, wearing my sharpest Smokey Bear suit, I greeted the camping public, collected fees, kept records and collated statistics, provided elementary guide service and occasional first aid—and kidnapped rattlesnakes.

Campgrounds and garbage cans attract birds and rodents; birds and rodents attract snakes. Part of our educational task was trying to encourage people to accept snakes as natural and useful inhabitants of the desert, not as monsters to be murdered on sight. Most of this went over well. Given half a chance park visitors are eager to learn what they can about a new environment. But many still balk and boggle at venomous reptiles, especially the noble rattlesnake. When a rattlesnake was spotted in the campground, therefore, it became necessary, for the rattlesnake's own good as well as that of the campers, to capture it alive and relocate it. For this purpose we used a tonglike instrument three and a half feet long, designed for picking up scraps of paper and other litter, but also handy for snatching snakes without harming them.

Holding the rattler in this gadget's firm but gentle grasp I would dump it in a garbage can, put the can in the back of a pickup truck and transport the snake out into the desert to the recommended minimum of five miles from the campground. There, always at the same site, I would stuff the rattlesnake down a gopher hole, always the same hole. (This was my own idea.) Over the course of three winter seasons I placed at least a couple of dozen in that one little hole, trying to create a true snake pit. They wouldn't stay.

Campground duty out of the way, the primary job was patrol. On foot and by four-wheel-drive vehicle I had the privilege of wandering the trails and back roads of desert, mountain and borderlands, all within the boundaries of Organ Pipe—a big place.

A grand place. Around 8 in the morning I'd saddle up the old government truck and set forth into the outback, following my assigned route for the day. No one could possibly patrol the entire park in a single day or even in a week; therefore the patrols were worked out in advance and fitted to a schedule in such a way that over the course of a month most of the park would come under observation at least once.

The procedure required so much time because I was the only full-time patrol ranger. The job fell to my lot because I was relatively inexperienced, not very bright, wore my sideburns long and was only a seasonal, not a career, man. The career men—the regulars—had to stick around headquarters and do the professional work: repair traffic counters, sell postcards, fill out report forms, answer the telephone. I exaggerate and oversimplify—but not by much.

One patrol might cover what is called the Puerto Blanco Drive. This is a 51-mile loop road that begins near park headquarters, close to the highway, and winds over the hills and across the flats of the western side of the park.

Winter mornings I liked, the sunlight slanting in from the southeast, long shadows over the rock and brush and sand—a cool, crisp and vivid world. The road I followed is rough, dusty, rocky, with tight curves and sudden deep descents into gullies radiating from the base of the mountains. Along these watercourses, always dry except after summer storms, grow the predominant trees of this desert: ironwood, mesquite, two varieties of paloverde. All are legumes, a family that includes the pea clan; none grow more than 20 feet tall, all have tiny leaves, thorny branches and look more like big shrubs than conventional trees.

Ironwood, as the name says, is an exceedingly hard and heavy wood. The core of it will blunt the edge of ax or saw, and a solid chunk will sink in water. Yet the wood when dead is very brittle and breaks easily against a rock or another ironwood branch. As fuel, especially for camp-fire cooking, it is unexcelled, burning slowly, smokelessly and very hot. There is no better way to broil a piece of meat than by laying it directly upon a bed of ironwood coals. South of the border in the state of Sonora, ironwood is much in demand as a household fuel and may soon disappear from the Mexican deserts. Year by year the professional woodcutters fan out ever farther across the land, hacking and hewing to supply the needs of the rapidly growing population. They too wish to eat, live and multiply, these woodcutters, and so the ironwood and after it the mesquite will have to go. Mexico is already in the swarming stage, that busy time that precedes destruction.

At a certain high point about three miles from headquarters I would stop to admire the morning sunlight on Pinkley Peak, a multicolored chocolate-vanilla-strawberry mass of compacted volcanic rocks standing more than 3,000 feet above sea level. Through field glasses, I would survey the mountainside for desert bighorn sheep, feral burro or—quite rare in this particular area—white-tailed deer or desert mule deer.

To the north is an almost level alluvial plain dominated by creosote bushes, with the dark green of mesquite, the pale yellow green of paloverde and the gray green of ironwood along the sandy washes. Nobody lives out there now, although someone did once; the ruins of a 50-year-old homestead still stand in a cleared patch of land near the northern boundary of the monument.

On the east the Ajo Range, on the west Kino Peak and the Growler Mountains wall in this valley. Twenty miles to the north I could usually see a thick plume of poisonous smoke rising from the stacks of the Ajo copper smelter, compliments of the Phelps Dodge Corporation. Coming up from behind a conical desert hill, it created the effect of a smoking volcano. When the wind was northerly, however, this banner of industry could not be seen, because then the smoke and sulphuric wastes were diffused through the air of Organ Pipe itself, obscuring the view in all directions.

My second favorite stop along the Puerto Blanco patrol was at a place called Redtail Well. Taking a dim jeep trail away from the main road, I would come after half a mile to the scattered remains of a miner's shack. Here were and maybe still are some rusted buckets and shovels, a midden heap of bean and sardine cans, and a hand-dug well. The well when I first found it was loosely covered with a few splintery boards; from the depths arose the unmistakable stench of decomposing meat. Taking my flashlight I peered down through the fumes into the well and saw a dim yellowish shape, too big to be a jack rabbit, maybe a bobcat, maybe a coyote, floating just below the surface of the oily water 20 feet below.

Hard to believe that an animal as agile as a cat or as intelligent as a coyote could have fallen into a well, no matter how desperately thirsty it might have been. The puzzle intrigued me for a while; finally I concluded that someone had shot the animal and dumped it in the well to hide it from the suspicious eyes of park rangers.

The smell of the decaying beast lingered around Redtail Well for the best part of my first winter season. Week by week I watched the remains slowly dissolve and disintegrate. Submersion in water retarded the natural process; had the animal been on the desert it would have been eaten up, dried out and rendered thoroughly clean and innocuous in a much shorter time.

A year later the corpse had disappeared, except for a few furry fragments. I nailed the boards together with cross members and weighted the cover with rocks, hoping to prevent another accident. If it was an accident. I didn't want to have to investigate smells again and find a jackass, a cow or a tourist down in there next time, presenting us with the forlorn sight, as Faulkner wrote in the novel *Mosquitoes,* of "that mute inopportune implacability of the drowned."

The jeep trail goes beyond Redtail Well to a natural basin in the rock called Redtail Tank; from there it forks, one road dead-ending at a copper mine deep in the hills, the other meandering on down a rough solid-rock gulch toward a place called Senita Basin, near the other end of the Puerto Blanco loop. In that area can be found a group of small abandoned gold and silver mines, including one known as Lost Cabin Mine.

The old copper mine, I've forgotten its name, was not so much a mine as a "diggings"—a prospect tunnel. It lay at the terminus of a two-mile hand-built road. I always walked the two miles, and it was a fine walk. Ocotillos 15 feet tall grew along the way; in March and April each spiderlike branch would be tipped with a scarlet cone of tiny flowers, looking from a distance like flames. Neither tree nor cactus, the ocotillo occupies a genus—*Fouquieria*—all its own. After each rain these plants take on a sheath of green leaves and do some hasty growing while the moisture lasts. When the inevitable drought returns, usually within a week, the leaves drop off, and growth is halted for a while until the next rain.

At times, walking that road, I'd hear a ghastly, spectral cough coming from above, as if out of the sky. A single powerful cough, like a giant clearing his throat. I could not imagine what it was, for looking up I would see nothing, no raven, no vulture, nothing in the air. Another mighty cough. I look again, my glance guided this time by the sound of clattering rocks on the hillside above, and see a shaggy little feral burro, ears up like semaphores, looking down at me. This burro is a footloose descendant of domestic burros lost or freed generations ago by pioneer miners. The cough is a warning sign, an alarm, a threat: I have invaded his territory. But I am no more willing to be intimidated than the burro; I walk on.

The feral burros are not exactly a blessing in the Southwest. Some biologists think that the burro is multiplying too fast and encroaching on the habitat of the bighorn sheep, consuming much of the latter's forage. The question at this time has not been definitely settled, but a burro control program—i.e., herd reduction by shooting—is carried on from time to time at Grand Canyon, where the competition between burro and bighorn is severe. The bighorn sheep was there first—thus the usual argument. But if the burro is better adapted to survive in desert areas, why not let it? An interesting issue. Perhaps the answer is that we need more predators, especially mountain lions, for whom the burro would be an easy prey. Or perhaps we should make the burro an official big game animal, so that every trophy hunter, sooner or later, can have the head of a jackass mounted on his rumpus-room wall.

Back on the Puerto Blanco road, the patrol continued to what is called Dripping Springs, one of the only two major natural and permanent water sources in Organ Pipe. At the end of a spur road I'd park the truck and take a short walk up a switchback trail to a shallow cave on the hillside. There in that cool little grotto was the spring, delphic, oracular, a deep oval pond under a dripping dome of rock. A small stream runs from the spring between succulent banks of watercress, purple asters and scarlet penstemon, dropping from there down into a rocky, brushy ravine where all of the surplus water is soon taken up by plant life or lost again underground. In the basin of the spring, swarms of mosquito larvae wriggle through the water; a few drowned honeybees float on the surface, others gather at the edge sipping up moisture. The water has a milky coloring, probably from minerals leached out of the rocks, but it always tasted clean and sweet to me.

The footpath beyond the spring leads to the saddle of a ridge, a big notch of rock with high walls of buff-colored volcanic rock on either side. This is the Puerto Blanco itself—the white gateway. From this high point you can look south over the granite hills and old mines of Senita Basin, far across the border to the jagged mountains of Sonora.

Toward the southeast the ridge rises gradually to the summit of Pinkley Peak. I climbed that mountain several times during my tour of duty at Organ Pipe, partly for the fun of it, officially to take rain gauge measurements. Once I found the dried-out hulk of a brown pelican close to the mountain's highest point. What was a pelican doing up there? No one knows. Blown astray, maybe, by the winds of a Gulf storm.

A few more miles of lovely primitive country, and the road leads past an old well, windmill, corral and line cabin. Still in use by rancher Henry Gray when I worked there, the corral had a trap gate that could

As majestic as the 16th Century Aztec Emperor for whom it was named, the towering butte called Montezuma's Head (center) dominates the landscape in the northeastern part of Organ Pipe Cactus National Monument. In this panorama, the 3,634-foot-high mountain, formed of various kinds of volcanic rock, resembles the upper half of a hulking giant seen from the rear. The "head" itself is a monolithic block of rhyolite, a rock formed from lava.

be rigged to open inward but not outward. Since the trough inside the corral held the only water for miles around, it made good and sufficient bait for catching cattle and horses. The old cabin across the road was used for storage and as a bunkhouse before the days of pickup trucks, when a ride of 30 miles on horseback or by team and wagon might take a whole day. A hitching rack, a table and a bench stood beside the cabin, under the welcome shade of a big mesquite tree.

Cattle grazing has been a major problem at Organ Pipe. Long before the area was made a national monument the Gray family had begun cattle operations here. Although they acquired title to only 157 acres, their long occupancy and use of the land has given them powerful squatter's rights, which the Park Service is bound by law and custom to respect. Year after year special appropriation bills have been introduced in Congress to buy out the Gray family—they would be happy to sell—but so far none has been passed. By 1972 the Park Service was seeking a solution through a court settlement, and it seemed likely that the issue would be resolved.

Meanwhile several hundred head of scrubby cattle have ranged the hills and plains of Organ Pipe, trampling the seedling cacti, stripping the soil of its natural cover, browsing on the mesquite and ironwood, and polluting the water holes with dung and parasites. Of course this has all been going on for a long time. Like corrals, cowboys and horses, the cattle business has been a basic part of the American West for a century. In part the usual story of greed and rapacity, there is also much that is good, honorable and beautiful in ranching as a way of life. Too much, more than we can afford to lose entirely.

For my part, if the only choice at Organ Pipe were between overgrazing by cattle or more asphalt trails for motorized tourists, I would prefer the cows. But there are better choices. The cattle can be removed with fair compensation to their owners. We can set aside most of the monument as permanent wilderness, wide open to any and all with interest enough to leave the security of their cars and try the will of their legs and feet and hearts.

Cattle grazing rates as a small misfortune at Organ Pipe compared to the catastrophe copper mining would be. National monuments are supposed to be off limits to commercial enterprise, but during the Second World War, under the guise of military necessity, several desert areas such as Death Valley and Organ Pipe were opened to mineral exploration. The war ended more than a quarter century ago, but what was supposed to have been a temporary measure has yet to be rescinded by

Congress. So far no metals or minerals of commercial value have been found at Organ Pipe, unless the mining companies are keeping their discoveries secret for the time being. But aerial surveys and on-site core drilling continue, and it is always possible that profitable ore deposits will be located and developed. Under present law there is nothing the Park Service can do about it except keep watch.

On with our Puerto Blanco patrol: After the corral-windmill-cowboy cabin come miles of open desert. I pass a cristate saguaro, so called for the tumorlike cross-shaped growth of tissue on the crown. Here too grows the Mexican jumping-bean bush, many of them, with reddish leaves, skin-burning sap and the autumn fruit that, when bored into by a moth larva, becomes the well-known jumping bean; its motion is caused by movements of the worm inside. Near the cristate saguaro is the biggest anthill I have ever seen in the United States: five feet in diameter and three feet tall crawling with a mass of red and black harvester ants. On such anthills as this the Yaqui and Apache, according to folklore, would crucify their enemies.

Down and across a broad sandy wash where the smoke tree, *Dalea spinosa,* flourishes. Well named, this hardy shrub seems to float on the air like a veil of wood smoke, like the mirage rather than the image of a living plant. Smoke trees grow only in washes primarily because more moisture is available here than on the harder, higher, stonier ground. But this is only a part of the explanation. Research has shown that, in order to break open and germinate, the seeds of the smoke tree must be rolled and tumbled along a rough sandy surface. The only force in nature that can provide such a service is the flash flood that rumbles down a dry stream bed during a summer storm. Stream action not only breaks open the seed coat, it also ensures that sufficient moisture will be present—at the right time of year—to sustain growth. What about winter storms? There are none in this desert—only drizzles.

In the far southwest corner of the park, within 100 yards of the Mexican frontier, the road brings us to the oasis called Quitobaquito, the other important natural water source in Organ Pipe. It is also the only place in the park where large deciduous trees, in this case cottonwoods, grow. Always a refreshing sight, bright green in summer, gold in the fall, they stand out for miles against the pastel tones of the desert.

Quitobaquito is a pond fed by natural springs. It was the home of small Papago bands for many centuries. Later it became a popular way station on El Camino del Diablo, the road leading from northwest Mexico to southern California. Aside from a few unreliable springs and water pockets in the low mountains to the west, Quitobaquito was the last good water supply available to travelers until they reached the Colorado River some 100 miles farther west. Many are supposed to have died on that trail, some of thirst, some at the hands of Indians known as Areñero or Sand Papago. In the days of the forty-niners, when the California Gold Rush was at its height, many Europeans and Eastern Americans attempted this route. On the map it looked like a good short cut. Today a few of their graves can still be seen along the traces of the old road, little mounds of stone and wooden crosses way out in the Cabeza Prieta wilderness west of Organ Pipe.

I would make my patrol of the pond, answering tourist questions, picking up litter, fishing an occasional tin can out of the water. I would pause at the inlet to the pond to look at the pupfish, lively, gleaming inch-long cyprinodonts adapted to life in the brackish water of desert streams; a rare sort of fish, they can be found only in Death Valley, in the Sonoita River (really a creek) south of Organ Pipe, here at Quitobaquito and in a very few other desert places such as Devil's Hole in Nevada. Fish experts say that pupfish are remnants of inhabitants of great inland seas that vanished a million years ago. This could be true.

I completed my patrol of Quitobaquito by emptying the garbage cans and cleaning out the rest rooms, then with my load of garbage reeking in the back of the pickup I would head eastward toward headquarters, rounding off the loop. If the sun was still high and the day young I usually made the turnoff at Senita Basin to check up on the cactus and our best elephant tree.

Senita cactus, also known as old man or grandfather cactus because of the graybeard spines at the crown of each branch, is one of the smaller giant cacti, reaching a height of 15 feet. Uncommon in Arizona, abundant in Sonora, senitas are rough, rank, shaggy plants, grotesque, sunburned, a little ridiculous but good to look at and think about, nice to know. Like its big brothers the saguaro, organ pipe and cardon, the senita cactus can flourish only where the climate is hot and the freezing periods infrequent and brief. High in moisture content, it would burst like unsheathed plumbing if exposed to a prolonged freeze.

The elephant tree is something else. At maturity it too may reach 15 feet in height, but the one in Senita Basin is no taller than a shotgun. Rare in the U.S. (Mexico is its more familiar habitat), the elephant tree has a thick trunk, wide-branching limbs and a scaly, dead white, sometimes brassy, leprous bark. Another useless plant, no doubt, like the senita, without anything of economic value for man or beast. It looks like a monstrous turnip trying to struggle up out of the ground. What good is it? You can't eat it, use it or sell it. True—but there it is.

Besides interesting plant life Senita Basin contains the densest cluster of old mines and prospect holes in Organ Pipe; most of them I visited at least once a week.

My favorite was the one called Bluebird, long ago forgotten, now the home of Mexican hognose bats. Once I walked deep into the pitch blackness, hearing the rustle of thousands of membranous wings in the gloom before me. As I advanced the bats retreated farther and farther toward the end of the tunnel, a thickening concentration of alarm.

I was the one, however, who was blind as a bat. The mine tunnel takes several turns and gradually all daylight, even the finest trace of illumination, is left behind. We really have no conception of the meaning of darkness until we enter such a place. The interior of an unlit house, or a clouded-over starless night, is nothing like it. The blackness of a mine or cave has a palpable quality; you can feel it, as if it were a sort of fluid medium denser than air, lighter than water. You stop and listen, you stop and feel, you find yourself immersed in a disorienting nothingness. For a certain temperament fear and then panic must be no more than a heartbeat away.

Closer to the bats. I could hear them shrilling and fluttering, the thick sound of crowded wings. I switched on my flashlight and there they were, milling around in the dusty stagnant air, others hanging in clusters upside down from the tunnel roof. I advanced a few more steps, pressing them back, and then they rebelled and as a swarm exploded, rushing past, over, and around me toward the entrance of the mine. Always wear a hat and an old shirt on such expeditions—I emerged from the mine, blinking in the glare, pretty well covered on shoulders and head by a mantle of bat dung and guano dust.

After the mines, after Senita Basin, there was little to do but go home, although during the all-too-brief desert twilight, loveliest time of the day, I was often impelled to stay out until nightfall. All too brief? In the desert, generally speaking, when the sun goes down the light fades very quickly because there is little moisture in the air to refract and reflect light. Only for a few magical minutes does the half light linger over the hills and washes, rocks and trees, shrubs and sand, before it melts away on the current of the evening.

The Puerto Blanco Drive was one of several regular patrols. Another followed the Ajo mountain route which took me into the high rugged eastern portion of the monument. In addition there were half a dozen other more difficult patrols requiring four-wheel drive and foot travel. One of the best of the latter was the hike to the edge of the hatchet-blade peak of cliff-bound Kino, accessible by only one narrow, tricky, hard-to-find route. This is bighorn sheep country, lion country, hiking and scrambling country. And centipede country.

The biggest centipede I ever met in my life was the one I saw slipping into a water hole, or *tinaja,* near the foot of Kino Peak. It was a splendid shining golden-mahogany beast about 10 inches long, a bold handsome centipede, a warrior, with the concentrated sleek viciousness of an engine designed for destruction and nothing else. I fished it out of the water with a stick and tried to count the legs—not easy, for this warrior would not hold still. There seemed to be about 80: 40 on each side. All other features were present: long probing antennae, complicated mouth parts of double mandibles and double maxillae, the front legs with their poisonous fangs, the feet like claws.

I know it's unjust and irrational, but I have never been able to overcome a definite sense of horror when confronting these armor-plated arthropods—scorpions, tarantulas, centipedes. This one below Kino Peak made me believe in the Devil. I turned it loose and watched it scurry off over the rock, a miniaturized tyrannic tank, bound for whatever happened in its way.

The best place to see bighorn sheep in the wild was up in the Ajo Range. Almost every time I went hiking there I'd see at least one or two. Always by chance. Once on Diaz Peak my friend John De Puy and I came upon a herd of nine. They were browsing on the brush, upwind from us, when we came around a ledge of rock and saw them. We stopped instantly and the sheep, unaware of our presence, continued to feed. We stood for what seemed like a long time but was probably only minutes, contemplating those lean, muscular, magnificent animals; one was an old patriarch of a ram, with massive horns curling back, around and forward in a full spiral; he must have been five feet long, three high at the shoulder, and weighed more than 200 pounds. May he live to reproduce his kind many times over and not end up, stuffed and glass-eyed, on the pine-paneled wall of some head collector's home.

Tiring a bit, one of us made a movement. At once the horned heads went up, the sheep saw us and sprang away in unison over the rocks with easy grace, vanishing down the mountainside. We were on the summit; they had nowhere to go but downhill.

A long-familiar landmark of Organ Pipe Cactus National Monument, the Bull Pasture (top center) juts out of the side of Mount Ajo like an immense hanging shelf. In years gone by this plateau's flat grassy terrain provided good grazing for cattle herds—after they had arduously climbed more than a mile above the desert floor to get there.

One day we climbed Montezuma's Head, a great eroded butte in the northeast corner of Organ Pipe. A first time for me, an oft-repeated tradition for the other rangers—Bill Hoy, Jim Carrico, Hal Coss. We started early in the morning, Jim and Bill leading the way. It is a technical climb, for which ropes and pitons are desirable, and my stomach was full of butterflies. Not too bad up to the shoulder of the monster, although there are certain hairy pitches on the route that make me sick to think about even now: I mean the sort of place on the rock where, if you glance down between your legs, you're likely to see a redtail hawk sailing past a hundred feet below.

We worked our way around the shoulder of the Head and came to a place called the Mantle. One look and I resolved to go no farther—but kept the resolution to myself for the moment. We had a choice of ascents: the first up a chimney, the second around and up the edge of the Mantle. The chimney looked much cozier to me, but the others agreed it took too long.

We roped up. A little numbly, for I'm no climber, I allowed myself to be attached to the rest of the party. Jim took the lead, stepping lightly along a slick ledge about six inches wide, about a thousand feet above the abyss. All that empty, vacant, fantastic space below, yearning toward our fragile human bodies with hypnotic magnetism. Jim reached a point where the little ledge petered out. From there the route led straight upward, by way of a single tiny handhold just a short distance beyond the reach of a man of average height. In order to gain that grip of solid rock it would be necessary for Jim to make a little leap up the face of the bulge before him.

We had him well belayed from the side and below. If he jumped and missed, we'd be able to stop his fall within 30 or 40 feet. He'd probably break no more than a few ribs, a leg, maybe a neck—nothing serious.

He jumped. And caught the handhold, as we all knew all along he would. He went on up, found a good belaying point and secured the climb for the rest of us. From there on it was a routine scramble. We reached the bald summit of Montezuma's Head, a dome of rock sloping away on all sides toward eagles' nests and the kinds of cliffs nightmares are made of.

"What's to do up here?" said Hal Coss, looking bored.

Things do not always turn out so well in this Organ Pipe desert, however. On February 3, 1971, we lost a visitor. On that day a young woman named Carol Turner, age 32, went for a solo walk up into an area of the

Ajo Range called the Bull Pasture, and disappeared, vanished as if from the face of the earth. She was an experienced hiker, in good bodily and mental health, a physical education instructor at the University of New Mexico—and her fate remains a complete mystery. So far not a trace of her has been found.

The case began with a ranger finding a note under the windshield wiper of Carol Turner's car, the note stating that she had gone for a hike up to the Bull Pasture and planned to return the same day. When she did not return on schedule a search was begun at once, expanded rapidly and continued for 12 days.

A second note was found in the trail register box at the top end of the Bull Pasture trail, addressed to anyone, unsigned but clearly in Carol Turner's handwriting:

"Hi, if you have binocs—look for a white shirt or yellow windbreaker across the way and say Hello."

The first day's search was carried out by the Organ Pipe ranger staff, but when the missing woman could not be found, reinforcements were called in, including Papago trackers, a United States Air Force helicopter, the Ajo town police, the border patrol, the county sheriff's department and the entire volunteer search and rescue team of Pima County. At the height of the search a total of 130 men were involved. But nothing was found. On February 15 Hal Coss and Bill Hoy, searching an area beyond a volcanic outcropping called the Sphinx, thought they detected the odor of decomposing flesh but could not find the source of the smell. On February 16 the search was called off officially, on the grounds that the woman could not possibly be still alive after 12 days without food or water in the desert mountains. The rangers and maintenance men of Organ Pipe have carried on periodic searches ever since then, in hopes of finding at least some bodily remains and solving the mystery, but without success.

In his official report on the matter Rod Broyles, now chief ranger at Organ Pipe, writes that "there is no evidence of suicide, foul play or a planned disappearance." The conclusion is that Carol Turner probably fell or slipped, injured herself and crawled into one of the many small caves or brushy crevices in the cliffs for shelter from the cold and wind. Since the searchers the next day heard no hint of a human cry for aid it also seems likely that she lost consciousness soon after her accident and died of shock, bleeding and exposure.

The walk up to the Bull Pasture is one of the loveliest and most rewarding in the entire monument. The trail climbs steeply from the Ajo Drive parking lot, winding through a narrow canyon, among boulders, past a great variety of desert plants, up over a ridge and along the base of great yellowish cliffs to a high point overlooking the place for which the trail is named.

The name is strictly historical, based on the fact that an early rancher kept cattle here, and conveys little of the character of the place. It is a grassy basin, walled in on the east by the ramparts of Mount Ajo and surrounded on all other sides except the trail route by precipitous drop-offs hundreds of feet high. It is a natural corral, requiring only some 20 feet of fence at one place to keep livestock penned in.

Worn across the bottom of the Bull Pasture are small ravines, with deep *tinajas* eroded in the red rock. Water can usually be found in the bottom of the deepest *tinajas*, even during the dry months of May and June, and sometimes, after summer storms or winter rains, the ravines come alive with running streams and brief, splashing waterfalls.

Since it has been free of cattle for many years the Bull Pasture is one of the few places in Organ Pipe Cactus National Monument where the visitor can see a bit of nature in its pure state. Here the grass grows knee high, the agave, the yucca and the ocotillo flourish, and the flowers, during the spring and autumn months, if the rains and temperatures have been propitious, brighten the fields with acres of color. The light seems a little more dramatic here than anywhere else in Organ Pipe —the sunrises, the sunsets, the moonrises, the stars a little more brilliant—and the air is almost always clean and good. There is something sweet, calming and benign in the general stillness, a quiet never disturbed by any sounds more harsh than those of the wind rushing through the tall grass, the music of falling water, the scream of a hawk. We have few places like this remaining in our poor, pillaged, squandered, ravished Arizona; there are not many that a man or woman could find better for a last long walk under the sun and sky, through the wind, into the earth.

The Lavish, Frugal Cacti

Though cacti are native to many corners of the Western Hemisphere, from Patagonia to Canada, they have reached a peak of development and diversification in the Sonoran Desert. Botanists have listed more than 140 species of cactus in this region, from the stately organ pipe (right) to the squat, spiny teddy bear cholla —and more are still being found.

The origins of the bizarre cactus family are shrouded in mystery. Botanists theorize that the first cacti evolved from roses, basing this conclusion largely on an outstanding feature of today's cacti: their lavish, showy flowers, which closely resemble roses in shape and structure. Some of the most beautiful flowers —and some of the most typical cacti —of the Sonoran Desert are shown on the following pages in pictures taken at Arizona's Organ Pipe Cactus National Monument. In the sheer variety of their forms and functions, these species sum up the present life style of the whole cactus family.

In adjusting to the desert, cacti have literally reshaped themselves to fit their environment, increasing their bulk and reducing the surface area they expose to sun and desiccating winds. In making this adaptation, cacti stopped bearing leaves; they could no longer afford these broad-surfaced appendages because of their spendthrift way with water; a leafy plant that has 100 times the surface area of a barrel cactus of equal weight loses moisture roughly 6,000 times as quickly.

When the cacti dispensed with foliage, their stems and branches, green with chlorophyll, took over the leaves' work of manufacturing food. This arrangement permits the cacti, drawing energy from almost constant sunlight and moisture from their water-storing interior pulp, to function all year round and to flower even during lengthy droughts.

Many other adaptations play a vital role in the frugal existence of the cacti. Their shallow, widespread root systems absorb maximum moisture in a region of brief rainstorms and thin, quick-draining soil. The waxy finish on their tough skins retards moisture loss, and their armament of sharp spines affords some protection from sun, wind and from the depredations of hungry, thirsty desert creatures.

Thanks to these ingenious mechanisms, the cacti, overcoming rigors that offer only a slender margin for life, are considered one of the greatest successes in the plant world.

A fusion of strength and grace, this large organ pipe cactus reaches a height of 20 feet with its tallest stems. Each expandable water-storing stem is supported by a woody framework and covered by a pleated skin with 12 to 19 vertical ridges resembling welts. The ridges are studded with dark areoles. Complex structures possessed only by cacti, the areoles produce clusters of spines and, high up on the organ pipe's stems, a scattering of fragrant night-blooming flowers.

A LOFTY ORGAN PIPE CACTUS

SPINES GROWING FROM AREOLES

FLOWERS THAT BLOOM BY NIGHT

A YOUNG PRICKLY-PEAR CACTUS

A RIPE FRUIT

NEWLY OPENED BLOSSOMS

PRICKLY-PEAR ARMOR

A BEE IN A DARKENING FLOWER

The Tough, Homely Prickly Pear

Prickly pears are the hardiest, most adaptable plants in the cactus family. Plain and unimpressive—though they have vivid red fruit and magnificent flowers that darken subtly from one day to the next—they grow in a sprawling succession of water-storing pads, protected by clusters of long spines and short barbed bristles called glochids. Capable of thriving in the poorest soil, these plants grow faster than their larger, handsomer relatives, reaching full size and strength in five to 10 years.

The prickly pears' vigor is based on a highly efficient root system. A tapering taproot anchors the plant, and a wide network of shallow roots rapidly soaks up rain water during the brief desert storms. In winter some species develop swollen roots; these take over the moisture-storing function of the pads, which are thus spared damage from freezing. The prickly pears' roots also help stabilize the thin, loose desert soil; the widespread roots of one species, the starvation prickly pear, are credited with keeping huge quantities of soil from being blown away by the winds that scour the arid Southwest.

Thanks to their toughness and adaptability, the prickly pears have achieved wider distribution than any other group of plants in the cactus family. They grow in sun-scorched flats and in chilly mile-high uplands, and can be found in all of the contiguous United States except Maine, New Hampshire and Vermont.

The Bulky, Pulpy Barrel Cactus

Tagged with as many nicknames as an aggregation of athletes, the family of barrel cacti—as their best-known common name suggests—are thick and squat. Even the tallest, which may reach 10 feet, look shorter than they are because of their water-bloated girth. The nicknames come from the many idiosyncrasies found among various species: some are called compass barrels because they naturally lean toward the sunny southwest or fishhook barrels for their long curved spines.

But few nicknames reflect the whole truth. Barrel cacti are not, as desert folklore would have it, filled to the brim with crystal-clear water, ever available to save the lives of dehydrated travelers. When the top of a barrel cactus is lopped off, the plant is found to be filled with a soft mass of tiny storage cells that hold moisture like the tissue of a sponge.

The shape of the barrel cactus —and of many other cacti—depends entirely on this soft cellular interior, whose changing moisture content causes the expansion and contraction of the plant's pleated skin. The pulp, scooped out and squeezed, yields a thick, sticky liquid that is slow to evaporate and so bitter that a traveler would have to be desperate to swallow a mouthful. But when the pulp is cut into cubes and boiled in sugar syrup, it makes a sweet that is something like watermelon preserves—hence another of the plant's nicknames: candy cactus.

A BARREL CACTUS BLOOM

A COVILLE BARREL CACTUS

MATURE FLESHY FRUIT

A CLOSE-UP OF SPINES

A CLUSTER OF NEW BLOSSOMS

A HEDGEHOG CACTUS' QUILL-LIKE SPINES

A MANY-STEMMED HEDGEHOG

A SMALL-BLOSSOMED FENDLER'S HEDGEHOG

The Hedgehog's Prickly Beauty

The hedgehog cactus, named for the resemblance of its long spines to a porcupine's quills, produces some of the most beautiful flowers in the entire cactus family. The blossoms of most hedgehog cacti are elegant, brilliant and spectacularly large in relation to the size of the plant. Few hedgehogs grow more than 10 inches tall, yet many species put forth flowers that measure three inches in diameter when fully opened. One species, the comb hedgehog, has blossoms five or six inches across —growing on a plant no more than nine inches tall. The hedgehogs' flowers may be white, yellow or pale green, but in most species the blooms combine red and blue in varying hues, producing almost every purplish tone from a pale lavender to a dark magenta verging on black. The petals have a delicate, satiny sheen that heightens the blaze of color, even in small-flowered species such as the Fendler's hedgehog *(opposite, bottom)*. Some species have hundreds of stems to a single plant, and each stem may have several flowers blooming at once.

As a further decorative touch, the flower color of many species is subtly shaded from dark at the base to light at the petals' tips. One species, the golden hedgehog *(left)*, sets off its pale lavender-pink flower with reproductive organs of contrasting color: dark green female stigmas at the center of the flower and male stamens of a delicate whitish yellow.

FLOWERS OF A GOLDEN HEDGEHOG

A RANK OF SPINES

A SENITA CLUMP

A BALD STEM TOP

A NIGHT-BLOOMING SENITA FLOWER

The Slender Gray-whiskered Senita

Seen from a distance, the rare senita cactus is easily mistaken for a towering organ pipe cactus. But the senita's columnar stems, armed with linear ranks of spines, are usually shorter (about 10 feet high), thinner and more numerous than those of the organ pipe. The senita's tapering tops are occasionally bald and sunburned, but usually they are tufted with gray whiskery spines. Like the organ pipe, the senita is a night-blooming species; but its flowers are smaller and more plentiful than the blooms of the organ pipe.

The senita's long, slender stems help to explain the species' local rarity. Except for their tough skin and woody framework, the thin stems consist entirely of spongy water-storing tissue that makes the plant highly vulnerable to damage from freezing, which can prune back the stems or even prove fatal to the plant. Partly because of this frailty, the senita's normal habitat is the frost-free desert region south of the Mexican border.

But in Arizona's Organ Pipe Cactus National Monument there are some senitas that manage to withstand occasional cold snaps. Their ability to survive freezing, a dramatic proof of the adaptability of cacti, is explained by the fact that senitas in Arizona have thicker stems than those in Mexico; these senitas have increased their mass in relation to their surface area in order to conserve enough warmth for survival.

A SPINY STEM WITH A HAIRY TOP

The Bristling, Brittle Teddy Bear

The chollas are the prickliest plants in the cactus family, and the prickliest of their kind is the small and shrubby teddy bear cholla. Paradoxically, the teddy bear's fierce armament accounts for its disarming nickname: its straw-colored spines and glochids are so numerous and close-set that the entire plant looks furry, especially when it glistens in a halo of bright sunlight.

To make the teddy bear even more formidable, it shares with the other chollas a brittleness that has proved painful to many a careless traveler. Its water-storing branches grow in short, thick segments called joints, which break off so easily on contact that they seem almost to leap up to impale a victim. Hence various species are popularly called "jumping" chollas, though of course they have no means of self-propulsion.

For all its spiky hostility to most creatures, the teddy bear provides protection for a few of them. The ingenious cactus wren constructs its nest securely in the heart of the plant; the pack rat fortifies its nest with piled-up cholla joints.

While functioning as a defensive weapon, the chollas' barbs also aid in the propagation of the species. By breaking off and hooking a ride on passing animals, the bristling joints are widely dispersed. Wherever a joint falls to the ground, it needs only adequate moisture and warm soil temperatures to put down roots and grow into a complete new plant.

A FLOWER GUARDED BY SPIKY ARMAMENT

A TEDDY BEAR CHOLLA

A FORMIDABLE DEFENSE

A FURRY CLUMP OF TEDDY BEAR JOINTS

TEDDY BEAR CHOLLAS UNDER A NOONDAY SUN

The Varied Tribe of Chollas

While all chollas share such basic characteristics as spiny joints, the various species differ radically in growth patterns and appearance. In contrast to the bristle-covered teddy bear cholla, the buckhorn cholla (so called because its water-storing branches resemble a deer's antlers) is only lightly armed with spines and glochids. Some full-grown cholla species are less than a foot tall, while the chain fruit chollas resemble trees, often measuring 12 feet in height and seven inches in diameter at the base of the woody trunk.

The chain fruit cholla is further distinguished by a striking peculiarity that inspired its name: the species bears its fruit in long festoons that sometimes touch the ground. The process that forms each chain begins with a flower that may vary in color from pink to purple, depending on the composition of the soil. After the flower withers away, an egg-shaped green fruit develops and usually remains on the plant; the next year—and the next—the fruit, still green and still growing, produces a flower and it, in turn, produces another fruit. Chains of fruit with 12 or 14 links are not uncommon.

Curiously, the fruit of this species contains only a few seeds, which are generally infertile, or no seeds at all. Yet the chain fruit cholla is in no danger of dying out; even a seedless fruit will take root just as readily as a broken-off joint when it falls on warm soil and is moistened by rain.

CHAINS OF CHOLLA FRUIT

A CHAIN FRUIT CHOLLA

A BEE ON A CHOLLA FLOWER

BUCKHORN CHOLLA IN BLOOM

A BUCKHORN BRANCH

SPRAWLING BUCKHORN CHOLLA

4/ The Sacred Peak

*Nearly every striking feature of this special world
...goes back ultimately to the grand fact of dryness—the
dryness of the ground, of the air, of the whole sum-total.*

JOSEPH WOOD KRUTCH/ *THE VOICE OF THE DESERT*

Papaguería, the Papago Indian Reservation in the heart of Arizona's Sonoran Desert, is a place of hungry cows and haggard horses, fat
buzzards and horned toads, flash floods and cactus forests. It is a place
of mud villages with names unpronounceable to the alien tongue:
Schuchk, Vaya Chin, Supi Oidak, Chukut Kuk, Kom Vo, Gu Komelik,
Sil Nakya, Pan Tak and Hickiwan. And it is a land of mountains.
Papaguería is the place of the Comobabi Mountains, the Quijotoa Mountains and, highest and most important, the number one holy one, home
of the god I'itoi, big green island in the desert sea, sticking up against
the sky like a great tooth—Baboquivari.

All my life I had wanted to ascend that sacred mountain, most wonderful of remote lost places on the maps of boyhood. (Those maps. I
used to read them as others read fairy tales, comic books and the funny
papers; for me maps were equally magical. Who or what for example
lived in Gunlock, Utah? Wolf Hole, Arizona? Bedrock, Colorado? Pie
Town, New Mexico? And what was life like there, how did it feel, how
did the morning light slant across the hills, what went on in the dead
heat of a summer afternoon, where were the people when the fool
moon rose at sunset like a great big platinum cymbal and simply hung
there for a while, mute, potent, an unstruck gong above the hills? Who
would record it all if I never got there in time? A serious question.)

So, a few years ago a friend, Dave Rehfield, and I staggered at midnight from a party, stumbled into a car, drove 80 miles south-southwest to the eastern base of Baboquivari, slept on the cold ground till dawn, woke up sick and beat, ate some tuna straight from a tin and started up the mountain.

We passed first a small ranch where yellow-eyed hound dogs barked passionately at our heels, earning their daily feed. We ignored them, plunged into oak thickets and juniper jungles, found a path and followed it upward to the crest of a ridge that seemed to lead to the base of the final peak. By the time we got that far it was late afternoon and the big granite tooth of Baboquivari seemed as far away as ever. Nevertheless we trudged on, up the ridge, into more thickets of scrub oak, tangles of thorny acacia, open places mined with prickly pear and Schott's agave. The October heat was sickening—a fierce, sullen resistance—and the trail petered out into an unfollowable maze of cattle paths and deer runs, through thorny tunnels under the brush. The sun was going down, a chill crept into the air and then into our bones. Hungover, exhausted, hungry, we gave up and retreated back down the long ridge to the ranch, the dogs, the road, our car.

Baboquivari had defeated our first expedition. But I knew that we would try again. I knew that Justice William O. Douglas had once climbed this mountain and if he could I could.

It was two years later, in the month of December, that another friend, John De Puy, and I drove to the western side of the mountain, in Papaguería, and camped at the foot of the trail, fortifying ourselves with steak and beer, coffee and cognac. Through the afternoon the skies had been cloudy, prophesying storm, but after sundown the clouds went away and all the desert stars came out.

There was a little formal campground here beneath Baboquivari's western flank, at the end of the road, with concrete picnic tables, fireplaces with grills, an abandoned ruin of what appeared to have been a caretaker's residence, and an official greeting sign from the Papago tribe in big bold hand-lettered red characters:

> Keep America Beautiful
> Pick Up Your Trash Before Leaving
> THIS means YOU!!
> Thank you!

Inevitably, all about were the tin cans and tinfoil wrappers, plastic plates, paper diapers, worn-out socks and old tennis shoes of those who come to where such signs are found. Through the garbage and under the spreading mesquite trees ran a trickle of a brook fed by melting snows above, a meager stream but musical, splashing over the rocks and sand and clods of old cow dung.

Cattle and cattle tracks were everywhere. The campground was badly overgrazed, as is the entire Papago Reservation. As is most of the West, come to think of it. When the grass is gone and the land becomes too tough for cattle we'll see herds of goats browsing on the cactus, as they do in North Africa, Mesopotamia, Crete—followed finally by teams of archeologists.

The starving had already begun. On hand to welcome us when we entered this derelict campground was a little yellow dog, a shaggy undersized mutt so obviously abandoned and unwanted, so wretched, so painfully servile, so conspicuously worthless, that even our cold hearts were faintly touched. We gave him the wax from our Edam cheese. He gulped it down without even tasting it. We gave him the butcher paper that had wrapped the steaks, nice and bloody and greasy, and he devoured it.

We stared at this voracious cur, impressed despite ourselves by his enthusiasm for survival. He stared back at us, the black shoe-button eyes shining with faith and hope, the stub of a tail wagging furiously. This was on December 20 and the spirit of Christmas stirred feebly in our bosoms. We retrieved one of the plastic plates nearby and poured the dog some beer. He lapped it up at once. We threw him a chunk of gristle and fat from one of the steaks and it vanished in mid-air, inside a sudden blur of yellowish hair.

I suggested then that the most merciful thing we could do would be to beat the little chap over the head with a rock until he was dead. My friend De Puy crossed himself, looking apprehensively at the mountain hanging above us, and muttered something about I'itoi the god of Baboquivari. He sliced off a portion of his steak and tossed it dogward. Again the miraculous disappearance. I was shamed into doing the same and so we had an unwanted dog on our hands and souls for the rest of the night and all the next day. We crawled into our mummy bags and dreamed of cheerful things.

Sometime before dawn we were awakened by the crowing of roosters from a nearby Papago rancheria. We rose and fumbled about in the dark, warmed up a sort of breakfast, packed our packs and shambled off up the trail. We figured on a long day; I carried a 120-foot rope, for use on rock, across my shoulders.

It would be a 3,000-foot climb from the big cactus belt where we start-ed to the piñon-juniper zone at the base of Baboquivari's bare peak. On the way upward I could mark the degree of our ascent not only by the trembling of my knees but also by the successive changes in the char-acter of the vegetation.

First, the mesquite forest, a dense jungle of thorny, scrubby little trees, their numbers a sure result of overgrazing. Good for firewood and fence posts, the mesquite tree also produces a kind of bean that makes a nutritious food for both animals and man; for many centuries it was one of the staples of the Papago diet. On the other hand, where the mesquite grows thick the grass cannot; when the cattle strip off the ground cover the mesquite forest moves in and takes over; the cattle de-part. Thus what is gained in beans is lost in beef, and which is better only time will show.

Towering above the mesquite is the great saguaro cactus. Burned by the sun and battered by storms, scarred by disease, bacteria, mammals and birds, some of these old giants have been here since the time of the American Revolution. They show it. Yet still alive, still flowering each May, they keep on reproducing. Or trying to. They produce their quota of seeds. The trouble is that swarms of hungry cattle, infesting so much of the Southwest, tend to trample out the young saguaro before they can take hold. Only those seedlings lucky enough to germinate and take root within the shelter of a nurse tree—a mesquite, ironwood or paloverde—where they are protected from foraging cattle and ro-dents and too much direct sunlight, are able to reach maturity.

The saguaro grows very slowly, sometimes taking nine to ten years to reach a height of six inches, about 30 years to reach five feet, 150 years to reach 35 feet. A saguaro may live, it has been estimated, for 200 years, grow to a height of 50 feet and weigh as much as seven tons. The weight of a particular saguaro varies from time to time, depending upon the amount of moisture available to the plant. Because of its flut-ed, columnar structure, the saguaro is able to expand when water is available for storage and to contract when the drought returns. The water-storing tissue of the plant makes up 75 to 95 per cent of its gross weight. Because of its great moisture-retaining capacity the saguaro can survive the most prolonged and severe dry spells, continue growth and carry on reproduction.

Like many plants the saguaro reproduces through flowering and pol-lination, a process that seems to require the agency of bees, bats and birds. The flowers usually appear in late May, large creamy-white blossoms clustered on the tip of the central trunk and on the tip of each branch. If fertilization occurs, the flowers produce an oval-shaped fruit about two to three inches long, without spines, resembling a watermelon in flavor, and containing over 1,000 tiny black seeds. This fruit is a popular item in the diet not only of birds and other flying creatures but also of man; the Papago Indians have traditionally harvested saguaro fruit by using long poles to knock the fruit to the ground. It can then be eaten raw or dried for storage, or ground up, allowed to ferment and made into a kind of cactus wine.

The saguaro's prospects for survival, as a species, seem only fair. Cattle grazing, even in national monuments like Organ Pipe and Saguaro (near Tucson), continues to take its toll. Near towns and cities, land-clearing projects, agriculture and housing developments have eliminated entire stands. Some botanists believe the plant is also being attacked by new forms of disease. Saving the saguaro will require more study and research and better protection, especially in the national monuments and national forests.

Up the trail we walked through thickets of ocotillo, that weird, Martian, spidery thing, and higher on the mountainside we entered the zone of the agaves. Here are the century plants, in various stages of development from baby rosettes close to the ground to the 15-foot expired stalks of last season's dead.

The century plant does not live a century; it only seems that way if you are sitting around waiting for it to bloom. Fifteen to 20 years is a normal lifespan, concluded by a flowering—the only one—and death. Year after year the plant has grown slowly, developing its base of heavy rigid leaves, each tipped with a sharp red spine. In the center of the plant the leaves remain folded together like the heart of an artichoke, concealing the agave's core. Finally one spring the supreme moment arrives: the inner leaves part and within a few days a great tumescent stalk rises to a height of up to 15 feet. Then it blooms—a loosely clustered pyramid of large, showy golden flowers at the tip of the stalk. This glorious blooming time is short. In only a few weeks the flowers fade, the stalk dries up and by the end of the summer the entire plant is dead. But it has accomplished the purpose for which the sacrifice was made: the flowers are succeeded by pods containing the hardy, dried seeds of the next generation.

Here at Baboquivari, the clock-face, or dollar-joint, prickly pear cactus, so named for the symmetric round shape of the succulent joints or

A mile below 7,730-foot-high Baboquivari, mesquite, acacias and looming saguaros share a rugged slope that rises from the desert floor.

pads, was perhaps the most prevalent of the cacti. The purplish fruit, which tastes a bit like pomegranate, is very sweet and seedy. The clusters of fine hairs on the skin of each "pear" can be removed by rubbing it through sand.

The trail paralleled a ravine for about half a mile and here we saw more typical desert plants like the hackberry, an evergreen shrub (sometimes growing to tree height) that provides occasional fruit for birds and small mammals. Also present was the acacia, both the white-thorn and the catclaw. The second is well named: the small curved claws, exactly like those of a cat, will sink themselves equally well into cloth or flesh and cling there, halting the unwary traveler in his tracks. Like mesquite, ironwood and paloverde, the acacias are members of the great pea family, the third largest group of flowering plants in the world (after the sunflower family and the orchid family).

We passed through stands of jojobas, shrubs that provide good browsing for deer and cattle. Among the jojobas grow other shrubs: white ratany, or crimson beak, the roots of which were boiled by Indians and pioneers to make a medicinal tea; coursetia, or baby bonnet, named for the shape of the small white flowers; and the fairy duster,

A JUNIPER TREE AND A SOTOL PLANT

LIVE OAKS, JUNIPERS AND PINONS

also known as false mesquite or calliandra, good browse for game and livestock. All of these shrubs are likewise members of the pea family.

Here also was the shrub called Mormon tea or Mexican tea or green ephedra, an odd plant because the stems appear completely leafless and because the seeds are contained in primitive cones that relate it to such ancient—and more common—forms of plant life as pines and other conifers. Unlike the pine, the Mormon tea shrub carries chlorophyll not in its scalelike leaves but in its green stems, a supply sufficient to maintain the food-producing process of photosynthesis. Mormon tea is thought to have therapeutic powers. I have brewed it myself, out of curiosity, boiling the stems and sipping the resultant tea. I found the flavor very bitter, which explains its curative reputation: anything that tastes so bad must be good for you.

The trail switchbacked still higher. Now and then we caught a glimpse of the great rock peak of Baboquivari soaring far above and far away, too far, seemingly inaccessible, a likely home for a desert god. We plodded onward, slowly and steadily, pausing at times to rest for a minute but not sitting down, which is much too tiring on a long uphill hike. Hard to explain but true. Only the slow and steady plod, based on

At different stages of the ascent to the top of Baboquivari, marked changes appear in the type and density of vegetation. A variety of tough plants and trees flourishes at about 4,600 feet (far left). The trees thin out around 6,000 feet (center) and diminish in size to shrubby dwarfs (below) at 7,000 feet, just below the bald, rocky summit.

SCRUB OAKS AND HARDY MOUNTAIN SHRUBS

heart and will as much as legs and lungs, can get you all the way.

Higher and higher. The vegetation continued to change. We saw a dark and scraggly thing called limber bush or, by the Mexicans, *sangre de drago*—dragon's blood—because of the reddish sap, sometimes used as a dye by the Indians. Here was the hopbush or switch sorrel, a member of the soapberry family, containing certain toxic substances that the Indians used as a poison to catch fish. A bright green shrub found in this zone is the red-berry buckthorn, with oily leaves and bright red fruit, sometimes utilized by the Papago in making a form of desert pemmican; they would mix the berries with meat into a highly nutritious, compact food easily carried on long marches.

From time to time we saw signs of coyotes, javelinas, jack rabbits, deer along the trail; red-tailed hawks and prairie falcons wheeled in the sky; flocks of piñon jays, juncoes and chickadees in the woods. We reached a saddle on the ridge below the peak and entered what seemed to me the most beautiful plant community on the mountain. Here, under the red and orange cliffs of ancient volcanic rocks, were green groves of Ajo oaks, piñon pines and junipers, with drifts of December snow stretching across the trail.

The Ajo oak was not classified until 1954. It seldom grows more than 30 feet tall but is nevertheless a true oak tree, producing acorns, nutritious and fattening for wildlife, and a good long-burning very hot fuel much in demand for heating and cooking among the Indians. Mixed with the oaks were two kinds of juniper: the one-seed, or monosperm, juniper and the alligator juniper, so called because of the hidelike texture of the bark. Beyond the junipers and oaks we walked gratefully into the shade of a pure stand of piñon pine, where the air smelled damp and resinous, and banks of ferns grew between the snowdrifts. It was a cool, dark place, high above the desert, refreshing after the wearying dust and glare below.

The trail now followed the shaded northern side of the ridge where the snow became a problem. The crust on the surface was not quite hard enough to support a man's weight; with every step we broke through the crust and sank in to the knees. Step-plunge, step-plunge —an awkward gait. But we carried on. The peak seemed much nearer and the day was still not old. We crossed over the ridge again into most welcome sunshine, a grassy slope with a vast view to the south, east and west. We stopped to eat our lunch.

Now we had to acknowledge that the yellow cur had followed us all the way; here he came, sniffing, whining, tail vibrating, eyes shining with a piteous hope. We had no choice but to share our lunch with him, suspecting that this dog might be much more than he appeared, might well be some disguised form of the spirit of the mountain—an avatar —sent down by I'itoi to test our souls. We gave the wretch the leftovers of our leftover steak.

Onward. The trail wound under thickets of oak and piñon pine, the snowdrifts became continuous and deeper. At places we sank in to our hips. On hands and knees we crawled over the largest of the drifts and came finally, at last, thank God, to the base of the great peak. Above was good, solid rock.

From here the route led along the base of a cliff, and then upward at 45 degrees toward the summit. After the brush and snow it was a great pleasure to plant our boots on real rock again and walk normally. We scraped the ice from the boot lugs and began to scramble. There was some ice on the rock, but it lay in patches and we found it easy to avoid, at least in the beginning.

At the first steep pitch we came to the ruins of a wooden stairway built in the 1930s by the CCC—the New Deal's Civilian Conservation Corps. The stairway now was nothing but fragments of splintered wood, studded with rusty spikes, more dangerous than the bare rock to which it was still partially anchored. We passed to the side of it, continued climbing over the rocks, traversed to the north side of the peak and encountered the combination of brush and snow again. More struggle, working through a tunnel of a path in the scrub oak thickets, until we came to the second rocky pitch. The little yellow dog was still with us, following close on our heels.

At this point the mountain assumed a more serious aspect. It began to look like rope country—not to say ice-ax country, and we had no ice ax. Not even a screw driver. We shuffled to the top of the last snowdrift and stood looking up at about 100 feet of rugged rock cliff, much of it glistening with ice, rising upward at an angle close to the vertical, with a little bench or shelf every now and then. Near the top we could see the remains of another wooden stairway built by the CCC—far beyond our reach this time. In between was an intricate puzzle of toe holds and fingertip grips that we had to solve in order to climb any higher. Since we were both strictly amateur rock climbers the prospect seemed dim. Was dim.

What were the stairways for? There was time for that question while we picked at the ice with our fingernails. The answer is that someone

An aerial view of Baboquivari, backed by the narrow, 40-mile-long range of which it is part, reveals sharp faults and almost perpendicular cliffs

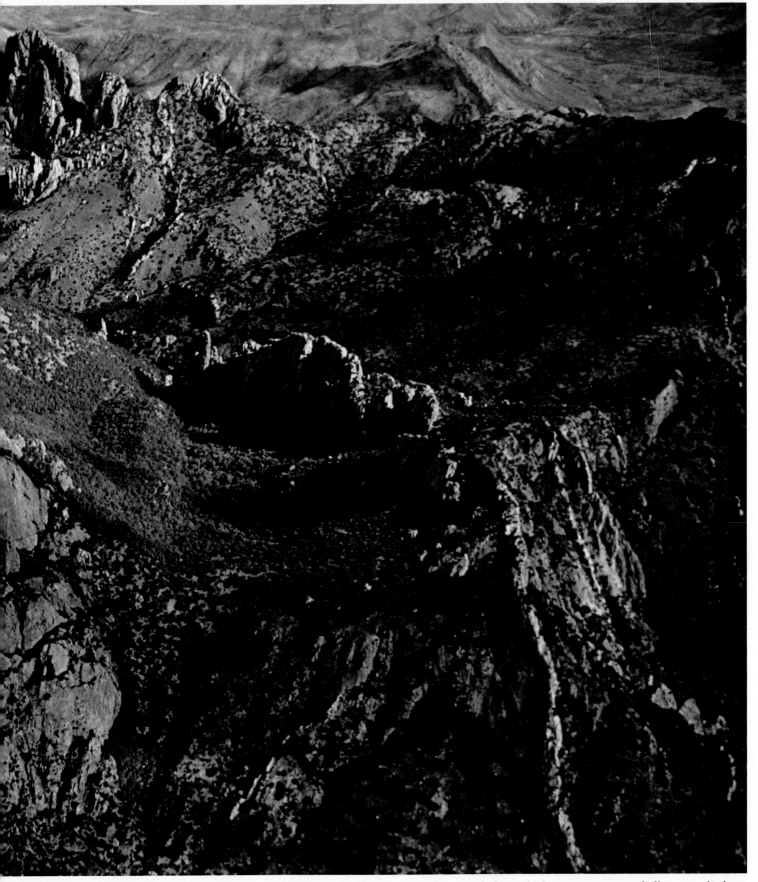

of the mountain's southeast face. Revered in Papago Indian legend as the home of a desert god, the peak also poses a strong challenge to climbers.

in the CCC decided that there should be a fire lookout station on top of Baboquivari. Lord knows it was high enough—7,730 feet above sea level, approximately 5,000 feet above the surrounding cactus desert. At great effort and expense the trail was built up the mountainside, the lumber for the stairways laboriously trucked in, carpentered together and hung on the cliffs, a frame shack erected on the summit of the mountain, and even a telephone line strung on poles the whole way from base to peak. The work was done.

Then someone realized that there was no forest to look at, or even to speak of, from the heights of Baboquivari. Nothing around and below, for hundreds of square miles, but the poor, overgrazed, trampled Papago desert. No trees but scrubby mesquite and paloverde, no grass but poverty weed and snakeweed, nothing worth setting fire to—or building a fire station to protect. One imagines the hush that must have fallen over the conversation as the government officials gazed out from the peak upon that lovely, forlorn, splendid and desolate wasteland. Since then, over the decades, the weather and the hikers have gradually taken apart all the laboriously constructed works. Nothing remains but boards and splinters, rusted anchor bolts and loops of telephone wire strewn across the trail.

Facing the next 100 feet of the mountain, John and I arranged the length of rope so that we were connected, and delicately worked part way up the cold and ice-streaked cliff. Halfway to the top we came to even more ice, too much ice, thick and treacherous ice. A pause. Cold, stiff, hungry and tired, we decided to give it up, try another day when the sun shone and little birds came out to sing. Taking turns—one descending while the other looped the rope around a rock—we belayed each other back down the bleak face, reencountered the yellow dog at the base of the cliff, and marched down the trail to camp and truck, defeated but looking forward to food and drink.

Next day the weather changed, the temperatures soared, the snow and ice began to melt. A week later I returned to Baboquivari and scrambled easily to the peak, standing where William O. Douglas had stood years earlier, and looking out over the desert.

The view from the peak is good, if not always perfect. When I was there I could see about half of southern Arizona and quite a parcel of Mexican Sonora and a lot of mountains: the Santa Catalinas, the Ajos, the Huachucas, the Agua Dulces, and the Pinacates and others down in Mexico. When the air is clear, I've been told, you can see the waters of the Gulf of California, some 150 miles away by line of sight. Unfortunately the air is seldom clear in Arizona any more and on that day I could not see the gulf.

Nearby on the peak was the scattered wreckage of the lookout shack, never used for anything but shelter for a generation of hikers and climbers, and now virtually demolished. In an ammunition box cached in the rocks near the ruined shack was a register book, which I signed, and where, as I ate some cheese and rested a while, I read the inscriptions and inspirations of previous signers.

Something about climbing a mountain, even a modest one like Baboquivari, brings out the poet, the exhibitionist or the clown in every man, woman and child. In this register book, for example, were several notations by a woman who called herself "the third best lady mountain climber in the state of Arizona." There was one by "the best 12-year-old climber in the Southwest." Someone wrote, "Easter Sunday: We did it for Jesus." There were the signatures of my friends John and Joanna McComb, who have climbed this peak, from all sides, more than 20 times each. And then there were several pages of sermonizing by some Mormon missionaries who had taken time off from their labors in the Papago Reservation to come climb this heathen peak. The sermons were followed by one line from Pete Cowgill, Arizona journalist: "Don't preach to me on mountaintops."

Okay, I thought, Amen, I'll go along with that. No more preaching on mountaintops. I closed the book. I finished my cheese. I relaced my boots and ate some snow and descended the mountain.

Dreams of Desert Treasure

In her desert classic, *The Land of Little Rain,* Mary Austin remarked on "the palpable sense of mystery in the desert air" that "breeds fables, chiefly of lost treasure." In the mountains of the Sonoran Desert, rumors of treasure contained some truth. Beginning before the Civil War and for more than 50 years—until copper became more prized than gold and silver—the Arizona hills echoed to the sound of the prospector's pick and the bray of his burro.

In the late 1850s news of gold on the Gila River drew thousands of fortune seekers, usually lone operators. The lucky ones found gold in river beds or in surface gravel, and usually extracted it by panning: the prospector would wash loose sand and pebbles from a panful of dirt, leaving the heavier rock to be sifted for nuggets of gold.

These surface deposits were all too quickly depleted. In 1858 prospectors at Gila City, site of the first gold rush, gathered as much as $100 in gold a day, but by 1864 "the color had played out," as the prospectors put it, and the town had dwindled, in the words of one observer, to "three chimneys and a coyote."

Mining for silver was more complicated: ore usually had to be hacked out of the rock and processed. By the mid-1870s hard-rock silver-mining operations had begun on a large scale in the Pinal Mountains north of Tucson. Most of the solitary prospectors gave way to small mining companies that hired gangs of men. Towns that started as a few shacks grew helter-skelter as increasing numbers of workers arrived, many with families. The smell of wealth—and the miners' need for food, drink and entertainment—attracted not only ranchers and farmers but gamblers and saloonkeepers.

Yet few of the miners and their hangers-on were really interested in settling. They came to get what they could from the land and then moved on. Most of the hastily built towns were abandoned. With the demonetization of silver in 1893 and the new-found importance of copper to the burgeoning electrical industry, dreams of riches in the desert became harder and harder for small entrepreneurs to realize. After the first decade of the 20th Century, the entrances of forsaken mines were, for the most part, left to the lizards.

Photographed around 1900, this prospector was one of the last of a breed of desert treasure seekers. His tough, sure-footed mules tended to be ornery like the burros—called Arizona nightingales for their high-pitched bray—favored by many prospectors. One contrary burro is even credited with helping to discover the richest gold deposit in Arizona: the Vulture Mine at Wickenberg. In a rage when the beast refused to be caught, its master pelted it with rocks—which fell far short of their target because they were so heavy with gold.

Hard-rock silver miners of the 1890s gather outside a tunnel entrance to the Gunsight Mine. A child—evidently too young for work, though children often toiled beside the grownups to augment family income—perches on a narrow-gauge railway truck used to haul ore from the mine tunnel.

On a steep cliffside, workers pause momentarily on the rocky path leading to a mine entrance. The buildings at upper left were storage sheds and living quarters. The long, sloping structure at lower left was used to funnel ore down the mountainside to trains that hauled it to the smelter.

Beams for shoring up tunnels lie in long stacks at the Silver King Mine in the Pinal Mountains. Hauled in by companies of mules and burros, a supply of timber was vital to mine operations because the excavated terrain was often a treacherous mixture of loose rock and soil. To prevent cave-ins, the beams were placed along the sides and ceilings of the tunnels.

5/ Wild Palms and Gold Mines

*...there is a special kind of beauty for every hour
the mountain knows, beauty which man perceives without
participating, beauty to which he feels himself a stranger.*

MARY AUSTIN/ *THE LAND OF JOURNEYS' ENDING*

Approaching the Kofa Mountains from the west, off Highway 95 in southwest Arizona, you see gaunt burned porphyritic cliffs rising from the desert plain like fortifications for a race of giants. Half buried in their own eroded debris, they look much older than the human imagination can comprehend, apocryphal, legendary.

They glow, these mountains, as if with an inner fire. The effect is caused by the coloration of the rock and its almost total nakedness. In one of the driest parts of a dry region, the Kofas support only the sparsest vegetation—brittlebush (blooming bright and yellow in January) teddy bear cholla and very hairy prickly pear, cotton-top mini-headed barrel cactus with its bloodshot-pink hooked barbs, here and there a mesquite or ironwood, an occasional creosote. And each plant is well separated from its neighbor, rationing not light nor space but water.

The aridity, even in midwinter, sucks at the pores of your flesh, dries the sweat as fast as it emerges from your skin, keeps you cool, dehydrates you mighty quick unless you keep gulping down water. Water, water, water.... You look for it everywhere you go, out here. Nothing so marvelous, so rapturous, so miraculous as water in the desert.

The dirt road winding eastward from Highway 95 leads toward a dark gap in the west façade of the Kofas. Huge buttresses of andesite and metamorphosed volcanic tuff stand on either side of the gap, which is actually the mouth of Palm Canyon. Beyond and above the gap are more tiers and terraces of rust-colored stone, surmounted by the 4,877-foot-high mesa called Signal Peak. A brutal hulk of rock, it looks like a titanic altar, rotten and corroded with the blood of gods. Like mangled iron from some cosmic collision. Or like the crumbling ruin of a Castilian castle. No, this is all poetical rubbish. The mountain looks like what it is, the eroded remnants of igneous intrusions, volcanic rubble, ash and cinder and sediment. Which is enough.

Kofa stands for King of Arizona, which in turn is the name of a gold mine, no longer operated, down on the southwest flank of the range. The original name for the Kofas was the S.H. Mountains. According to one story, early prospectors named the range S.H. because of prominent quadrangular rock formations near the summit that resemble old-fashioned outhouses. Later, out of courtesy to pioneer ladies, S.H. was interpreted to mean Short Horn instead of the real, but unmentionable, name. Government map makers settled the controversy in their characteristic Bowdlerian fashion by choosing the present official name, although the original initials can still be seen on the earliest Geological Survey maps.

As in the Superstition Mountains, the Kofas have attracted more than a proportionate share of fortune hunters, gold seekers, those who come to search for whatever it is they lost a long time ago. We, on the other hand, have come to see the wild palm trees, the California fan palms, *Washingtonia filifera,* which grow in various oases in southern California and Baja California but in Arizona only in this one area, the northernmost and easternmost limit of their range.

Nine miles of dust and gravel bring us to a dead end, a sort of parking lot bulldozed out of the side of a slope, where the trail into Palm Canyon begins. We are now in what is called the Kofa Game Range, a national wildlife refuge area, an extensive portion of public real estate administered by the U.S. Fish and Wildlife Service, Department of the Interior. Once a wildlife sanctuary, the Kofas were opened in 1955 to hunting on a restricted basis, a move that sizably increased the revenues of the Arizona Game and Fish Department through the sale of licenses. The chief attraction here for hunters is the desert bighorn sheep, and perhaps now is the right time and place to say what must be said about trophy hunters:

I am not against hunters or hunting. Many of us who call ourselves conservationists or wilderness nuts or nature freaks have been hunters too. Born and raised on a Pennsylvania farm, I spent much of my boyhood in the pursuit and slaughter of small mammals. I was a trapper and familiar with the sight of a muskrat frozen in ice or the look of a gnawed-off fox's leg in the steel jaws of one of my Victor traps. As a boy such things troubled me only slightly. I thought nothing of killing rabbits, squirrels and ringneck pheasants for the table, and badgers, groundhogs and skunks for sport. We were helping to rid the world of "varmints"—an honorable undertaking.

Later, in the Southwest, in the glory of youth, I became an avid deer-slayer, often by jack light under the stars, often the day before the season opened (hiding my kill in the woods for 24 hours), and sometimes even fair, square and legally. I didn't care. It was all for the sake of putting meat on the table and deerskin gloves on my sweetheart's hands. Honorable work, nothing a man need be ashamed of.

But I discovered gradually that I no longer found much pleasure in killing for the sake of killing. The more I hunted the more I found it necessary to justify my activity by convincing myself that I was doing it for the sake of the meat. I could no longer kill anything I did not intend to eat. Why? Over a period of years the answer came to me: I was growing up. Even the meat was only a pretext, I realized, not a genuine need. There were others whose need for venison was far greater than

Signal Peak

mine: Indians, for example, and out-of-work copper miners, and students and Mexicans living a submarginal existence. And mountain lions. Yes, most especially the lions, for whom deer meat is basic, the staple of their diet. (And who needs lions? We all do—including the deer. Most especially the deer. For their own evolutionary good.)

Therefore I gave up even the annual deer hunt. Not however on absolute moral grounds—please note that. When and if I ever need the meat I shall load up the old .30-30 and go trudging off again into the mountain dawn. As for all my friends and countrymen who continue to hunt deer, or anything else that is good to eat, in plentiful supply, in no danger of extinction, I say *buena cacería*—good hunting. I see nothing wrong in it; I perceive no moral superiority in the position of the ethical vegetarian who exploits cattle and goats for their milk, uproots harmless carrots, mutilates innocent turnips, violates cabbages and plunders fruit trees to keep body and soul conjoined. All must eat to survive; all must kill in order to eat. The system demands it and our only moral obligation under this system is to do what killing we must in the proper spirit of humility, gratitude and grace.

Trophy hunting, however, is another matter, one that lacks the most

Summit Peak   Squaw Peak

Sharply outlined against the sunset, the jagged crest of the Kofa Mountains in southwest Arizona resembles the skyline of a primitive metropolis of palaces and turrets. The range, whose principal peaks are identified in the picture, is volcanic in origin, and covered with a layer of lava that is 2,000 feet thick in places. The discovery of veins of ore-bearing rock around the turn of the century set off a flurry of gold and silver mining and also won the Kofas their name, after the King of Arizona, a gold mine abandoned in 1910. Today the mountains are best known as a refuge for bighorn sheep.

elementary justification. No one kills bighorn sheep or mountain lions or javelinas because he needs the meat. (Which is not to say that these animals cannot be eaten if the need arises.) Nor can anyone honestly claim to kill such animals in self-defense; none of them are ever likely to attack humans, unless cornered or molested. The only reason these animals are still subject to hunting is because some men—not many —find a weird sort of psychological gratification in the slaughter of them. It does not even appear to be a question of establishing a sense of manhood through the killing, because other more legitimate game, deer for example, are amply available. The purpose of trophy hunting seems to be no more than the collection of heads for the sake of the heads. It is a hobby then, admittedly one sometimes involving skill and always great expense of time and money, pursued with the passion other men reserve for the pursuit of women, gold, power or fame.

Bighorn sheep have become particular victims of this head-hunting mania. Among the collectors of sheep heads there is a magical achievement called the Grand Slam—which means the killing of one full-grown ram from each of four distinct kinds of wild sheep found on the North American continent. The four are the desert bighorn, the Rocky Mountain bighorn, the Stone sheep and the Dall. If you can kill all four you have hit a Grand Slam—a homer with the bases loaded. Four stuffed sheep heads to mount on your rumpus-room wall.

Perhaps none of this would matter much if bighorns (and lions and javelinas et al.) were as common as jack rabbits and mule deer. So long as the animal kingdom can bear it, the peculiar hobbies of trophy hunters would get no argument from me. The harm lies in the fact that they hunt most eagerly the very animals that are most in danger of extinction, such as polar bears, leopards, jaguars, grizzly bears and ibexes, as well as the North American bighorn sheep. It appears that the very rarity of an animal makes its dead head all the more desirable.

True, the desert bighorn is supposed to be protected by law. The hunting of it is severely regulated, with only a limited number of permits issued each year. In theory, at least, the bighorn population should be sustained. Unfortunately a considerable amount of poaching goes on, mostly by wealthy hunters who fail to obtain one of the much-prized official permits, then pay exorbitant fees to unscrupulous professional guides and willingly risk a fine if caught. Luxury poaching has become so common, as the bighorn become harder and harder to find, that one guide recently announced he was quitting the business altogether rather than participate any longer in the extermination of a species.

Other factors contribute to the decline of the desert bighorn. The specimens most prized by the trophy hunters are the hardy and vigorous old rams—the best breeding stock in each herd. At the same time predation by the natural enemies of the bighorn, such as mountain lion and coyote, has been greatly reduced because of decades of poisoning and trapping predators. In the ordinary course of events, natural predators eliminate the weak and the ill among the bighorn, the least competent and alert, thereby increasing the quality of the sheep herd as a whole. Only the best survive. Now, between the depredations of the trophy hunters and the nonpredations of the predators, the opposite effect from that achieved by evolution results: the inferior survive, the breed declines.

Finally the bighorn sheep are being squeezed toward extinction simply by the general advance of our industrial culture. Hordes of nature lovers (such as myself) invade their sanctuaries, linger about their water holes and interfere with their grazing and browsing habits. Noisy aircraft disturb their privacy. The military's use of much of the Southwest as a bombing and gunnery range may be producing deleterious if not precisely known effects upon the stability of the species. Most serious of all, the ever-growing extension of fencing by the cattle raisers obstructs the free migration of the bighorn herds from one mountain range to another when their feed or water conditions require a change of location. Nevertheless they still survive, the wild bighorn, and may yet be saved. All they need is a fair chance.

Back to the wild palms of the Kofas. Leaving our jeep, the two of us walked a well-beaten trail into the mouth of Palm Canyon and followed it up and across a boulder-strewn wash until we reached a point where we could see the first group of palms. They grow in a deep, narrow little side canyon, high up a very steep pitch between the towering walls. There is no water visible on the surface, so that the area does not resemble what we think of as an oasis, but there is evidently enough water trickling through the rock just below the surface to keep the palms alive and thriving.

Some of these palms are 30 feet tall, but because of the mountainous terrain surrounding them they appear, from a distance, much smaller. The dangling dead fronds of the trees form a thatch about the trunks, very dry and flammable. One group of palms that we inspected seemed to have been set on fire in the recent past, perhaps by lightning, perhaps by man, for the trunks were completely blackened. The trees were

Flourishing in an improbable habitat, California fan palms brighten the bleakness of a cragged canyon deep in the Kofa Mountains.

alive, however, green and flourishing above the fire line. According to Peggy Larson in her book *Deserts of America,* the palms not only are able to survive an occasional fire but may even benefit from it; fire clears away the underbrush surrounding the palms, giving the young seedlings an opportunity for unobstructed growth. Destruction of competing shrubs also leaves more water for the fire-resistant trees.

The idea that fire plays a beneficial as well as inevitable part in the growth and regeneration of trees is gradually gaining some acceptance among professional foresters; what is good for wild palms may also be good for the ponderosa, the spruce, the fir and the aspen. After all, as is readily apparent to common sense, both lightning and great forests have been around for a long time, and the forests have survived.

These Arizona wild palms do not produce dates, but they do produce a fruit that used to be eaten by the desert Indians. Botanists guess that an individual palm lives from 150 to 200 years, and in favored locations —not in the inhospitable Kofa Mountains—will grow as tall as 50 feet. The annual crop of seeds remains dormant until temperature and moisture conditions are suitable. Where palms and water are present in ample number and quantity, a special kind of plant and animal community is formed, essentially different in character from the surrounding desert; this ecologists term a micro-habitat—the oasis.

We walked farther up Palm Canyon, climbing steadily toward the sunlit ramparts beyond. On the way we saw more palms, some in groups, some alone, but almost always—we saw only one exception—growing on the sunny, south-facing side of the canyon. The canyon was very silent that evening; we saw or heard no sign of animal life except now and then a little gray bird flitting through the brush.

It might have been wiser, so late in the day, to turn back to our jeep and make camp. Instead, under the spell of the mountain and the desire for the new, we continued scrambling up the narrow canyon, climbing over and around boulders and up little scarps of bedrock, until finally we emerged from the canyon to find ourselves in a basin a mile wide, walled in by more cliffs on the east and south. To the north we could see a notch or pass in the surrounding wall. Traversing the steep talus slope of loose rock, richly studded with teddy bear cholla, we made our way toward the opening.

Teddy bear cholla, *Opuntia bigelovii,* makes a formidable obstacle in rough terrain. A shrubby sort of cactus, usually growing no more than four feet high, it is so densely covered with inch-long silvery-golden

Through steep-walled Palm Canyon, seen at center in this aerial view, a narrow, precipitous path winds into the Kofa Mountains.

spines that from a distance it presents a soft, furry aspect. Thus the common name. But this plant is anything but cuddly. The spines are attached to stubby joints of woody material, and the slightest contact is enough to remove an entire joint—easily detachable from the branches —and hang it on your skin. Once attached to skin or clothing, the joint is not easily removed, for if you try to pluck it loose with your hand the joint merely transfers its allegiance to the hand, giving you a palmful of spines. The usual solution is to get a pair of sticks or stones and brush the joint away; afterward you pluck out the spines, one by one, from your flesh or clothing.

A half hour's scramble brought us to the pass on the north. From there we could see what looked like a fairly easy descent, down a long sloping shelf of rock, to the desert floor a couple of thousand feet below. The sun was already hovering on the horizon and a decision had to be made quickly: to return the way we had come, a long but certain route, or take a chance on what looked to be a much faster way down, but one that might hold difficulties not visible from above.

We elected to gamble. Equipping ourselves with dead agave stalks for balance and support in the brush and scree, we started down. For a while, as the darkness settled in, all went well. The route was clear, lessening the danger of a sprained ankle or a fall on the head. We found a half dozen young fan palms growing in a secluded place, hiding from the world, from us tourists. We found a sheep trail and piles of mahogany-colored pellets at lookout and resting places; examining the droppings, breaking them open, I guessed they might have been a month old. So the sheep were still around—somewhere. Watching us, perhaps; bighorns are notoriously curious, like cats. Which often proves to be their undoing. But they were all out of sight. Or maybe had left the Kofas for the Castle Dome Mountains, across Stagecoach Pass and King Valley to the south. Or maybe north into the New Water Mountains. Who knew? Who knows? But someone should. Some benevolent eye should be on these creatures, guarding them from harm.

In the lavender gloom, rapidly thickening to night, we approached the foot of the mountain. Here we discovered that our sloping shelf terminated in a series of deep, narrow canyons quite inaccessible from above. We seemed to be rimmed up, trapped in a place where further descent was impossible. If we had had 200 feet of rope with us we might have been able to rappel down into the canyons. But we had no rope.

We began thinking about gathering wood and starting a fire. It would be a tedious cold night, on this desert mountain in January, with nothing to protect us from the weather but our clothes and maybe a cave in the rock if we could find one. Wandering about on that rocky promontory, the shadowy depths on either side, I found a little niche in the rim and a rubble-filled channel leading down. The way out? We took it, proceeding cautiously, and discovered with pleasure that the route did indeed go clear to the bottom of one of the side canyons below.

Fighting our way through the thorny brush, stumbling over loose and unbalanced rocks, we finally reached the solid rock of the canyon floor. Here we came upon a series of three shapely water-filled natural tanks in the stone, each about three times the size and depth of a conventional bathtub. By this time we were thirsty as well as tired, hungry and a bit worried; we named the pools Salvation Tanks. There are many such tanks—some a lot larger—in these otherwise barren mountains: scoured by the rare but powerful summer floods, they will retain water for days, sometimes weeks or months, wherever the depth is great enough and the shade adequate to prevent rapid evaporation.

We drank our fill of the cool, stagnant but potable water, then worked our way out of the canyon and around the base of the mountain, another three or four miles, to the road and the jeep. Under a sky all dazzling with stars and sliding meteors—there seemed to be a shower of them that night—we built a fire and made our supper of bacon and beans, then bedded down in the welcome luxury of old Army surplus mummy bags for a good and well-earned winter night's sleep.

The next day we went forth to inspect some of the old-time gold mines in the foothills of the Kofas. Back to the highway, south, east on a dirt road through King Valley and north at Zero Zero Junction brought us after 20 miles of hard, rocky, dusty jeepherding to a group of abandoned mines: the King of Arizona, the Rob Roy and the North Star.

The remains consisted of a few old weatherbeaten shacks, the ruins of many more, a scattering of ancient rusted mining machinery, and on the hillsides the mine entrances and the huge gray tailing dumps. I should not say that these mines have been completely abandoned; although none have been in operation for many years, they do remain private property and active mining claims have been staked out around each. Both the King of Arizona Mine and the North Star Mine are protected by resident caretakers.

Neither mine looks like much now, since they have been picked over for so long by rock hounds and souvenir hunters. But the King of Ar-

In the shadow of the Castle Dome Mountains a deep tinaja, or natural water basin in the rock, reflects the morning sunlight.

izona, discovered in 1896 by one Charles E. Eichelberger, is supposed to have produced three and a half million dollars' worth of gold from 1897 until 1910, by which time the vein was worked out. The ore was milled near the mine by what is called the amalgamation process, with cyanide treatment added later, both methods requiring much water. Water was a serious problem in this barren area, but the miners solved it by drilling deep wells nearby, where the water was pumped out with power supplied through a wood-burning boiler plant. This pumping system consumed so much firewood that the land for miles around was largely stripped of mesquite and ironwood, the only fuels available.

Even today, more than six decades after the operation was discontinued, these trees are rare among the foothills on the south side of the Kofa Mountains. But one well the miners dug was a good one; still in use, it supplies the domestic needs of the half dozen individuals who now live in the area. The milling job was also very thorough; according to the caretaker whom I interviewed on the site, the gold ore from this mine was crushed, amalgamated and acid-treated so completely that no one has ever succeeded in attempts to rework the tailings—even though in most other places, with improved methods of refining ore, miners have found the tailing dumps of old silver and gold mines to be one of the most valuable sources of those precious metals.

Two miles north of the King of Arizona is what remains of the North Star Mine, another allegedly fabulous producer. (Some regional historians believe that the production of these old mines was greatly exaggerated at the time by their owners, for the purpose of luring more investment capital.) Like the King of Arizona, the North Star is largely a ruin now; a great deal of the machinery and iron rails have been removed by commercial scavengers. The mine is said to have produced a little over a million dollars' worth of gold ore. This figure refers of course to the gross value of the production; costs were so high in mining and milling in this remote and nearly waterless location that the net profits were probably not great, if there were any at all. By 1911, one year after the King of Arizona was closed down, the North Star too reached its "economic limits"—meaning that miners and geologists believed more gold was present, but that current prices were not high enough to justify the expenditures required to recover the ore. This is the chief reason spokesmen for the mining industries are always pressuring Congress to raise government prices for gold and silver; in effect they are asking for public subsidies to make it profitable for them to extract these metals from the ground. From *public* ground, by the way: most mining in the West takes place in what are supposed to be public lands, presumably the property of all Americans.

There was once a spell of fine romance attached to prospecting and mining, especially in the realm of gold, as anyone will testify who has read such books as J. Frank Dobie's *Apache Gold and Yaqui Silver,* or that marvelous novel by B. Traven, *The Treasure of the Sierra Madre.* But the romantic period in metal and mineral extraction has long since passed. The eccentric and fiercely individualistic types who worked alone, towing a burro over the hills, are mostly gone; the legendary Seldom Seen Slim of Death Valley, for example, will never be seen again —he died a few years ago.

Today almost all serious prospecting is carried out by teams of college-trained geologists on the payroll of giant world-girdling corporations such as Kennecott and Anaconda. Nor do they waste much time seeking out gold and silver; today's prospectors are after things more basic: copper, zinc, iron, manganese, coal, oil shale, sand tars, molybdenum, titanium, uranium. When they locate something salable they will butcher whole mountains to remove it from the earth.

Fortunately no such dismal fate has yet overtaken the ancient stony battlements of the Kofas. As we discovered in two more days of exploration, this range still remains essentially undamaged by man or his works. Perhaps it cannot be considered pristine wilderness, because trails, jeep roads and mining ruins are many, but it surely belongs in the category called primitive. What these mountains really need from us is to be mostly left alone, neither exploited nor—perhaps equally dangerous in the long run—loved to death. That the sheep may safely graze. That the lion may lie down with the lamb. (In order to eat him.) That islands of relative peace, order and sanity may remain amidst the chaos of a mindless industrialism. Tranquillity, I reckon, like water or money or seed corn, can usefully be stored away in safe places.

The Water Misers

ILLUSTRATED BY BARRY DRISCOLL

Much of the Sonoran Desert averages less than 10 inches of rain a year, but despite the aridity some wildlife manages to survive—and even thrive—there. The species that succeed are those that have found ways to cope with the long periods of drought, employing a variety of mechanisms to ensure the fullest use of the water available to them, venturing onto the desert floor only after the sapping sun has set, and in general husbanding their energies.

Among the animals that have adapted to desert life, eight of the most intriguing appear on the following pages in paintings by the eminent British wildlife artist Barry Driscoll, based on his researches both in the field and at the Arizona-Sonora Desert Museum near Tucson. Perhaps fittingly, the portrait gallery begins with the kangaroo rat (right), which its admirers acclaim as "the rodent that never drinks water." This diminutive creature—three inches of body and seven inches of tail—is totally geared to conserving liquid.

The kangaroo rat has no sweat glands; it cools off by breathing. Moreover, its nasal passages are at a lower temperature than the rest of its body: when warm exhalations circulate through the passages, some moisture condenses and is retained by the animal. Another built-in aid to survival is the strength of the kangaroo rat's kidneys, among the most efficient possessed by any mammal. While all animals must flush out uric wastes with water, this rat rarely urinates. It can concentrate its uric wastes until they are less a fluid than a kind of paste. The amount of water thus expended is very small.

Diet and habitat also help the kangaroo rat combat the desert's dehydrating effects. Its primary source of nourishment is the carbohydrate in dry seeds. Although these contain only 4 per cent water, the animal metabolizes moisture as well as energy from the seed particles.

Its burrow provides added insurance. The rat digs it deep enough so that a year-round temperature between 46° F. and 85° F.—and a relative humidity between 30 and 50 per cent—is maintained, especially when the occupant plugs the burrow entrance with dirt.

The beneficent protections that nature has afforded the kangaroo rat seem nothing less than a marvel. But it is one that is matched in the cases of the seven other creatures portrayed, each with remarkable survival techniques of its own.

As agile as the large mammal for which it is named, the kangaroo rat is well protected not only against desert dryness but also against the host of predators that find it a tempting tidbit. Using its oversized hind legs and a bipedal form of locomotion (most rodents run on all four legs), it can leap almost two feet in any direction, including straight up, and execute mid-air pivots. The rat's huge inner ears and long tufted tail help provide the balance such acrobatics require.

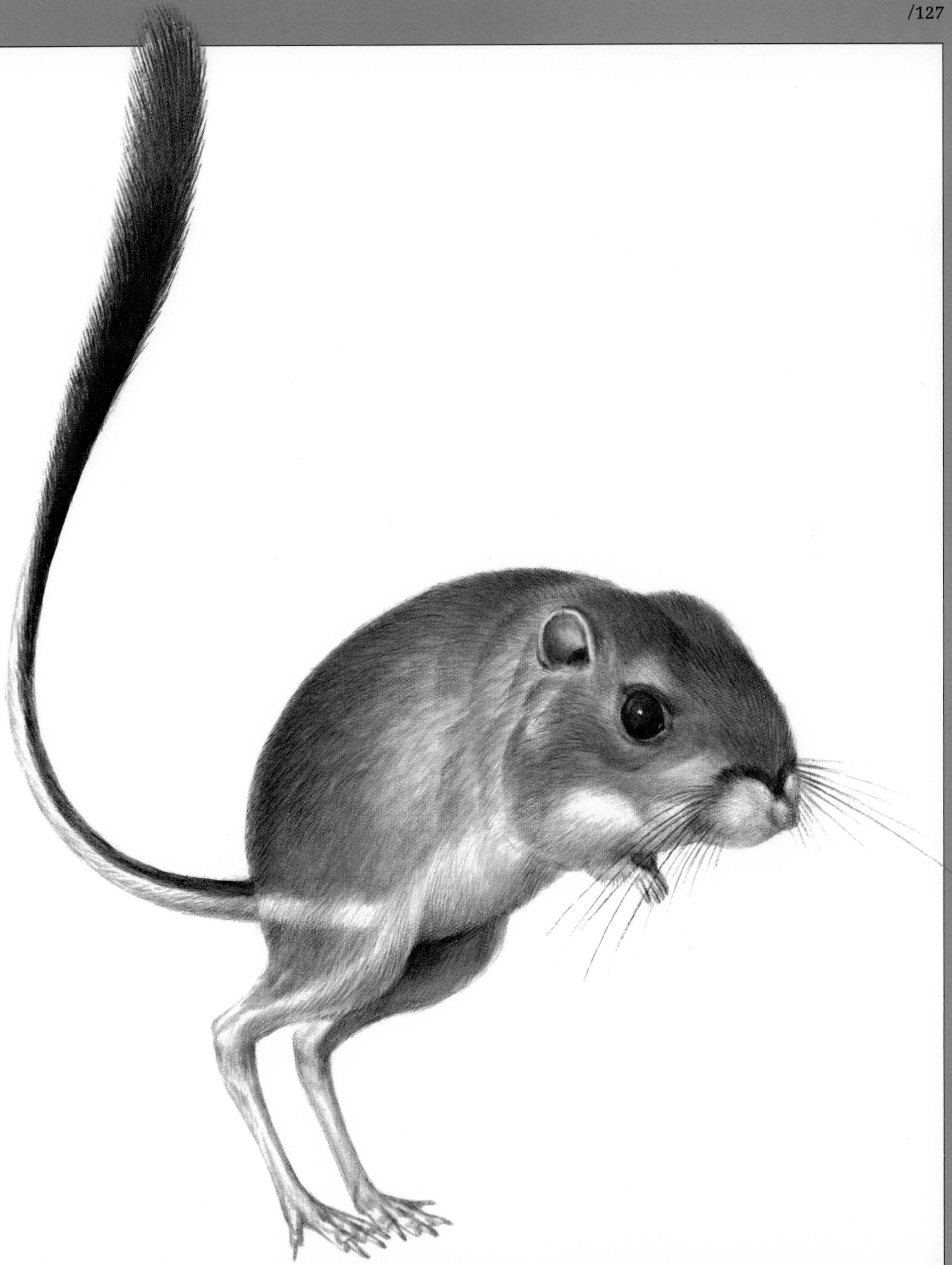

The Case for a Much Maligned Reptile

Endowed with a stubby low-slung body, which measures about a foot and a half long at maturity, and a rough, irregular orange-and-black skin, the Gila monster is the most fearsome-looking member of the desert animal kingdom.

For all its dire aspect, which has led to the widely held notion that this lizard is lethal to man, the Gila monster is too sluggish and timid to offer a real threat to humans. True, it is one of the world's only two poisonous lizards (the other is a relative, the Mexican beaded lizard), but the Gila rarely unleashes the painful venom secreted by glands in its lower jaw. Unlike the rattlesnake, which may strike with minimal warning at the unwary passerby, the Gila avoids man and rarely bites unless handled or otherwise provoked—holding on bulldog fashion and grinding with its powerful jaws. It uses its venom primarily to stun the other reptiles and birds whose eggs constitute much of its normal diet and provide both the protein and fluids it needs. Even so, the Gila rarely fights for its food, invariably retreating from danger.

In the seasons when other animals are busy laying eggs, this lizard emerges to conduct solitary hunting forays. In winter it snuggles into a humid burrow in a state of decreased metabolism, drawing on fat stored in its tail. Thus the Gila spends part of its life in a stupor, a shy, inoffensive creature that belies the malevolent myths surrounding it.

A Gregarious Desert Pig

A distant kin of the domestic swine and the European wild boar, the collared peccary, or javelina, can grow as big as a fox hound. A social animal, it protects itself against predators by traveling in groups.

An essential—but little understood—means of communication between members of a group of these animals is a musk gland, located on the javelina's hindquarters and exposed by raising its bristles (far left). A pungent odor exuded by the gland may serve individuals within the group as a means of asserting their dominance; but some biologists also think the whole group may use the smell to stake out its collective territory in the desert—warning other javelinas not to encroach.

A bunch of javelinas—about a dozen in all—will wander ceaselessly through cactus country scrubland to appease their prodigious appetites. The animal's favored foods are cactus and roots, which it is able to shovel up by means of its sizable snout. In times of drought when water holes evaporate its diet of cholla and prickly-pear cactus provides water as well as food. Consuming these spiny plants poses no problem for the javelina. It can mouth a pad of cactus to blunt the largest spines; then, ignoring the smaller spines, it gobbles the pulp.

If javelinas sense the presence of potential danger from animals or humans, the herd may charge, but more often it will flee.

A Nimble and Resourceful Bird

Pioneers crossing the Sonoran Desert in the late 19th Century often found an odd two-foot-long bird trotting tirelessly on the ground beside their wagon wheels. They dubbed this seemingly earthbound creature the roadrunner.

Actually, the roadrunner can take to the air if necessary, but it prefers to jog on "X"-shaped clawed feet that provide traction on the desert sand. It is capable of going as fast as 15 miles per hour and uses its foot-long tail as a combination rudder and flap, swiveling it in order to change course or raising it upright, like a feathered exclamation point, in order to come to a stop.

Unlike many desert birds, the roadrunner does not migrate during dry seasons, depending for fluids on its omnivorous diet—which even includes small rattlesnakes. One delightful cactus country legend has it that the bird fences in a sleeping rattler with the prickly joints of the cholla cactus; upon awakening, so the story goes, the snake, finding itself hopelessly ensnared by spines, bites itself to death.

A real confrontation between a roadrunner and a rattler is dramatic enough. Relying on its great ability to move nimbly, the bird dances about the rattler, which strikes uselessly at the gyrating bird, expending its venom. Then, stunning the rattler with powerful thrusts of its beak, the roadrunner proceeds to stuff the victim down its gullet.

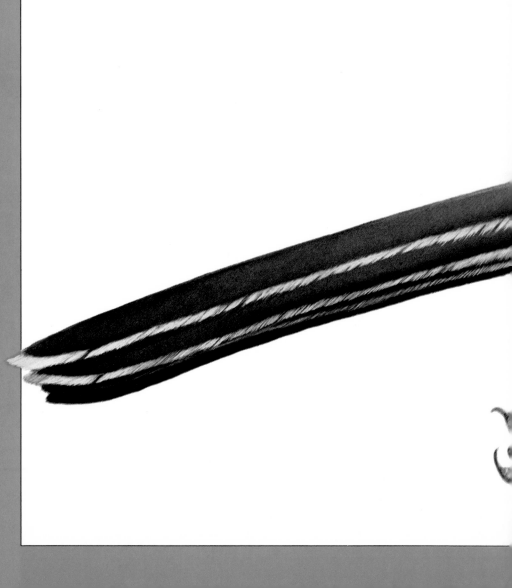

The Incongruous Coatimundi

Encountering a coatimundi is like coming upon a bizarre jigsaw puzzle. The first glimpse is of an apparently disembodied furry brown tail, aimed skyward, bobbing across the horizon. Then the animal comes into full view, and from its long nose to its fluffy banded tail it looks thoroughly implausible: a seeming amalgam of pig, bear cub and raccoon.

This creature, called the coati (ko-AH-tee) for short—and known locally to Arizonans as the chulu—is a tropical relative of the raccoon; the coati drifted from South and Central America north to the mountains dotting the cactus country. It is an omnivorous feeder and a skilled climber, scaling trees to doze both night and day. In the cooler hours of dawn and dusk it descends to forage for meals, which, depending on the time of year and its own prowess, range from small rodents and lizards to berries and roots.

Like javelinas, coatis band together for survival, segregating themselves by sex, with the mature males in groups separate from the females and their offspring. But despite the safety they seek in numbers, coatimundis have a baffling reaction to danger. Agile and comfortable in the trees, which would therefore seem their safest refuge, they will jump to the ground when threatened and take to their heels across country —where they are capable of surprising speed but are no match for a hungry bobcat.

A Sturdy, Retiring Turtle

For nine months of the year, the desert tortoise hoards liquids like a miser pinching pennies, storing water in a bladder inside its upper shell; next to the kangaroo rat it is the desert's best conserver of moisture. Like the kangaroo rat, it concentrates uric wastes to conserve vital body fluids, though unlike the kangaroo rat it will drink its fill of water when it gets the chance. Between drinks, its leathery skin and hard shell help keep evaporation loss to a minimum.

During dry seasons the desert tortoise retreats to a cool, moist den and stays put there for the better part of the day, subsisting on a diet of herbs and grasses. It livens up only in the summer rainy season, when succulent annuals in bloom and frequent rain pools tempt it out of its den to feast and drink.

It also mates at this time, a process often preceded by jousts between rival males. After some nipping, the contenders begin to ram each other with shovellike extensions of the lower shell. The goal is to immobilize the opponent by flipping it over on its back.

In this species of turtle growth is slow; a mature desert tortoise measures about nine inches long. The model for the 13-inch specimen shown here was perhaps 25 years old, and is in museum captivity. Had it been left to live in the desert, its tough carapace would have been scarred from digging burrows in the rocky desert soil.

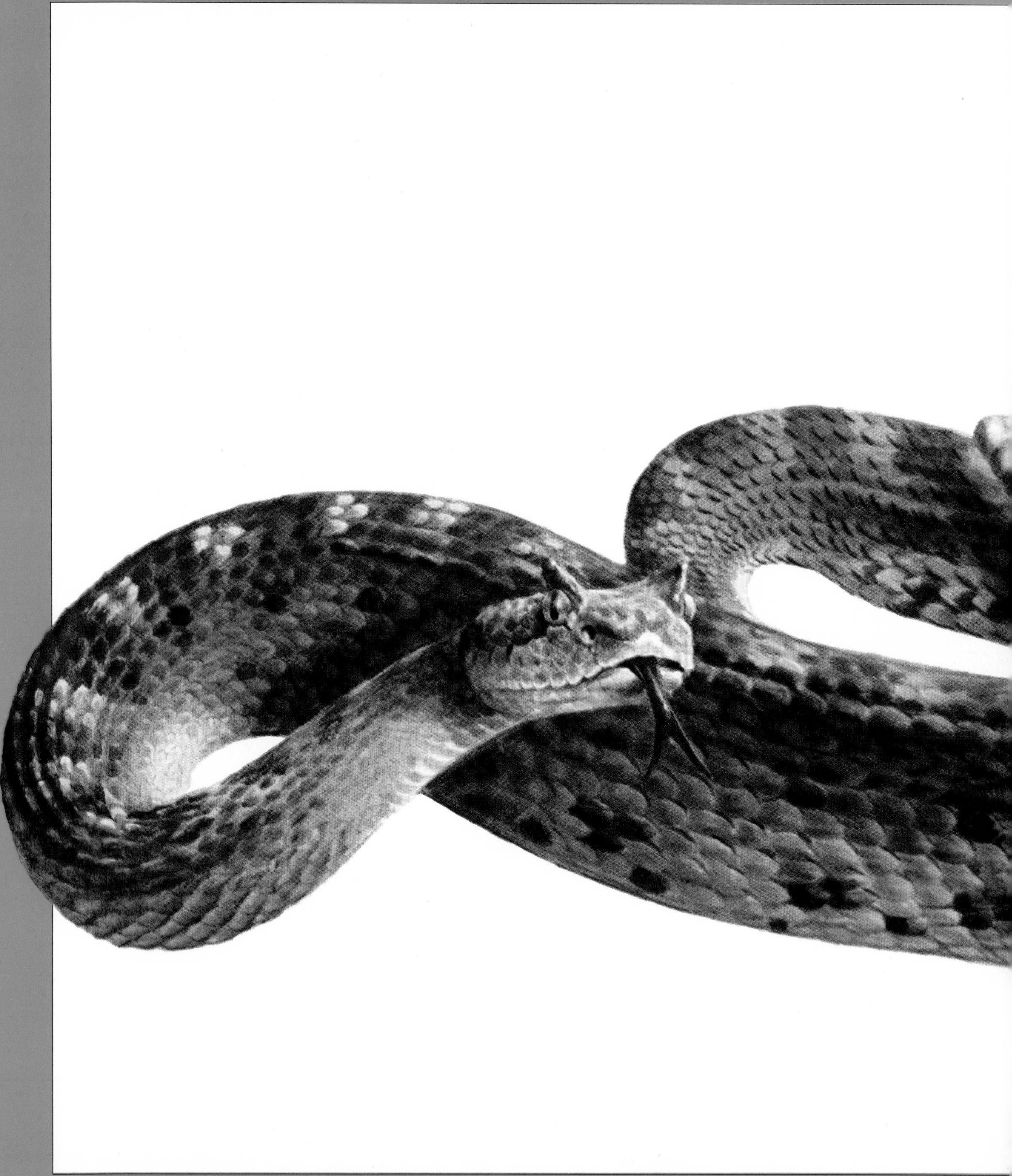

The Snake with a Telltale Signature

Parallel slash marks in the sand lead across the dunes and end abruptly in a circle. Inside it lies what from a slight distance appears to be a coil of rope: it is the Sonora sidewinder, lurking in ambush.

One of the smaller rattlesnakes, averaging about 18 inches long, the sidewinder—shown life-sized at left—is named for its unique shimmying movement. It moves across the desert by hurling itself forward obliquely, looping its body in successive "S" curves. This rapid, sinuous motion leaves the snake's distinctive trademark: a series of separate straight lines, each ending in a "J" curve made by the snake's neck and head, the curve sweeping in the direction of the snake's forward progress.

The sidewinder hunts only when the sun is down, preying on lizards, kangaroo rats and other rodents, and utilizing a set of highly efficient hunting tools: a mottled buff skin ideal for desert camouflage; two pits located on each side of the head, which sense heat from nearby bodies; a forked tongue that picks up even the faintest odors; and a fast-working venom—injected through the snake's one-quarter- to one-half-inch-long fangs—that weakens the coagulants in the victim's blood and causes fatal hemorrhage.

Once it has caught the prey, the sidewinder swallows it whole. The victim is reduced by the snake's strong internal acids and absorbed as both food and water.

A High-Speed
Quick-Change Artist

The antelope jack rabbit has made its own superb adaptations to desert life. It can speed across its open habitat at 35 miles an hour, bounding along like its namesake and easily outdistancing its predators. Lacking sweat glands, it keeps cool through the unusual means of its eight-inch-long ears: arteries carry blood saturated with body heat to the ears, from which the heat is then dissipated into the air. But this mechanism will work only if the animal spends as much time as possible facing north—a mysterious habit that may enable the rabbit to take advantage of minute temperature differences in air striking its ears from a northerly direction. Whatever the reason, a jack rabbit facing south absorbs heat through its ears.

But perhaps the most fascinating of this animal's adaptations is its ability instantly to turn the color of either one of its flanks from tan to white (right). Called "flashing" and used to befuddle pursuers, this quick change appears when the jack rabbit employs muscles that pull its skin over its flank so as to expose the white underfur.

As it takes off in a full-speed zigzag that a football halfback would envy, the jack rabbit always whitens the side visible to its pursuer. By this maneuver, known as directive coloration, the hare deliberately draws attention to its changes of direction, thereby adding confusion to the chase and aiding its escape.

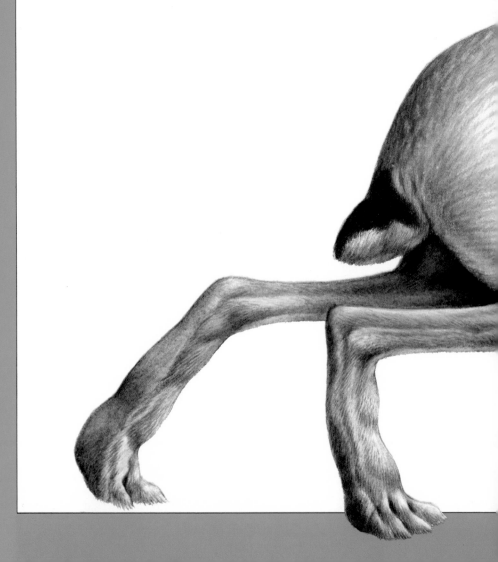

6/ Down to the Sea of Cortés

*No, the desert cannot be fought successfully; and to join it
...one must walk in it. It is then...we gradually find
ourselves in the comforting company of other living and
warm-blooded creatures.*   ANN WOODIN/ *HOME IS THE DESERT*

From the terrace of my old stone house in the Santa Catalina foothills, we've been circling outward, farther and farther from the crowded haunts of Americans, into the wilderness. Each expedition—to the Superstitions, Organ Pipe, Baboquivari, the Kofas—took us a little greater distance from the cities and from what Thomas Wolfe called "the manswarm." And now we come to one of the largest remaining wild areas in the Sonoran Desert, the northwestern corner of old Mexico where the desert meets the Gulf of California.

The northern part of this area, called El Gran Desierto on Mexican maps, includes the great sea of dunes and the numerous volcanic craters and lava flows of the Pinacate region—a place so strange and grand that it will be an appropriate climax to this exploration of the Sonoran Desert. But first, in this chapter, we will have a look at the southerly region, the gulf coast and the largely uninhabited desert that bounds it.

As my guide I invited my friend and neighbor Richard Felger, a botanist who has specialized in the ethnobotany—people and plants—of northwest Sonora. We made our preparations and one January day got off to an early start at the crack of noon—early for us, anyhow—and headed south for the border. Avoiding the slow-moving entry at the city of Nogales, we took a little-traveled dirt road farther to the west and entered Mexico by way of the village of Sasabe, barely detectable on the maps, which is one of the nicer things about it.

"Alto," says the road sign by the Mexican border station. We halted, entered the station, obtained our tourist cards and tipped the inspector the customary dollar's worth of pesos. Leaving, I savored those smells characteristic of Mexico—refried beans, burning lard, mesquite and ironwood smoke, wine, manure, hot sheet iron, old adobe baking under the heat of the desert sun.

We drove south by southwest over a rough, rocky, winding dirt road, past mile after mile of burnt adobe brickworks (apparently the chief local industry, after cattle raising), and then into the open desert. Buzzards circled overhead—there always seem to be more buzzards in the sky on the Mexican side of the border. Why? Because both life and death are more abundant down in Mexico. It's the kind of country buzzards love. A candid country, harsh and bare, which is no doubt why it strikes us overcivilized Americans as crude, vulgar and dangerous.

Scrub cattle ranging through the bush galloped off like gnus and wildebeests at our approach. I never saw such weird, scrawny, pied, mottled, humped, long-horned and camel-necked brutes trying to pass as domestic livestock. Most looked like a genetic hash of Hereford, Charolais, Brahman, Angus, moose, ibex, tapir and nightmare. Weaned on cactus, snakeweed and thistle, they showed the gleam of the sun through the translucent barrel of their rib cages. But they could run, they were alive, not only alive but vigorous. I was tempted to think, watching their angular hind ends jouncing away through the dust, that the meat on those critters, if you could find any, might just taste better than the aerated, water-injected, hormone-inflated beef we Americans get from today's semiautomated feed lots in the States.

For most of the afternoon we rambled toward the setting sun through the rolling desert of mesquite, creosote, paloverde and cactus. The saguaros were sparse and stunted-looking; even the prickly pear and cholla do not seem to do too well down here. But the mesquite thrives, growing in dwarf forests over what used to be grassy savanna, according to some ecohistorians. (Overgrazing—the old story.) Every now and then we'd descend into a wash or arroyo where the vegetation was much denser and more varied. Here Felger would stop to beat through the brush, searching for various shrubs and annuals. Some people collect stamps or beer bottles or wagon wheels; professional botanists collect weeds, press them between wooden plates, and store them away in museum files never to be seen by light of day again.

In the evening we paused for an hour to cook our supper on a heap of incandescent ironwood coals. Coyotes wailed the sun down, heavy-footed cattle stumbled through the chaparral, somebody turned on a few stars. We were down in the Mexican desert and pretty pleased with ourselves; it seemed like a retreat through time—of about 50 years.

The January nights are very long and chilly, however, even in Sonora. We drove on to the town of Caborca and put up at a motel beside a stream of freight trucks, buses and California cars rumbling greasily through the gut of the city. This part of Mexico is well assimilated into the industrial-highway culture of North America, and it was without regret that we left it in the blue dawn and headed southwesterly again into the backlands.

Into the backlands, the back of beyond, the original and primitive Mexico. For the next three days we would see very few other human beings and not a motor vehicle of any kind, nor a gas station, nor a telephone pole. On all sides the sun-baked glare of the rock, the dull pallor of the dust, the sunburned trunks of century-old saguaros, the olive drab of mesquite, creosote and ironwood. On the horizon, ancient and crumbling granitic mountains. The inevitable vultures soaring overhead reminded us, though, that somewhere in this brushy wilderness was life, sentient creation, living meat. Hard to see, of course, during the day, for most desert animals keep themselves concealed in the bush or in burrows under the surface of the ground. But you could see their tracks: birds, lizards, rodents, now and then a coyote, here and there the handlike footprints of raccoon, the long claws of badger, the prints of ringtail cat, the heart-shaped hoofmarks of deer and javelina, the rounded pads of bobcat, the more unusual long narrow tracks of chulu.

I have barely begun to name the immense variety of mammals, large and small, that inhabit the desert. There are, for example, dozens of species of little rodents—rock squirrels, pocket gophers, pocket mice, grasshopper mice, cactus mice, kangaroo rats, wood rats, prairie dogs —and a large assortment of skunks, cottontail rabbits, jack rabbits, porcupines, kit foxes and gray foxes.

Some of these animals, especially the rodents and other smaller mammals, may never drink free water in their entire lives. Instead they get by on what moisture they can obtain from plant food and through the internal manufacture of what is called "metabolic water." Particularly distinguished in this regard is the kangaroo rat, which subsists almost entirely on a diet of dried seeds, bathes itself in sand, ignores green and succulent plants, and shuns water even when it is available.

But of all these Sonoran beasts surely the most curious is *Nasua nar-*

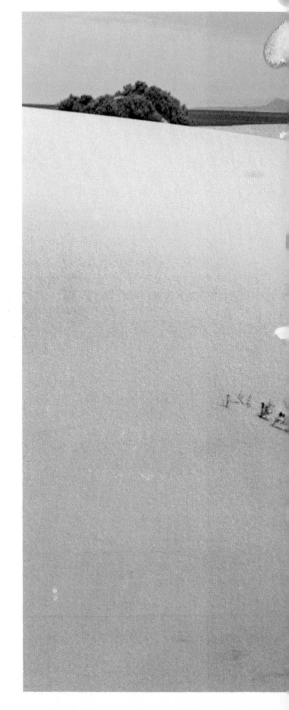

Saguaros and salt-tolerant shrubs fringe the dunes that mark the encounter of desert and sea at Desemboque on the Gulf of California.

ica, the chulu, or as it is also called, the coatimundi. Generally chulus travel in bands of a dozen or more, sometimes as many as 200, according to report. But the first one I ever saw was a loner—the older males are often solitary—prowling in a garbage dump near the town of Nogales. Preoccupied with its search for something to eat, the chulu ignored me, or perhaps did not perceive me, and I had ample opportunity to observe it closely.

It was an old one, a grandfather no doubt, unable to keep up with its band, which would also explain why it had been reduced to scavenging in a dump for survival. It was about four feet long, including the two-foot tail, which in the chulu is almost always held upright, at right angles to the body. The fur was rusty brown, the tail marked with light and dark rings like that of a raccoon, which the chulu resembles somewhat. But it looked a little like a small bear, too, with long hind legs and shambling gait. In fact it looked like a mixture of several mammals, with the tail of a raccoon, the gait of a bear, the nose of a pig, a face masked like that of a badger, long wolflike canine teeth, and the lean slab-sided body of a fox or coyote.

As I watched this chulu I saw it turn over rocks, tin cans, boards and other junk with its front paws, exhibiting the manual dexterity of a human. It was probably searching for insects, grubs, arachnids and snakes, as it spent a great deal of time rooting about underneath things with its long and flexible snout. I have learned since that chulus, like coyotes and javelinas, will eat most anything they can find or catch; like us, they are omnivorous.

To see what it would do, I walked toward the chulu, whistled and held out one hand. It looked at me with soft brown eyes, seemingly full of trust, but a snarling grin that exposed long yellow fangs conveyed a different impression. I would not have cared to tangle with this animal barehanded, but before I got close enough to risk attack it turned tail and scurried as nimbly as an old tomcat up the trunk of a big juniper. I left it then in peace.

My favorite desert animal, I think, after such obvious choices as coyote, vulture, cougar, ringtail cat, Gila monster and gopher snake, is the whimsical, cockeyed, half-mad, always eccentric, more or less lovable *Pecari angulatus sonoriensis,* otherwise known as javelina or peccary. A herd of them scampered across the road in front of us as we bounced over the backlands toward the sea. We stopped and watched them go, crazy as crickets, up a hillside and over the crest, the dust flying from their busy hoofs.

What are javelinas? Piglike animals, but they are not true pigs. They look more like razorback hogs, but they are not true razorbacks either. Someone has likened them to a child's notion of what a pig should look like. They are comical, myopic, vicious and excitable. They have sharp little hoofs, pointed ears, small square bodies and huge heads mounted on massive necks; neck and head appear to take up nearly half the total body volume. The tail is so small as to be ridiculous, but the teeth are sharp. Javelinas are capable (it is said) of inflicting severe—even fatal—damage upon anyone unlucky enough to find himself between a charging javelina and an immovable wall.

I remembered my first encounter with javelinas. I was blundering about in the Sonoran hills, daydreaming as usual, when I gradually became aware of a snorting, snuffling sound ahead, accompanied by the shuffle of many active hoofs. The terrain was brushy, the lilac twilight falling about me, so that I could not see much, and besides I was listening primarily to the melancholy chorus of red-spotted toads in the canyon below. I crashed on through the thickets. The nearsighted javelinas did not notice my approach until I almost stumbled over them. At that point the herd exploded in all directions at once, two of them stampeding past me so close on either side I felt the friction of their bristles. They must have been even more startled than I was. A moment later I stood alone in a now-quiet little clearing, among uprooted roots and overturned stones, and sniffed at the curious musky odor in the air. Off in the distance, at 16 different compass points, I could still hear the panicked scramble, the outraged snorts, squeals and grunts, of the shattered herd of javelinas. It must have taken them hours to get properly reassembled and back to their evening feed.

As with humans and chulus, javelinas will eat anything—snails, locusts, roots, berries, clams, truffles, mushrooms, garlic, bugs, birds, eggs, general assorted garbage. This is reputed to be an indication of intelligence. Living in the Sonoran Desert, however, the javelina specializes in the consumption of cactus—spines, barbs, hooks, needles, thorns, hair and all; its favorite cactus is the succulent pad of the prickly pear.

The javelina also fancies the barrel, or compass, cactus, that bloated monster of a vegetable that rises up like an overgrown green fireplug, leaning south, all over the sunny sides of hills. But the barrel cactus, armored by an intricate network of rosy claws, cannot easily be approached, except for the yellowish fruit on top, which the javelina and other creatures will extricate and consume in due season. The only way a javelina can get at the tender insides of a barrel cactus is from the base, exposed occasionally when excessive growth, or a storm, or a weakened root system, causes the plant to keel over. Then the javelina, seizing its chance, drops to its knees and burrows headfirst into the bottom of the now defenseless plant. I have never actually seen this performance but I have seen barrel cactus fallen over and hollowed out, and all around the scuffle marks and scat of the javelina.

On to the sea. All day long Felger and I rattled through the desert; we passed a few small rancherias where mesquite-branch corrals, idle windmills and small mud huts attested to the part-time presence of our fellow men. But we saw no one. We passed other ranches obviously abandoned. Herds of starving cattle appeared from time to time but not so frequently as north of Caborca.

Ahead the horizon was cactus-studded. Eventually we topped a rise and came to our first cardon, a cactus related to and resembling the Arizona saguaro, but with many more branches, greater mass, a more bronzed, massive and *sculptured* appearance. And "sculptured" seems the best word. The older, properly aged, wind-blasted and sun-scorched cardons do indeed look as if they'd been hammered out of bronze and old iron by some demented junkyard genius from Hoboken, New Jersey. The biggest cardons grow just as tall as the noblest saguaros, maybe a little taller; they must weigh three times as much. In girth, near the base, where all the mighty branches start out, they could equal the biggest oak or cottonwood I ever saw. Like the saguaro, the cardon is basically columnar in structure, with flexible, expansible fluting in trunk and branch to permit gains and losses in moisture content. Compared to the cardon the saguaro seems slender, even graceful, almost elegant; compared to the saguaro the cardon is a crude hulking brute of an organism. I'll take the cardon.

Tastes differ. I asked Dr. Felger to name his favorite vegetable. "I am a scientist," he said. "I refuse to make value judgments." Spoken like a true scientist. Then he added: "They are all my friends."

Finally we went through a pass in the desert hills, and there off on the western horizon lay an infinite band of blue, a misty shimmer of vapor and sky that merged one with the other far off beyond the end of land. We were coming at last to the sea, El Mar de Cortés, or, as it is identified on most maps, the Gulf of California.

As we approached the sea the cacti began to peter out, becoming smaller and sparser. Apparently the damp sea air does not entirely

Not far from its rich larder of fish food in the Gulf of California, an osprey approaches its nest in the coastal Mexican desert. The nest, a bulky affair built of dead sticks, perches atop a cardon cactus, a Mexican cousin of the saguaro; the cardon can grow 10 feet larger than its stately relative.

ered through the dusk, a horned owl hooted from the top of a nearby cardon, coyotes and bobcats, skunks and badgers, serpents and tarantulas were all on the prowl for supper. We fried our bacon, warmed up our beans, drank our wine and slept.

The next day we took off for points still farther south. We were now entering the most magnificent and varied desert garden I had ever seen. First and predominant were the great cardons, towering 50 and 60 feet. Here and there were the familiar saguaros, organ pipes and senitas, and one new to me, what the Mexicans call *agria,* an ugly, sinister reptilian thing that crawls and twists over the ground in knots with itself. Then there were the many kinds of prickly pear and cholla, including such unusual varieties as Schott's cholla and the purple staghorn cholla, which conceals its chlorophyll beneath a purplish skin.

Some of the agave plants, we noticed when we stopped to inspect them at close range, were about ready to erect their mighty stalks and burst into the one great efflorescence of their glorious and tragic careers. Now is the time, said Dr. Felger, to eat them. When the center leaves begin to part, he explained, that is the time to dig up the agave, cut out its heart, roast the heart on slow coals and eat it. Especially delicious, he continued, when seasoned with a bit of wild garlic—and he knelt and with his fingers dug up a tiny, obscure little green plant that I had not even noticed. He scraped the dirt from the small white bulb at the end of the roots and offered it to me. I ate it. It was good, although it tasted a bit more like scallion than garlic, I thought.

We stayed that evening with friends of Felger's, a missionary couple, in the Seri Indian village near the mouth of the usually dry Río San Ignacio. Beyond the village lay miles of open beach, unimproved by a single visible work of man, curving south toward a craggy headland called Mount Tepoca. Behind the beach were high dunes of white sand, adorned with flowering vines that I could not identify. I wandered across these virgin sands, marveling at their beauty, picking up and casting aside sea shells, each of them a natural work of art. I paused for a good look around. There was the loveliness of the dunes, the sea, the sky; there was the squalid village in the distance, and across the gulf, dimly apparent through the mist and clouds and radiance of the setting sun, rose the dark mountains of Baja California.

The next day we tooled across mile-long ceramic dry lake beds, then through more of the lonely, lovely, delectable wilds, with giant cacti thriving all around and in the background rugged peaks of granite and agree with them. First the cardons disappeared, then the saguaros, then the others. Last to hold out, sometimes on the dunes behind the beach, were the senita and a few scrubby specimens of cholla.

The road we were following brought us to a fishing village called Puerto Libertad, inhabited by half a dozen families of Seri Indians and on occasion by American tourists and fishermen. We could see the huts of the Indians, at the northern end of the bay, and two houses built by American colonists, near the beach, but since we had no business with any of those people and needed no supplies, we turned south on a road —a single-lane sand track—paralleling the shore.

After a few miles we turned off and took a seaward trail to inspect the beach and the gulf. What we found first was a natural water hole, or *pozo,* within half a mile of the beach. From this water hole, lined with tules and Olney bulrushes, innumerable trails radiated, revealing the visitation of not only the usual starving scrub cattle but also many of the more common desert mammals. I tasted the water: saline, but evidently not so much that the animals would not drink it. At some point the hole or seep had been enlarged and fenced in with a few strands of barbed wire, long since broken through.

Dr. Felger found much of interest around this well: more weeds. But I was aware of something else, something I hadn't heard for nigh on to a year: the clamor of the sea. It came from over the brow of the dunes, where saltbush and marshgrass shivered in the wind, where gulls circled, screaming, where a lone osprey searched for its supper.

I climbed the ridge and descended through hot sand to a splendid beach. The glare of the sun, the glittering waves, dazzled my eyes. A strong wind blew onshore, roiling the water onto the beach; the gush of foam, the steady roar of the waves, the moan of the wind combined in most pleasing symphony, filling the air with that constant vibration of the elements in action.

The beach curved in unbroken crescent north and south, perhaps 15 miles long, empty of any human company. Felger caught up with me and we walked the strand and hunted souvenirs. We found shark eggs, sand dollars, kelp, starfish, rotting sponges, the shell of a fiddler crab. I looked inside: nobody home. We found bleach bottles, tequila bottles, cans, fragments of boat and fishing tackle, and other jetsam, mostly non-biodegradable but all somewhat modified by passage through the salty sea. Strange to find such garbage on this lonely shore. Reassuring, no doubt, to some people: nothing is far away these days.

Better to make camp for the night deep in the cactus land. Bats flick-

This is not meant to suggest that the desert rat is necessarily tougher than other rats. He is certainly not nearly so tough, for example, as the *Rattus rattus urbanus,* that highly specialized breed that thrives or at least survives on cement and steel, clamor and crime, lethal gasoline fumes and the deadly double dry Martini. Compared to him the desert rat is a delicate, fastidious epicene, tender as a water lily. But the desert rat carries one distinction like a halo: he has learned to love the kind of country that most people find unlovable. Call the desert barren, harsh, bitter, dreary and gloomy, acrid and arid, lifeless, hopeless, ugly as sin, foreboding as the gates of Hell—he will happily agree with you. Because in his heart lies the secret belief that the awful desert is really sweet and lovable, that the ugly is really beautiful, that Hell is Home. And if others think he's crazy so much the better; he is reluctant to share his love anyway.

Even for desert rats, however, there are limits. Some think that the blood-sucking cone-nosed kissing bug is too much of a good thing. Some draw the line at centipedes that drop from the ceiling into your cooking pots. Some hesitate at six-foot diamondbacks coiled on the "Welcome" mat in the evening. But these are petty annoyances. More serious divisions of opinion between desert rats concern places. Some, for example, feel that Death Valley, in the summertime, at 130° F. in the shade, is going too far. Most would agree, however, that the ultimate among the various provinces of The Great American Desert is Sonora's Pinacate region, at the head of the Gulf of California. This region is the bleakest, flattest, hottest, grittiest, grimmest, dreariest, ugliest, most useless, most senseless desert of them all. It is the villain among badlands, most wasted of wastelands, most foreboding of forbidden realms. At least in the Southwest, the Pinacate desert is the final test of desert rathood; it is here that we learn who is a true rat and who is essentially only a desert mouse.

One cannot claim that Pinacate is a scenic area in any common sense of the word. The deserts of northern Arizona and southern Utah feature sheer-walled canyons, thousands of feet deep, entrenched for 500 miles through great plateaus; the biggest "canyon" in Pinacate is a gulch about 40 feet deep and 10 miles long. Almost anywhere else in the Southwest you will see real mountains with snow fields and alpine flora; but in Pinacate country the highest point is Pinacate Peak itself, a tired old dome-shaped volcano (extinct) rising only 3,957 feet above sea level. Hardly enough elevation to cast a shadow or float a cloud. Vol-

canic phenomena are a Pinacate specialty, but even in this aspect its cinder cones, craters and lava flows do not equal in color and drama those of the Sunset Crater volcanic region of northern Arizona.

Well then, you ask, what *is* the attraction? Why should anyone go out of his way to contemplate the Pinacate country, El Gran Desierto, this ultimate wasteland?

One answer might be that very few people ever do go out there. A few Mexican woodcutters; a few hardened hot-country fanatics from the States. But this is not an answer, only an evasion. Perhaps the explanation is that the appeal of the Pinacate country lies in its total lack of any obvious appeal. In its emptiness. In its vast, desolate nothingness. At its heart is a 750-square-mile volcanic field, an iron-hard iron-hued wilderness of craters, cones, congealed lava flows, with tired old Pinacate Peak in the middle. To the south lie the empty salt marshes, the sandy hummocks that border the Gulf of California coast. On the north and east are rugged little granite ranges and more cactus and creosote desert, inhabited only by a few starving scrub cattle and wild animals. On the outskirts of this desert are the towns of Sonoita, San Luisito, and Puerto Peñasco, with a combined population of maybe 20,000 Mexicans. Which isn't much for an area the size of Connecticut.

And then there is the erg.

The erg (a term borrowed from the Arabic) is a sea of sand, an ocean of dunes stretching from the base of Pinacate Peak all the way to what is left of the Colorado River and its now mostly lifeless delta at the head of the gulf. From peak to delta is a distance of about a hundred miles by line of sight, interrupted only by a few small, isolated, waterless desert mountains. In all of the region there is nothing that can be called man-made except the highway skirting its northern edge and on the south the single railway line that runs along the coast from Mexicali to Puerto Peñasco.

The sand dunes, like the volcanic field and the glittering sea that form so much of the horizon here, have one quality more overwhelming than any other: a great brooding solemnity, compounded of equal parts of distance, space, emptiness and silence. "Nothing is more real than nothing," wrote Samuel Beckett, thinking of the human soul; he could have said it of Pinacate. Thomas Hardy, too, would have found something familiar in this moorland among deserts. And desert rats, like all romantics, are half in love with that abyss that yawns over yonder, beyond the world's rim.

A belt of rolling sand dunes, as much as 40 miles wide in places, borders the Gulf of California in El Gran Desierto in Mexico.

"There's something about the desert," a friend once said to me, trying to explain why he loved the desert. Rather, why he loved it so *much*. And try though he would, he could say no more. I have often wondered what the answer would have been from one of the most famous of Death Valley oldtimers, a prospector named Seldom Seen Slim. But he never answered his telephone. He didn't have a telephone. And he was never home. Didn't have a home.

I have tried to analyze my own emotions on this subject: why am I so much in love with the desert? I love also the sea and the seashore, the mountains, lakes and glaciers, the soft blue-green hills of my Appalachian boyhood, the plains of Oklahoma, the blue grottoes of Capri, the dark forests of Bavaria, the misty golden hills of Scotland, yes, even the back alleys of Hoboken, New York City, Berlin, Naples, Barcelona, Brisbane, Pittsburgh. There's beauty, heartbreaking beauty, everywhere. Still, after all, when I think of where I want to be, in the end it's the old hot dusty eyeball-searing head-aching skin-blistering throat-parching boot-burning bloody goddamned desert. Why?

"There's something about the desert . . ." my friend had said. And paused. And halted. And could say no more. He might of course have mentioned the obvious things: the bracing aridity of the air, the clarity of the light (where industry has not yet shoved its brutal snout into the hinterlands), the elegant neoclassic simplicity of the landscape, the landforms, the relative scarcity of man and his works, the queerness of the plant life, the admirable hardiness of the animal life, the splendor of sundown after an August storm, the rare oracular miracle of dripping springs in a nearly waterless land, the human history—the Indians fighting against cruel and hopeless odds, the Euro-American whites driving onward the frontiers of expanding empire. All of this is true enough, but every other particular region, anywhere on earth, has its distinctive features too.

Yet none quite fulfills the peculiar appeal that the desert scene has for some of us. There is something more in the desert, something that has no name. I might call it a mystery—or simply Mystery itself, with a capital "M." Unlike forest or seashore, mountain or city, plain or swamp, the desert, any desert, suggests always the promise of something unforeseeable, unknown but desirable, waiting around the next turn in the canyon wall, over the next ridge or mesa, somewhere within the wrinkled hills. What, exactly? Well . . . a sort of treasure. A kind of delight. God? Perhaps. Gold? Maybe. Grace? Possibly. But something a little more, a little different, even from these.

So there you are. The secret revealed, the essence uncovered, we come right back to where we started. The desert rat loves the desert because there is something about it that he cannot explain or even name.

Which brings us full wobbly circle back to Pinacate, because here is the secret allure of the desert in its purest form—simply because there is so little to compete with it: no great canyons, no mighty mountains, no spectacular flora or fauna, no weird and colorful rock formations, no winy spirits in the air. Only the bleak and brooding badlands, the shimmering sea of sand, the watery rim of the salt sea.

After the generalizations come the qualifications. As I've noted, the plant life in the Pinacate country is sparse. But the first time I visited this area was in March of 1968, a great year for desert wild flowers; the winter rains had come in just the right amounts and at proper intervals. Guided by ranger-naturalist Bill Hoy of Organ Pipe Cactus National Monument, our party approached from the east, off the Puerto Peñasco road, and drove to the end of a woodcutters' truck road at a waterless dead end called Paloverde Camp. Except for the lone paloverde that gave the place its name, there was a dearth of shade as well as water; even in March the daytime temperature was in the high 80s.

But this mattered little. What we saw, looking up from that forlorn spot among the rocks, was the 2,000-foot-high slope of a cindery mountain all covered with a rash, a fuzzy golden coat, of blooming brittlebush, *Encelia farinosa,* yellow flowers spread across a panorama 20 miles wide. Proceeding on foot, we found other early spring flowers in bloom: the pinkish fairy duster, or *Calliandra eriophylla;* the golden Mexican poppy, *Escholtzia mexicana;* the scarlet-flowered hummingbird's trumpet bush, *Zauschneria californica;* and the coral-colored globe mallow, *Sphaeralcea ambigua.* Masses of bloom. Drunken honeybees, sick with joy, zigzagged crazily from bush to bush, flower to flower, having the time of their lives.

That was the day Bill Hoy rappelled down into the well-like opening of a 60-foot fumarole in the heart of a lava flow and nearly never emerged. We watched him go down—his Argentine wife, Marina, a friend, myself —and saw him fade into the gloom at the bottom of the fumarole. He poked around for a while in the ancient dust, hoping to find Indian artifacts, the pelvic bones of sacrificial virgins, a further opening to the underworld, anything novel, literary, scientific. There was nothing but darkness and dust.

He started back up the rope, pulling himself upward and out with the aid of a pair of jumars—clamplike metal devices that grip a rope with many times the leverage of human hands. This particular fumarole, however, has a pronounced overhang on its inside rim. When Bill reached it he found himself hung up. His weight pulled the rope tight against the face of the overhang so that he couldn't move the clamps up the line. He was dangling, and could not claw his way around the overhang. Nor could we risk pulling him from the top by the upper end of the rope, even though it was firmly attached to a rock near the rim of the fumarole. Bill's weight on the rope, its friction on the rock and the added strain of our tugging from above might have broken the line. The only thing we could do was lower a second line. Long, sweaty, hard-breathing minutes followed, while we let down the second rope, and Bill succeeded—one-handed—in securing it around his chest. We had him belayed. Then we pulled him out into the middle of the fumarole and away from the overhang, so he was able to use his jumars, and clamber over the lip of rock.

Next day we visited Crater Elegante, the deepest and one of the most spectacular of Pinacate's collapse calderas, to use the precise geological term, formed by the sinking of subsurface magma. The result in the case of this caldera is an almost perfectly circular depression over a mile in diameter and approximately 850 feet deep. The walls slope at a moderate grade, so that it is possible to scramble down to the interior. Here you find a sparse growth of typical Sonoran Desert shrubbery —creosote bush and cactus—and a small population of mice and lizards and birds. There is no permanent water in Crater Elegante; the inhabitants therefore must manufacture their own water, metabolically, as kangaroo rats do, for example, or obtain it from the blood and tissue of their occasional prey.

We left the volcanic field by a northerly route, skirting the frontal edge of a lava flow 50 feet high and several miles long. Here too the brittle-bush was in massed bloom, and under the flowers we glimpsed the collared lizard, the leopard lizard and the fat chuckwalla, once much prized by Papago gourmets. A fierce-looking lizard a foot long, the chuckwalla will, when threatened, crawl into a rock crevice and inflate itself, wedging its body tightly in place. This helps as defense against hawks and coyotes but not against hungry Indians. The Papago would deflate the lizard with a knife or sharpened stick and drag it out, squirming, to meet its fate. Which was not good, from the chuckwalla's point of view: it would be boiled alive, like a lobster, or eaten raw.

Among the Indians and Mexicans of Sonora the Pinacate desert is considered a *mal país,* an evil land, a place better to be avoided.

The dangers once were quite tangible. More than a century ago Pinacate was the territory of the Pinacateño Areñero, a subgroup of the Indian tribe known as Sand Papago. They were thought by other Indians to be proficient in the magical arts, especially the malevolent variety. Whether this was so or not, the Pinacateño were definitely hostile toward outsiders, perhaps because their homeland was so hostile to them. Dependent for survival upon the meager fruits of cactus and mesquite and such scattered, hard-to-take game as bighorn sheep, jack rabbits and whitetail deer, they understandably resented intruders: more competition for an already marginal food supply.

When strangers did appear, passing through or along the edges of Pinacate toward El Dorado of Southern California, the Pinacateño ambushed them at the few water holes. Many missionaries, traders, gold seekers and other gamblers died in the blue hours of dawn, their bodies studded with arrows, their guns not even in their hands. But as always the white men soon got the best of the Indians: the next to the last of the Pinacateño died of yellow fever in 1851, and the last one simply vanished in 1912.

Today the vestiges of the Indians and traces of their forebears who roamed the region for thousands of years before can still be seen. It was they who made the delicate but definite pathways that follow the contours of the land and wind across the level desert. Near the *tinajas,* or natural water tanks, of the area you will see potsherds; if you are lucky you may find, hidden among the rocks, a complete clay pot, intact. Out in the open, along the ancient foot trails that lead from water hole to water hole, from the hills to the dunes, from the desert to the sea, is other evidence of the former inhabitants: heaps of broken sea shells, cairns that may have been trail shrines, campground clearings and sleeping circles. The latter are small cleared places on the ground, enclosed, sometimes only partially, by low stone walls that functioned as windbreaks; despite the intense heat of the days the nights can be cold in the Pinacate desert, especially when a wind is blowing. These Indians may or may not have had blankets; they probably kept themselves warm at night with one another's bodies—"body heaps."

Even if the Pinacateño had never lived here, there is sufficient in the region itself—the grim landscape, the iron hills and bluish basaltic arroyos, the brooding sky, the scarcity of even the simplest forms of life—to suggest magic to a certain cast of mind, thoughts of the supernatural and the occult. It's the kind of country old veteran witch doctors would like.

I found myself thinking about this on our second trip to the Pinacate country, a year after the first, in the awful heat of May. We came down from Los Vidrios on the north for a look at the western side of the desert, and on the way we stopped near what appeared to be no more than a modest rise. We climbed it and found ourselves peering down into a ghastly pit of jagged black basalt 650 feet deep. Sykes Crater. Much wider than it is deep, this crater makes a more vivid impression on the senses than the more accessible expanse of Crater Elegante. Here at Sykes the precipitous walls, the pitlike proportions, the angular exposure of the rock, the shadowy depths, combine to suggest something hostile, evil, the ruthless violence of the underworld's mostly dormant but always potent vulcanism.

From Sykes Crater, we drove southward for some 20 miles and three hours over the roughest, rockiest jeep trail this side of Baja California. Eventually we reached the dead end of the trail at a place called Tule Tank, where we made camp for several days and nights.

Tule Tank isn't much to look at, merely a bench of lava rock with some scrubby paloverde and saguaro growing out of it, low buttes and ridges forming the horizon, but in the gulch close by is one of the few usually reliable *tinajas* in the entire region, a deeply corroded watertight basin in the basalt bedrock. It is not a spring; there are no springs in Pinacate. The *tinaja* is filled by thunderstorms and flash floods, after which it may be 10 to 15 feet deep, depending upon the amount of gravel and rocks washed into the tank. Because of the high walls on either side, which shade it from the sun and retard evaporation, this *tinaja* almost always contains some water.

A few words on water-hole etiquette: where they are rare, as in Pinacate, it is considered bad form to bathe in *tinajas,* especially by the next person who comes along needing a drink. A good desert rat prefers to scrub himself with sand and sunshine anyway.

Once comfortably set up in the shade, what there was of it, with a couple of canvas bags of *tinaja* water hanging from a limb of a paloverde, cooling and evaporating in the hot breeze, we began to think about climbing a mountain, such as it is, i.e., Pinacate Peak. There wasn't any other mountain immediately available. We thought about it all day long, reclining in the shade with our bird books and lizard books, waiting for the sun to decline to a bearable angle. In the evening we went for a long walk over the flats and thought about it some more. Off

Nearly a mile across and 450 feet deep, MacDougal Crater in the Pinacates supports a growth of plants where a volcano once spewed fire.

in the west, paralleling the rim of the sea, the rippled erg glimmered at us, blazing with light and heat, endless and depthless. Perhaps we should investigate the dune world. We strolled across the desert pavement, under a fat rising moon, and thought about the moon and the dunes and the mountain.

Desert pavement is aptly named. Very small volcanic stones and cinders, worn smooth as tile by millennia of weathering and closely packed in a matrix of silt, form a regular, level surface where few plants ever gain even a nominal foothold. Chemical reactions among soil, rock and air, continuing through the centuries, have given the "pavement" a varnishlike patina of black. Some of these pavements extend for a mile, as wide as they are long, God's own natural parking lots for spiritual shopping centers.

The old fool moon drifted along above, soft and silvery and well worn as a peon's last peso, shedding its indifferent light upon the grand desolation around us. Pinacate, the sleeping volcano, sloped upward on the east, half in moonlight, half in shadow. Becking? Not really.

A "moonbird" called from some dark crevice in the petrified lava: "Poor-will . . . poor-will . . . poor-will. . . ." The Southwest's small relative of the Eastern whippoorwill, the moonbird or poorwill or *Phalaenoptilus nuttallii* has kept me awake for half of many a desert night. Especially when the moon was up. The only recourse is to crawl out of your sack and pitch rocks at the bastard till he flutters off to go haunt somebody else for a while.

Risky, though. There's something a little weird, a bit supernatural about those moonbirds, most of all when heard in the eerie emptiness of the Pinacate country. We looked again at the mountain. One way to exorcise any evil spirits here might be through direct confrontation, face to face, human to inhuman, upon the summit of their territory.

We would climb the mountain. Why not?

But first we spent a day out on the billowing sea of sand, a picnic in the erg. The only erg in the Western Hemisphere, someone told me once. Which may well be true. Arabia, the Sahara, that is where ergs belong. We jounced down the trail in our hardy Toyota, following a sandy wash under giant mesquites and lovely graceful paloverdes covered with the golden bloom of spring toward those pale brownish yellowish reddish dunes that rimmed the western horizon. (The color of them changes from hour to hour, from place to place, with the declensions of the sun.) A few miles to the north were granite mountains, low but rugged, all rock, like miniature Tetons, half buried by the encroaching sand. Nobody lives out there but a few bighorn sheep, the usual rats, lizards, birds and snakes. The sand became deeper and softer, too much even for four-wheel drive. We got out, shouldered our packs, and marched out of the shade and into the heat, out and up and into the erg.

On the dunes nothing is simple. From the distance we had seen nothing but sand. But once out on it, in it, we discovered forms and signs of life everywhere. Most worthy of honorable mention were the mesquite trees, small and scattered but quite beautiful in their fresh green spring leafery; they too were in bloom, with a fragrance faint but sweet, smelling like apples. We saw saltbush, the four-winged variety, and clumps of smoke tree, that ghostly shrub. There was locoweed, sand verbena, coyote gourd and other plants I could not recognize. Occasionally we saw dead trees, both mesquite and paloverde, which had been smothered by parasitic mistletoe. All over the sand were the tracks of rats, mice, lizards, birds, snakes, beetles and butterflies. Butterfly tracks? Why not? Butterflies have feet too, just like you and me.

We saw all of this on the edges of the erg. As we tramped farther in, following the cornices of the great firm dunes, the plant life and with it the animal life became more and more scarce, until finally, maybe a mile into that silent oven of sand and sky and sun, we came to where there was no more life. Except us, alien and awed.

A zephyr of wind came up, stirred the loose fine sand on the immaculate edge of the dune we stood on, and pushed it over the brink. Lying on our bellies, we could hear a delicate tinkling sound as the grains of sand drifted off the cornice and tumbled down the slip face of the dune. We rolled over and looked up at the sky, that mad dome of blue with its solitary fanatic star. I let my head hang back over the edge of the dune and studied the world upside down. Always a wise and refreshing practice.

About then I noticed two pairs of black wings soaring casually, nonchalantly, without effort, somewhere halfway between us and the sun. Vultures. Patient, and hungry as always. We decided to get back to camp before our brains got roasted and our eyeballs plucked.

Next day we climbed the mountain. No great climb, really, not even a scramble, just a long hike, up the lower slopes and up a ravine where we passed La Tinaja Alta, the highest natural water tank in Pinacate. We noticed as we trudged by that it contained only a few inches of water. We took a long thirsty pull—from our canteens instead—left the ravine and began the tedious ascent of the peak. Hot up there; gravity dragged at our boots. Through scattered saguaros, stands of shiny teddy bear cholla, we tramped on, crazy as crickets—"Why are we doing this?" "My God I don't know, why are you doing it?" "My God, I don't know, I guess I'm crazy, what's your excuse?"—until, four hours from Tule Tank, we reached the summit of Pinacate Peak.

There was nobody there but us mountain climbers. No gods, no spirits, no ghosts that I could see, only the wind and the brittlebush and a great deal of loose scaly rock.

It was not even a first, our conquest of the mountain. We found a canister and inside it a register book filled with names and dates: half the hiking clubs of Southern California had been here before us. Also the third-best lady mountain climber of Arizona. We added our names to the list. Half the point of climbing a mountain is to be able to say you did it; the other half is getting back down.

But first we took a good survey of the world around us. Even though it was a hazy day we still could see for close to 50 miles in all directions. There was obvious Arizona on the north, mantled in smelter smog and progress, as usual. The state of Sonora to the east did not look much healthier. South we could see a range of granitic mountains called Sierra Blanca; a friend named Larry May, an ecologist and a hopeless, incurable desert rat, would take me there later to show me a valley where he had measured the temperature, one day in June 1971, at 134° F., which equals the highest reading ever recorded at Death Valley and is exceeded only by a figure of 136° taken at a weather station called Azizia in Libya.

We gazed southwest and west, beyond the craters and the cones toward the erg, which forms a golden crescent on the verge of the sea. Both the blue sea and the sea of sand extended farther than our vision could carry, fading off into the western haze and a vague suggestion of the mountains of Baja California.

We descended, down the broken rock and unstable cinders, through the ocotillo jungles and the saguaro groves. Here and there little mahogany pellets, sure sign of bighorn sheep. But the pellets were old, and dry as dust. Are there any bighorns left in this place? I don't know; Larry May says there are. Even mountain lions, or at least *a* transient mountain lion—he saw it.

The heat became greater as we went down, down from the mountain into the waiting inferno. In the middle of the afternoon we paused for an hour's rest in the shade of an ironwood by the side of La Tinaja

Alta, the high tank. It seemed to us that the water in the little basin had gone down since we had seen it last, two or three hours earlier. We stared at the stagnant oily water, its surface coated with dove feathers and a scum of dust and dead and living bugs, bees, flies, fleas. After the climb, our canteens were empty. The water looked good. We drank some and felt much better.

It was most excellent to lie there on the cool blue-gray basalt under the tough old tree—ironwoods may be almost as long-lived as Methuselah—and watch the bees buzzing and sipping at the water's edge. The heat and glare beyond our little sheltering bower was terrific, stunning, exhausting; the heat waves looked dense enough to float a boat on. But here in the shade we knew peace of a sort, a happy bliss, ease of limb and mind. While my companion filled his canteen, straining the insect-filled tepid water through a bandana, I watched the insouciant birds creeping and flitting through the brush. *Phainopepla nitens, Pyrrhuloxia sinuata, Pipilo fuscus,* all my desert favorites were there, stoking their furious metabolisms with bug and seed, stuffing their greedy gizzards.

We prepared to go, but paused for a last look at the little water hole. Our drink and filling one canteen had plainly lowered the water level another two inches. Only a bucketful or so remained. La Tinaja Alta is a very small *tinaja* to begin with and this was the dry season. The bees crawled over the damp rim of the basin, bedraggled and puzzled. Now the bird cries seemed forlorn.

Out in the rocks and brush somewhere crouched other small animals waiting for us to leave, waiting their turn for a drink. We didn't see them, we didn't hear them, but we felt them.

Four miles to go, a good two hours' march (on that terrain) before we reached camp and the big *tinaja* of Tule Tank. We thought about the birds and bees and animals, the injustice of life, the general harshness of existence. I know, it's tough all over, but nowhere tougher than on the blackened slopes of Pinacate, under that pitiless Sonoran sun.

All the water we had was in the one canteen. We emptied it back into the little stony basin. Not in charity but out of caution. It seemed, after all, no more than a prudent sacrifice to the spirit of the desert.

Rock, Sand and Solitude

PHOTOGRAPHS BY ERNST HAAS

Long an ardent desert buff, photographer Ernst Haas was recently drawn to El Gran Desierto in Mexico by its reputation as the emptiest, grimmest part of the vast Sonoran Desert. Haas confirmed the superlatives after a two-week trek through hundreds of square miles of barren, jagged mountains, shiny black lava fields and enormous sand dunes. "But," he added, "my strongest impression was of strange, solemn beauty and immutable peace."

According to plan, Haas met his young desert guide, John Woodin, and set out across the moonlike wasteland in late November, when the weather promised nothing worse than chilling nights and midday temperatures in the 80s. Their trip soon settled into an easy routine. They would set up camp for a day or two and explore on foot for miles around. Then they would drive on to a new campsite in a versatile vehicle that was equally capable of traversing razor-sharp lava beds and climbing steep sand dunes.

With only a drizzle and a rainbow as brief diversions, Haas grew increasingly aware of the desert's brooding majesty and disconcerting size. A caldera that seemed merely large from a distance proved to measure three miles around. Every vista was immense and remote, and in scanning the void for a typical plant or an unusual lava formation Haas found himself observing more acutely than ever before. As he later explained, "If you look at nothing long enough, you see something, and it is beautiful."

Always the desert posed picture-taking problems. The blinding glare of the sun in a bleached cloudless sky limited Haas's working day to early morning and late afternoon. Yet even in those periods, deep shadows and the ruddy light played tricks with his subjects, distorting their usual shapes and disguising their somber colors.

And above all there was the silence and solitude. Haas had expected the days of lonely work to make him eager each night for campfire conversation—just for the sheer relief of hearing another human voice. But he and his guide—by tacit agreement—talked less and less as the two weeks passed. Haas felt himself sinking deeper and deeper into a mood of isolation—and enjoying the sensation more and more. When the time came to go back to the frantic pace of the crowded city, he felt altogether refreshed and renewed.

A RAINBOW OVER A LAVA BED NEAR THE PINACATES

WIND-RIPPLED SAND IN A SEA OF DUNES

A SUN-WASHED OCOTILLO SHRUB

BRITTLEBUSH (FOREGROUND) AND LIMBER BUSH GROWING IN LAVA CINDERS

A PATTERN OF SAND DUNES

WHITE BRITTLEBUSH AMID CREOSOTE SHRUBS

A SHRUB-STUDDED CRATER IN THE PINACATE REGION

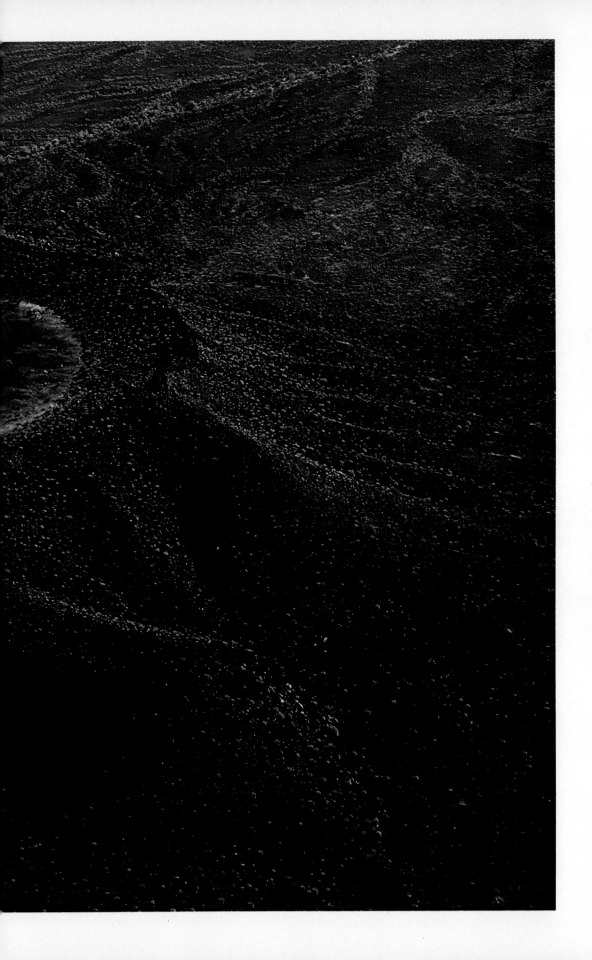

THE "STANDING WAVE" DUNES NEAR THE HORNADAY MOUNTAINS

A LAVA FORMATION NEAR MAC DOUGAL CRATER

THE PINACATE BEETLE AND ITS TRACKS

Bibliography

*Also available in paperback
†Only available in paperback

Barnes, William C., *Arizona Place Names*. University of Arizona Press, 1960.

Bates, Marston, *Animal Worlds*. Random House, 1963.

Benson, Lyman, *The Cacti of Arizona* (3rd ed.). University of Arizona Press, 1969.

Borror, Donald J., and Richard E. White, *A Field Guide to the Insects of America North of Mexico*. Houghton Mifflin, 1970.

†Dodge, Natt N., *Flowers of the Southwest Deserts* (4th ed.). Southwestern Monuments Association, 1965.

†Dodge, Natt N., *100 Desert Wildflowers in Natural Color*. Southwestern Monuments Association, 1965.

†Dodge, Natt N., *Poisonous Dwellers of the Desert* (12th ed.). Southwestern Monuments Association, 1970.

Dunbier, Roger, *The Sonoran Desert*. The University of Arizona Press, 1968.

Earle, W. Hubert, *Cacti of the Southwest*. Arizona Cactus and Native Flora Society, 1963.

Hastings, James Rodney, and Raymond M. Turner, *The Changing Mile*. University of Arizona Press, 1965.

Howes, Paul Griswold, *The Giant Cactus Forest and Its World*. Duell, Sloan and Pearce; Little, Brown, 1954.

*Jaeger, Edmund C., *Desert Wild Flowers*. Stanford University Press, 1967.

*Jaeger, Edmund C., *Desert Wildlife*. Stanford University Press, 1961.

Jaeger, Edmund C., *The North American Deserts*. Stanford University Press, 1957.

Kearney, Thomas H., and Robert H. Peebles, *Arizona Flora*. University of California Press, 1960.

Klauber, Laurence M., *Rattlesnakes* (2 vols.). University of California Press, 1956.

Klots, Alexander B., *A Field Guide to the Butterflies of North America, East of the Great Plains*. Houghton Mifflin, 1951.

Klots, Alexander and Elsie, *Insects of North America*. Doubleday, 1971.

†Krutch, Joseph Wood, *The Desert Year*. The Viking Press, 1952.

*Krutch, Joseph Wood, *The Voice of the Desert*. William Sloane Associates, 1955.

Larson, Peggy, *Deserts of America*. Prentice-Hall, 1970.

Leopold, A. Starker, *The Desert* (rev. ed.). TIME-LIFE BOOKS, 1967.

Manning, Reg, *The Cactus Book*. Reganson Cartoon Books, 1969.

Murphy, Robert, *Wild Sanctuaries*. E. P. Dutton, 1968.

†Olin, George, *Mammals of the Southwest Deserts* (2nd ed. rev.). Southwestern Monuments Association, 1959.

Peattie, Donald Culross, *A Natural History of Western Trees*. Houghton Mifflin, 1953.

Peterson, Roger Tory, *A Field Guide to Western Birds*. Houghton Mifflin, 1969.

Putnam, George Palmer, *Death Valley and Its Country*. Duell, Sloan and Pearce, 1946.

Schmidt-Nielsen, Knut, *Desert Animals: Physiological Problems of Heat and Water*. Oxford University Press, 1964.

Shreve, Forrest, and Ira L. Wiggins, *Vegetation and Flora of the Sonoran Desert* (2 vols.). Stanford University Press, 1964.

Sloane, Howard N. and Lucille L., *A Pictorial History of American Mining*. Crown, 1970.

Smith, Hobart M., *Handbook of Lizards*. Comstock, 1946.

Stebbins, Robert C., *A Field Guide to Western Reptiles and Amphibians*. Houghton Mifflin, 1966.

Wallace, Andrew, *The Image of Arizona*. University of New Mexico Press, 1971.

Welles, Philip, *Meet the Southwest Deserts*. Dale Stuart King, 1964.

*Woodin, Ann, *Home Is the Desert*. Collier Books, 1964.

Writers' Project, *Arizona* (rev. ed.). Hastings House, 1966.

Acknowledgments

The author and editors of this book wish to thank the following persons. At the Arizona-Sonora Desert Museum, Tucson: Betty Berg, Executive Secretary; Robert Craig, General Curator; Donald Ducote, Curator of Plants; Charles L. Hanson, Curator of Birds and Mammals; Merritt S. Keasey III, Curator of Small Animals; Larry May, Research Associate; Gale Monson, Resident Supervisor; William H. Woodin, Director Emeritus. At Organ Pipe Cactus National Monument: Karon Bege-man, Park Aid; Rothwell P. Broyles, Chief of Interpretation and Resource Management; Larry Henderson, Assistant Chief of Interpretation and Resource Management; Matt H. Ryan, Superintendent. Also, Jim Carrico, Superintendent, Great Sand Dunes National Monument, Alamosa, Colorado; Harold T. Coss, Park Interpreter, Saguaro National Monument, Tucson; John DePuy, Oracle, Arizona; Gerald Duncan, Acting Refuge Manager, Kofa Game Range; Richard Felger, Tucson; Sidney S. Horenstein, Department of Invertebrate Paleontology, The American Museum of Natural History, New York City; Bill Hoy, Fort Bowie National Historic Site, Willcox, Arizona; Ned Jackson, Recreation and Land Staff Officer, Tonto National Forest; Dr. William H. Loery, Pathologist, Medical Center at Princeton, New Jersey; Larry G. Pardue, The New York Botanical Garden, New York City; Douglas Peacock, Tucson; Ann Schlumberger, Tucson; Margaret Sparks, Arizona Pioneers Historical Society, Tucson; Floyd Werner, Professor of Entomology, University of Arizona, Tucson; Ann Woodin, Tucson; John Woodin, Tucson.

Picture Credits

The sources for the pictures in this book are shown below. Credits for the pictures from left to right are separated by commas; from top to bottom they are separated by dashes.

Cover—Dean Brown. Front endpapers 2, 3—Dean Brown. Front endpaper 4, page 1—Harold T. Coss. 2, 3—Dean Brown. 4, 5—Harold T. Coss. 6, 7—David Muench. 8, 9—Larry A. May. 10, 11—Ed Cooper. 12, 13—Larry A. May. 18, 19—Map by R. R. Donnelley Cartographic Services. 24—Ernst Haas. 28 through 41—David Cavagnaro. 45—Dean Brown. 48—Dean Brown. 53 through 61—Wolf von dem Bussche. 68, 69—Dean Brown. 74—Dean Brown. 79—Al Freni except bottom right Harold T. Coss. 80—Al Freni, Richard Weymouth Brooks—Bob Waterman, Al Freni. 81, 82—Bob Waterman. 83—Al Freni, Bob Waterman. 84—Al Freni—Bob Waterman. 85—Bob Waterman. 86—Al Freni—Bob Waterman. 87—Al Freni. 88, 89—Bob Waterman, Al Freni, Bob Waterman—Al Freni, Al Freni. 90—Al Freni except bottom right Richard Weymouth Brooks. 91—Bob Waterman—Al Freni. 96 through 103—Dean Brown. 107 through 111—Arizona Pioneers Historical Society. 114 through 123—Dean Brown. 127 through 141—Drawings by Barry Driscoll. 144, 145—Wardene Weisser. 148—Bob Waterman. 155 through 179—Ernst Haas.

Index

Numerals in italics indicate a photograph or drawing of the subject mentioned.